Contemporary Class Piano

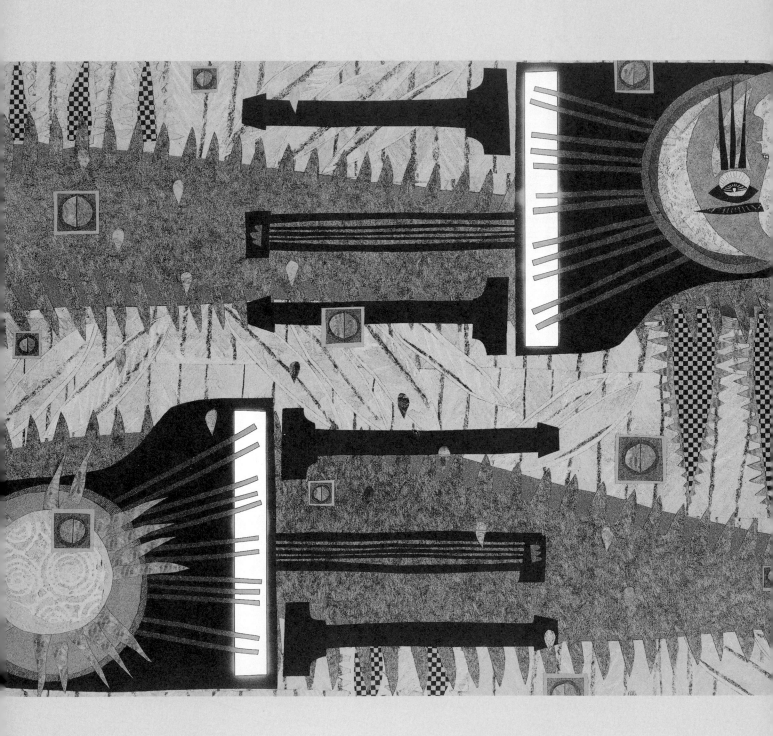

Contemporary Class Piano

SIXTH EDITION

Elyse Mach
Northeastern Illinois University

New York   Oxford
OXFORD UNIVERSITY PRESS
2004

Oxford University Press

Oxford   New York
Auckland   Bangkok   Buenos Aires   Cape Town   Chennai
Dar es Salaam   Delhi   Hong Kong   Istanbul   Karachi   Kolkata
Kuala Lumpur   Madrid   Melbourne   Mexico City   Mumbai
Nairobi   São Paulo   Shanghai   Taipei   Tokyo   Toronto

Published by Oxford University Press, Inc.
198 Madison Avenue, New York, New York 10016
http://www.oup-usa.org

Oxford is a registered trademark of Oxford University Press

ISBN: 0-19-516688-4

Text design by Cathleen Bennett

Printing number: 9 8 7 6 5 4 3

Printed in the United States of America
on acid-free paper

Contents

UNIT 3 *Pieces with Easy Accompaniments* 241

UNIT 4 *Tonality and Atonality* 377

UNIT 5 *Letter-Name Chord Symbols* 457

Preface

Contemporary Class Piano, Sixth Edition, is an introduction to the keyboard designed for college students who are enrolled in a class piano course, whether or not they are music majors and whether or not they have prior keyboard experience. It is suitable for non-piano majors who must gain keyboard proficiency, for prospective elementary teachers, and for any student who wishes to learn how to play the piano for the sheer fun of it.

The book's creative and multidimensional approach made earlier editions great successes in class piano courses throughout the country. Besides offering a well-rounded and abundant solo and ensemble repertoire—including classical pieces from the baroque to the contemporary period and folk, jazz, pop, and blues tunes—the book teaches students to sight read, to transpose, to improvise in various styles, to harmonize folk and popular songs, and to compose simple accompanied melodies. In addition, students learn the fundamentals of theory and musical form. Throughout, all materials are presented with a logical progression in difficulty. For instructors, there is a wide selection of material that will accommodate a variety of individual teaching goals and keyboard requirements. This abundance of material also allows the teacher to pick and choose—tailoring keyboard experiences in a fresh new way each time—rather than using a page-by-page approach throughout the book.

The text is divided into six units with four appendixes. Unit 1 introduces keyboard basics and the five-finger position. The emphasis is on learning to play by touch, without looking down at the keys. Note reading is taught by interval study, and a multi-key approach to reading is stressed. Sections at the end of this and subsequent units are devoted to special repertoire pieces, sightreading studies, improvisation, rhythmic studies, technical studies, creative music and harmonization, ensemble pieces, and written worksheet reviews—all of which reinforce techniques and skills introduced in Unit 1.

Unit 2 contains many simple pieces based on the five-finger position. A register guide appears at the beginning of every piece in this unit to help students quickly locate the correct starting position for both hands. Five-finger studies in all major and minor keys and their respective major and minor triads are presented, along with added practice studies and pieces in all the major keys.

Unit 3 extends the five-finger position and offers students an unusually large variety of accompaniment patterns for improvisation and creative writing.

Unit 4 contains minor and modal materials, but it is largely devoted to twentieth-century pieces, introducing students to jazz, pandiatonicism, clusters, innovative notations, and polytonal, atonal, and twelve-tone pieces and techniques.

Unit 5 provides students with practice in harmonizing folk and popular melodies with various accompaniment patterns. The interpretation of letter-name chord symbols is an important feature of this unit.

Unit 6 is an anthology by representative composers as well as newer twentieth-century composers of repertoire pieces that vary widely in difficulty, length, and style. The compositions are presented in their original form with no changes except for fingerings and slight editing where necessary to aid the player. For students who advance quickly, these pieces will become "stretcher pieces" in the special challenge they present.

Appendix A provides students with an introduction to score reading both three- and four-part textures.

Appendix B contains major and harmonic minor scales in two octaves.

Appendix C gives students easy-to-play arrangements of selected patriotic songs.

Appendix D offers a list of performance terms and symbols.

The Sixth Edition retains all the strengths of the first five editions, and it has been enriched in numerous respects:

- Standard MIDI File (SMF) disks that feature a wide range of accompaniments that extend to full orchestrations have been prepared especially for this text by composer Phillip Keveren. Each piece that has an accompaniment on the disks is identified by an icon that shows the track number. Ultimate performance tempos are illustrated. However, teachers will probably want to use slower tempos at first for classroom teaching purposes.

002

- An instructor's manual that accompanies the text may be found at www.oup.com/us/classpiano and contains suggested daily lesson plans and teaching tips, as well as serving as a guide to curriculum development.

- Thirty-one new solo repertoire pieces of master and twentieth-century composers have been added, along with new-age styles of today that students will find exciting to learn and to play.

- Sixteen new ensemble repertoire pieces—arranged for four to eight hands—providing students with more easy arrangements of appealing ensemble repertoire that they can learn to play immediately. For wider scope and style, these pieces now include "Spring" from *The Four Seasons* by Vivaldi, "Canon" by Pachelbel, "Amazing Grace," "Story Time" by Dello Joio, "Boogie Woogie Treat" by Goldston, and others.

- Unit 5 includes thirteen new songs to harmonize, six of which comprise the new "Famous Themes" section with such student favorites as *Für Elise* and *Liebestraum* themes.

- Unit 6 has an expanded selection of eight new repertoire pieces that includes a rich mix extending from Rameau to Starer, from J. C. Bach to Hovhaness, and from Mozart to Miller to Tingley.

- All major and harmonic minor scales in two octaves with provided fingerings appear in Appendix B for quick and easy location to use.

- Easy-to-play arrangements of three patriotic songs—*America, America the Beautiful,* and *The Star-Spangled Banner*—are presented in Appendix C.

- Eighteen new teacher accompaniments have been added, to be played with selected repertoire and ensemble pieces, and with the major five-finger patterns.

- New techniques—such as easy formulas for learning and playing various chord progressions more quickly and preparatory studies for learning and playing both the chromatic and major scales more effectively—are presented with clear and concise illustrations for quick and easy understanding.

- A new Dorian mode accompaniment provides students with more varied ways to improvise using this mode in Unit 1, while the addition of several new chord progressions in Unit 3, featuring secondary chords, helps to reinforce and expand these particular theory concepts and techniques.

- There has been a "fine-tuning" of the entire text, which includes changes of harmony, updating of markings, and more clearly defined terminology—hopefully, everything that can make the book a stronger and better one for both teachers and students to like and use more effectively.

Upon completing this book, students will have built a strong foundation of keyboard skills, techniques, theory, and repertoire, and will be ready to move to the next level of keyboard study.

No book is ever done without the generous help and assistance of others. I am doubly grateful to have a number of special individuals to single out and thank in the preparation of this Sixth Edition.

For direction, focus, and production of this book, my thanks to the team at Oxford University Press: special thanks to Jan Beatty, executive editor, whose professionalism is exceeded only by her personal warmth; gracious thanks to Christine D'Antonio, senior project editor;

Cathleen Bennett, text designer; Eve Siegel, cover art director; Elyse Dubin, director of editing, design, and production—all consummate professionals and the best team I could possibly have to work with; and many kind thanks to Talia Krohn, editorial assistant, for her diligence and willingness to be of help when an extra hand was really needed.

For their gifted and creative talents, my deepest respect and gratitude to Phillip Keveren and Ken Iversen, composers and arrangers whose work is indispensable to the book, and to Andrew Lidgus, whose magnificent art piece graces the cover.

For thoroughly scrutinizing the manuscript and offering ideas and pertinent suggestions that were instrumental in preparing a better book, my never-ending gratitude to the prerevision reviewers: LeGrand Andersen, Southern Utah University; Peter Collins, Southwest Missouri State University; Cassandra Hanna, Miami-Dade CC, North-Miami; Irene Kim, Los Angeles City College; Roberta Kraft, Hope College; Nanette Lunde, University of Wisconsin–Eau Claire; and Tammie Walker, Western Illinois University; and to the final manuscript reviewers: Angeline Case-Stott, University of Memphis; Patricia Carter-Zagorski, University of Tennessee; Barbara English Maris, Catholic University; Carol Heinick, SUNY, Potsdam; Terrie Manno, Minnesota State University, Moorhead; Sandra Stewart, University of North Florida; and Vincent Trauth Parkland College. And thanks to Marienne Uszler for her counsel and David Hernandez for his insight.

Finally, for continuing to bring new and fresh perspectives to the learning process, and for making the joy of music-making continue to be such a great and rewarding passion, I offer eternal heartfelt thanks to all of my students.

Contemporary Class Piano

Keyboard Basics

You see my piano is for me what his
frigate is to a sailor, or his horse to an
Arab—more indeed: it is my very self,
my mother tongue, my life. Within its
seven octaves it encloses the whole
range of an orchestra, and a man's ten
fingers have the power to reproduce the
harmonies which are created by hun-
dreds of performers.

Franz Liszt (written in 1838)
Romantic Period Composer, Master
Teacher, and Concert Pianist

*L*earning to play a keyboard instrument is an
exciting adventure and challenge. Equally
exciting is to know, as Liszt so aptly pointed out,
that the ten fingers we use in playing this instrument have the capability of taking us on countless
musical excursions of sound. Music is, after all,
sound—not just some notes, signs, or terms.
Playing a keyboard instrument, however, isn't just
about the fingers that strike the keys. It's also
about a strong supporting cast that is used to
assist the fingers in the music-making process.

For instance, the body is involved—that is, the shoulders, arms, wrists, and hands are frequently called upon to assist the player in producing the many kinds of sounds that are musically required. Even the feet get involved from time to time when one or both of them are called upon to do the pedaling.

The aural facility plays a key role as well. The ears are needed and used by the player to hear and listen to how the musical sounds are being produced, projected, and shaped, and they are essential to the player in determining what to do next.

The visual aspect is also important. The eyes assist the player in reading, learning, and, often, memorizing the music. In addition, sometimes the player will have to glance down at the keys briefly to make sure that they are struck with greatest accuracy, for example, when there are large jumps from one note to another.

Therefore, before starting to learn about the basics of keyboard playing, the first important step should be to learn some of the dos and don'ts about the basics of keyboard posture that include the correct use of the arms, wrists, hands, fingers, and even the eyes.

This figure illustrates keyboard position for the body, arms, wrists, hands, and flexed fingers.

SITTING AT THE KEYBOARD

Body

Place your **body** directly in front of the middle part of the keyboard where the name of the keyboard appears. Both feet should be kept flat on the floor. Keep your body far enough back from the keyboard so that it bends slightly forward at the waist.

Allow your **arms** to hang loosely and rather quietly at your sides.

Wrists

Your **wrists** should be level with the keys so that your hand can fall from the wrist. Do not allow your wrists to slump below the keyboard level.

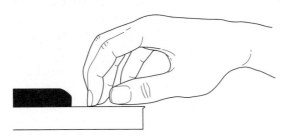

Hands

Your **hands** should be slightly cupped as if you were holding a bubble in each hand.

Fingers

Flexed (correct position)   *Unflexed (incorrect position)*

Your **fingers** should be curved so that each key is struck with the ball or fleshy part of the finger. Remember to keep your fingers **flexed** as you strike the keys. Flexing means not allowing the first knuckle of the finger to collapse on striking the key.

Eyes

Your **eyes** should be on the music. Learn to develop a "feel" for the keys—that is, learn to play by touch.

FINGER NUMBERS

Practice various finger-number combinations by tapping on the wood panel over the keyboard, first with each hand separately, then with both hands. Remember that the two thumbs are 1, the two index fingers are 2, the two middle fingers are 3, and so on.

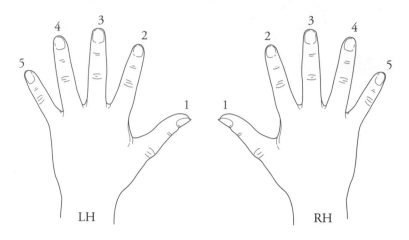

BASIC NOTE VALUES

Whole note	o	= 4 beats
Dotted half note	♩.	= 3 beats
Half note	♩	= 2 beats
Quarter note	♩	= 1 beat

The combination of note values is called **rhythm.**

Measures

Beats are part of a recurring pulse that continues like the ticking of a clock throughout the music. Beats are grouped together to form measures.

Measures may contain two, three, four, or more beats. The beats are counted 1, 2 or 1, 2, 3 or 1, 2, 3, 4, and so on.

Bar lines divide the regular beats into measures of equal duration.

Double bar lines are used to indicate the end of a piece.

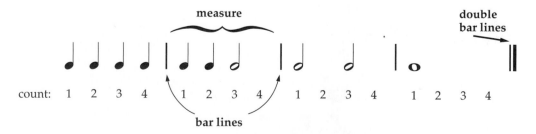

Contrary Motion

Tap various finger-number combinations where both hands use the same finger numbers. When both hands are playing the same finger numbers, the patterns will be played with both hands moving in opposite directions (**contrary motion**). For example:

Right Hand tap 1–5   Then tap both hands together: RH 1–5

Left Hand tap 1–5   LH 1–5

Parallel Motion

Tap finger-number combinations where both hands move in the same direction (**parallel motion**). For example:

RH tap 1–3–5   Then tap both hands together: RH 1–3–5

LH tap 5–3–1   LH 5–3–1

Practice Strategies

Tap the finger-number combinations, which will move in **contrary motion,** with the indicated hands and finger numbers.

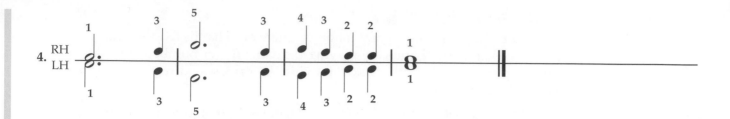

Next, tap finger-number combinations, which will move in **parallel motion**, to the right-hand finger-number combinations given.

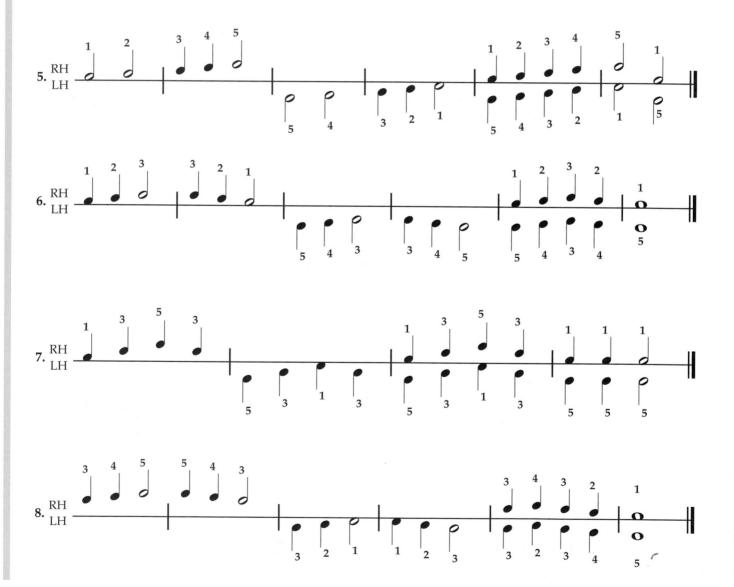

THE KEYBOARD

The standard piano keyboard has 88 keys, but only the first seven letters of the alphabet—A, B, C, D, E, F, G—are used to name the white keys.

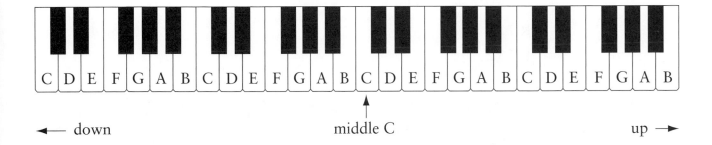

← down   middle C   up →

Location of White Keys

Practice playing the musical alphabet up and down the keyboard, saying the letter names as you play, until you are familiar with the names and locations of the white keys. Do this first with the right hand, then with the left, using whatever finger is most comfortable for you. As you move to the right, you will be playing higher **tones** or **pitches.** As you move to the left, you will be playing lower pitches.

Registers

Next, play the musical alphabet in different **registers**—segments of the total range of the keyboard—lower register, middle register, and upper register, as in the following diagram. (Middle C is the C nearest the center of the keyboard.) Use whatever finger or fingers are comfortable to use. Use LH for keys below middle C and RH for keys above middle C.

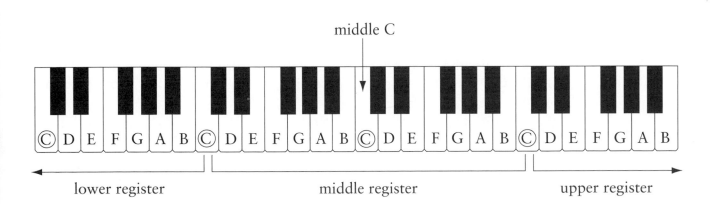

lower register   middle register   upper register

Using Black-Key Groups to Locate White Keys

Play all the groups of two black keys on the keyboard, both upward and downward, using the RH fingers 2 3 together, first, and then the LH fingers 3 2 together, next.

Two Black-Key Groups

or RH 2 3
   LH 3 2

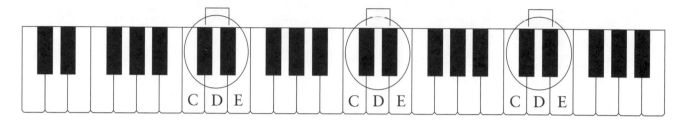

C-D-E Groups

Notice that three white keys—C, D, E—are located around the groups of two black keys.

Using the groups of two black keys as reference points, play all the C's and E's, then all the D's.

Next, use the right hand, beginning on middle C, to play all the C-D-E white-key groups, observing the fingerings and rhythmic patterns given.

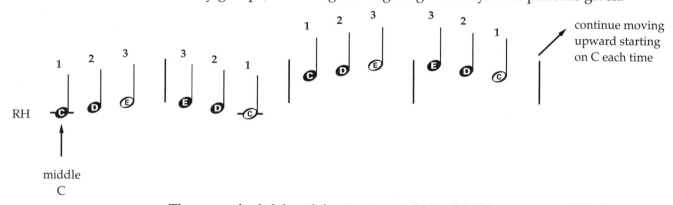

Then, use the left hand, beginning with the **third** finger on middle C, to play all the C-D-E white-key groups, observing the fingerings and rhythmic patterns given.

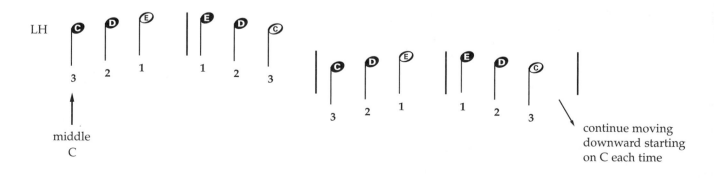

Three Black-Key Groups

Next, play all the groups of three black keys on the keyboard, both upward and downward, using the RH fingers 2 3 4 together, first, and then the LH fingers 4 3 2 together, next. Finally, see if you can improvise some melodies using the black keys only.

or RH 2 3 4
LH 4 3 2

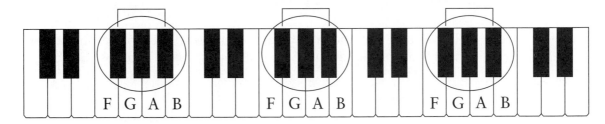

F-G-A-B Groups

Four white keys—F, G, A, B—are located around the groups of three black keys.

Using the groups of three black keys as reference points, play all the F's and B's. Practice the rest of the tones in the same manner.

Next, use the right hand, beginning with the thumb on F below middle C, to play all the F-G-A-B white-key groups, observing the fingerings and rhythmic patterns given.

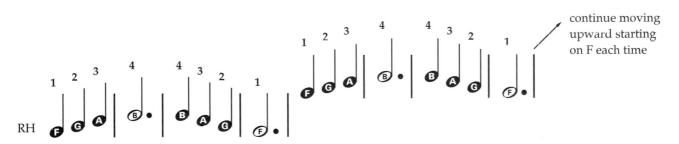

Then, use the left hand, beginning with the **fourth** finger on F below middle C, to play all the F-G-A-B white-key groups, observing the fingerings and rhythmic patterns given.

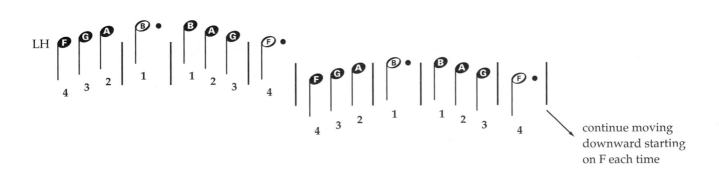

Playing by Touch

After you have learned the keys by sight, start to locate them by **touch**—that is, learn to find any key without looking down. First, without looking down, play all the groups of two black keys. Next, play all the groups of three black keys. Using these black-key groupings as reference points, start picking out individual tones.

Practice Strategies

Locate and play the following pitches. Next, using the groups of two black keys and three black keys as reference points, locate them by touch.

1. middle C
2. F above middle C
3. F below middle C
4. a low B

5. a high E
6. any D
7. any A
8. using both hands, **two** C's in different registers at the same time

Sharp and Flat Signs

A **sharp** (♯) raises a pitch one half step. A **flat** (♭) lowers a pitch one half step.

Half Steps

A **half step** is the distance from one key to the very next key, whether it moves up or down, whether it is a black key or a white key.

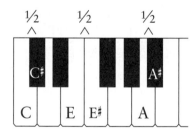

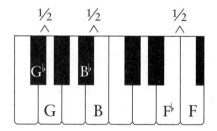

Sharp: one key up (to the right). This can be a black key or a white key.

Flat: one key down (to the left). This can be a black key or a white key.

E♯ and B♯ are white-key sharps.

F♭ and C♭ are white-key flats.

Practice Strategies

1. Practice playing half steps from middle C upward to the next C and then back down again. State the letter names aloud and their half-step relationships in sharps as you play them.

2. Practice playing half steps beginning on middle C downward to the next C and then back up again. Call aloud the letter names and their half-step relationships in flats as you play them.

Natural Sign

A **natural sign** (♮) cancels a sharp or flat. For example, D♯ will be lowered one half step when it becomes D♮ to go back to its natural state. B♭ is raised one half step when it becomes B♮ so it can go up to its natural state.

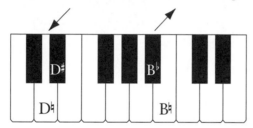

Enharmonic Tones

Enharmonic tones have the same pitch but are referred to by different names. For example, the black key between F and G is called either F♯ or G♭. F♯ and G♭ are enharmonic tones.

What are the two names of the black key between G and A? between A and B?

Letter Names for All Twelve Tones

The seven white-key pitches and the five black-key pitches make up the total of twelve tones with which our music is written.

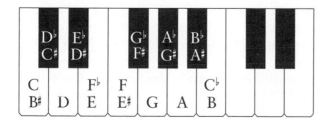

Practice Strategies

Play the following tones, and say the names aloud. Then name the pairs of tones that are enharmonic:

1. G,   G♯,   G♭
2. C,   C♯,   C♭
3. F,   F♯,   F♭
4. A,   A♯,   A♭
5. D,   D♯,   D♭
6. E,   E♯,   E♭
7. B,   B♯,   B♭

Whole Steps

A **whole step** is a combination of two half steps. For example, E♭ to F is a whole step, A to B is a whole step, and C♯ to D♯ is a whole step. Notice that one key is skipped in building a whole step.

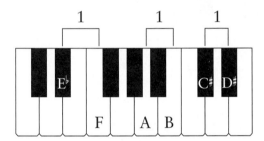

Practice playing and saying whole steps up and down the keyboard.

THE MAJOR FIVE-FINGER PATTERN

The **major five-finger pattern** (also called a **major pentachord** or **pentascale**) is arranged in the following pattern:

The major five-finger pattern can be constructed on any of the twelve tones. The first tone of the major five-finger pattern is referred to as the **tonic**. If we build the pattern on C, C is the tonic. If we build the pattern on G, G then becomes the tonic.

The major five-finger pattern is the first five tones of a major scale (as discussed in Unit 3).

Practice playing the five-finger patterns given, first starting with the one in C, and then in G, F, and D.

Play the patterns first with each hand separately ascending and descending.

Legato

Next, play the patterns with both hands moving in parallel motion. Play all the patterns **legato**—that is, connect the tones so they sound as smooth as possible.

C Major Five-Finger Pattern

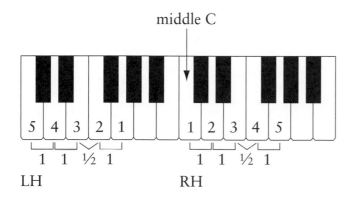

G Major Five-Finger Pattern

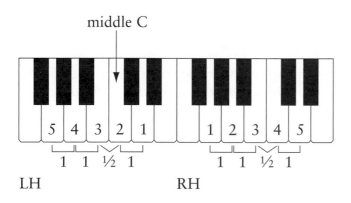

F Major Five-Finger Pattern

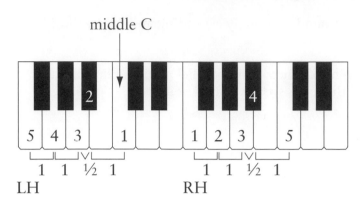

middle C

LH   RH

1	1	½	1			

1	1	½	1			

RH
1 F 5
2 G 4
3 A 3
4 B♭ 2
5 C 1
4 B♭ 2
3 A 3
2 G 4
1 F 5
LH

D Major Five-Finger Pattern

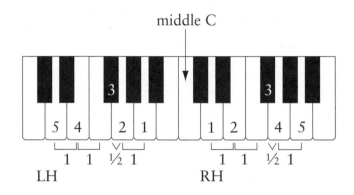

middle C

LH   RH

1	1	½	1

1	1	½	1

RH
1 D 5
2 E 4
3 F♯ 3
4 G 2
5 A 1
4 G 2
3 F♯ 3
2 E 4
1 D 5
LH

Practice Strategies

Build and then begin playing the major five-finger patterns on the starting tone (tonic) given. Be sure to use **five** different letter names in building your pattern.

1. A MAJOR

A

2. E MAJOR

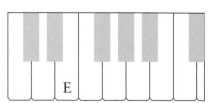

E

3. G♭ MAJOR

G♭

4. D♭ MAJOR

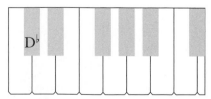

D♭

DYNAMICS

Dynamics are the degrees of softness and loudness in music. Common dynamic markings are

Sign	Italian Name	Meaning
p	piano	soft
mp	mezzo piano	medium soft
mf	mezzo forte	medium loud
f	forte	loud

Ryan's Song can be played using the tones of the five-finger pattern. Here is the five-finger pattern of C.

Five-Finger Notation

C MAJOR
FIVE-FINGER
PATTERN

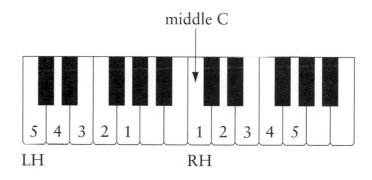

middle C

5 4 3 2 1   1 2 3 4 5

LH   RH

PRACTICE DIRECTIONS

1. Clap or tap the rhythm while counting the beat before playing the melody.
2. Place your hand (or hands) in the correct five-finger position. Try not to look down at the keys once you have found the correct position.
3. Do an **abstract** of the melody—that is, go through the finger motions of playing the music in each hand without producing any sound. As you do so, say or sing aloud the finger numbers. Next, go through it saying or singing the letter names.
4. Next, play and sing aloud the letter names of the notes. Do not stop or hesitate to find the notes. Remember to keep the beat moving!

First play *Ryan's Song* with the right hand, and then with the left.

RYAN'S SONG

Student

E. M.

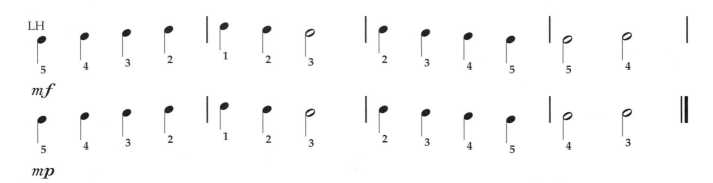

RYAN'S SONG

Accompaniment

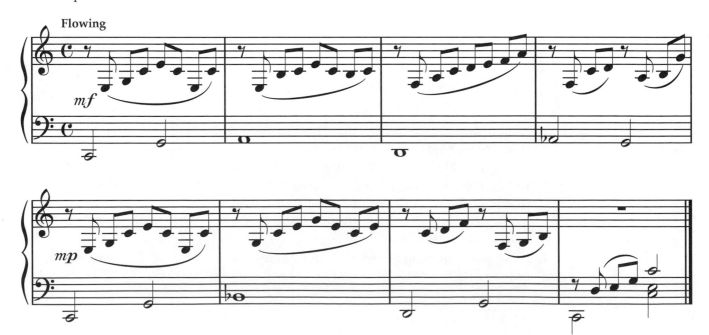

Next, sing and play the melodies of *Ode to Joy, In Praise,* and *Aura Lee,* first with the right hand, then with the left, and finally with both hands. Use the same practice directions as given on page 15.

ODE TO JOY

Student

Ludwig van Beethoven
(1770–1827)

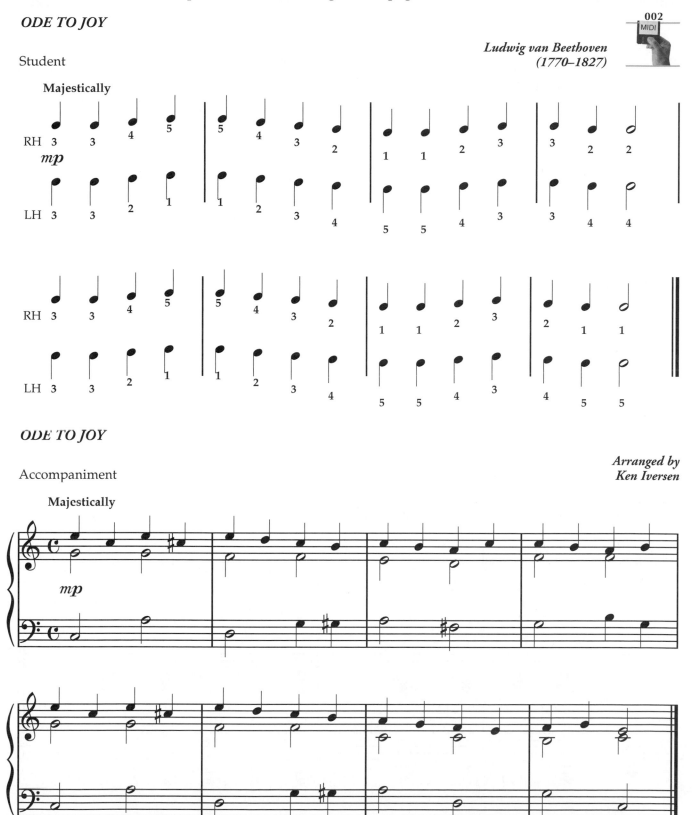

ODE TO JOY

Accompaniment

Arranged by
Ken Iversen

IN PRAISE

Student   *E.M.*

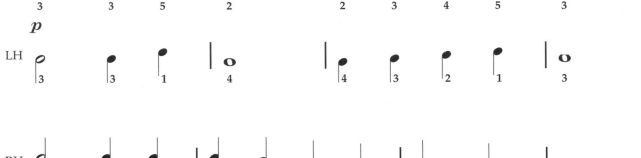

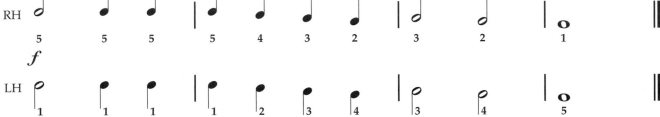

IN PRAISE

Accompaniment

AURA LEE

Student

George Poulton

Play each of these tunes in the five-finger patterns of G, F, and D.

AURA LEE

Accompaniment

Arranged by
Ken Iversen

READING NOTES

The Staff and Clefs

A **staff** consists of five lines and four spaces.

A **clef** is added to indicate the pitches of the notes.

The **treble clef** is placed at the beginning of the staff and is called the **G clef** because it circles around the second staff line, designating that line as the note G. (The right hand usually plays the notes in the treble clef, to the right of middle C.)

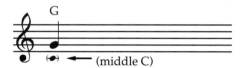

The **bass clef** sign is placed at the beginning of the staff and is called the **F clef** because the fourth staff line is enclosed by dots, designating that line as the note F. (The left hand usually plays the notes in the bass clef, to the left of middle C.)

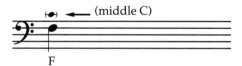

Grand Staff

The **grand staff**, also called the **great staff**, is made up of two staves, one with a treble clef, the other with a bass clef. The short lines above and below the staff are called leger lines. Their purpose is to extend the range of the staves when necessary.

The darkened notes (♩) are landmark notes which will help you learn the notes more quickly.

In 𝄞 clef, use the C's and G's as landmarks.

In 𝄢 clef, use the C's and F's as landmarks.

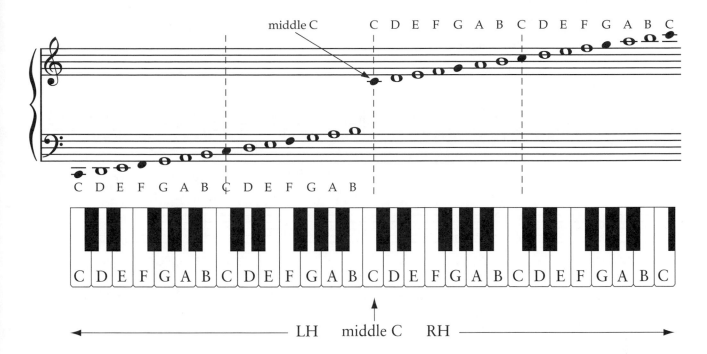

Practice Strategies

1. Beginning on middle C, play and name the notes in the treble clef, moving upward to the next C and then back down again. Next, beginning with C, third space in the treble clef, play and name the notes up to the next C and then back down again.

2. Beginning with C, second space in the bass clef, play and name the bass-clef notes up to middle C and down again. Then, beginning with the lowest C given on the staff, play and name the notes up to the C, second space in the bass clef, and down again.

3. Using the graphic chart given below, practice playing and naming the notes in the spaces and then the notes cutting the lines in the treble clef. Follow the same procedure in the bass cleff.

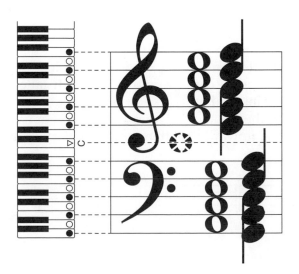

Name and play the following treble-clef notes with the given right-hand fingerings:

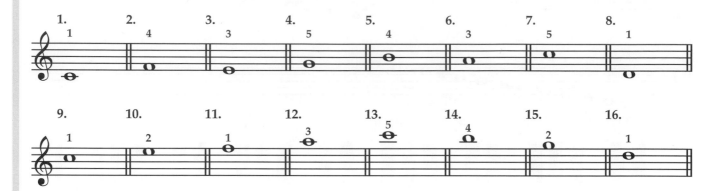

Name and play the following bass-clef notes with the given left-hand fingerings:

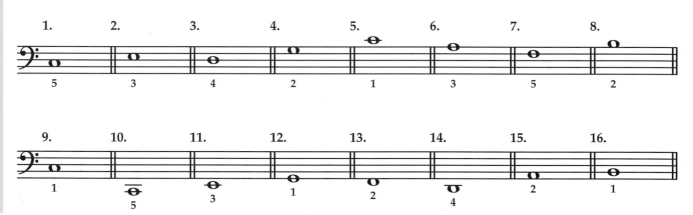

INTERVALS

Good reading habits in music are developed by learning to read notes in relationship to each other—that is, recognizing the distance between notes. This is called reading by interval.

An **interval** is the distance between two notes. For example: C to F is a fourth because, counting upward by letter name, C is 1 and F is 4.

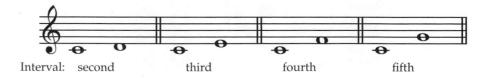

Interval: second   third   fourth   fifth

Melodic Intervals

Melodic intervals are written and played one note following the other:

Harmonic Intervals

Harmonic intervals are written and played together:

Harmonic intervals are also called **blocked intervals**.

Practice Strategies

Practice playing the following intervals, which are given both melodically and harmonically. First, practice hands separately, and then with both hands.

Interval Studies

Read the following intervals and then play them without looking down at the keyboard as you move from one note to the next—that is, concentrate on developing a "feel" for the distance between the various intervals.

A. Right-hand examples

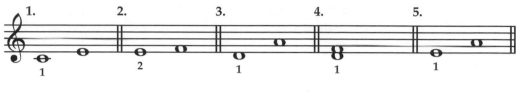

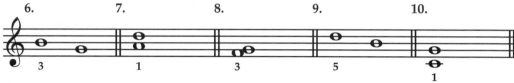

B. Left-hand examples

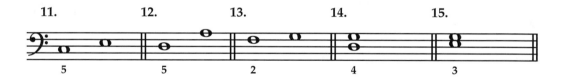

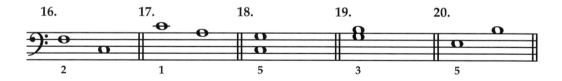

KEEPING TIME

Meter Signatures

At the beginning of a piece you will find a **meter signature**—two numbers that look something like a fraction. The top number indicates the number of beats in a measure, and the bottom number indicates the kind of note that receives one beat.

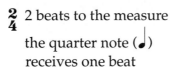 2 beats to the measure

the quarter note (♩)
receives one beat

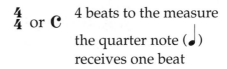 4 beats to the measure

the quarter note (♩)
receives one beat

3/4 3 beats to the measure

the quarter note (♩)
receives one beat

Tempo

Tempo is the rate of movement or speed. Note values are always relative, depending on the tempo. For example, a quarter note would be held longer in a slow tempo than it would in a fast tempo.

Rests

A **rest** represents a silence of the same length as the value of its corresponding note.

Notes	Rests		
𝅝	▬	Whole rest	4 beats or any whole measure
𝅗𝅥	▬	Half rest	2 beats
♩	𝄽	Quarter rest	1 beat

PRACTICE DIRECTIONS

1. Clap or tap the rhythm while counting the beat aloud.
2. Place your hand in the correct five-finger position. Try not to look down at the keys.
3. Study the interval patterns of the melody.
4. Abstract the melody (finger motions but no sound).
5. Play and count aloud.
6. Play and sing aloud the note names. Remember to keep the beat moving!

Five-Finger Melodies for the Right Hand

Five-Finger Melodies for the Left Hand
Follow the same practice directions as given on page 26.

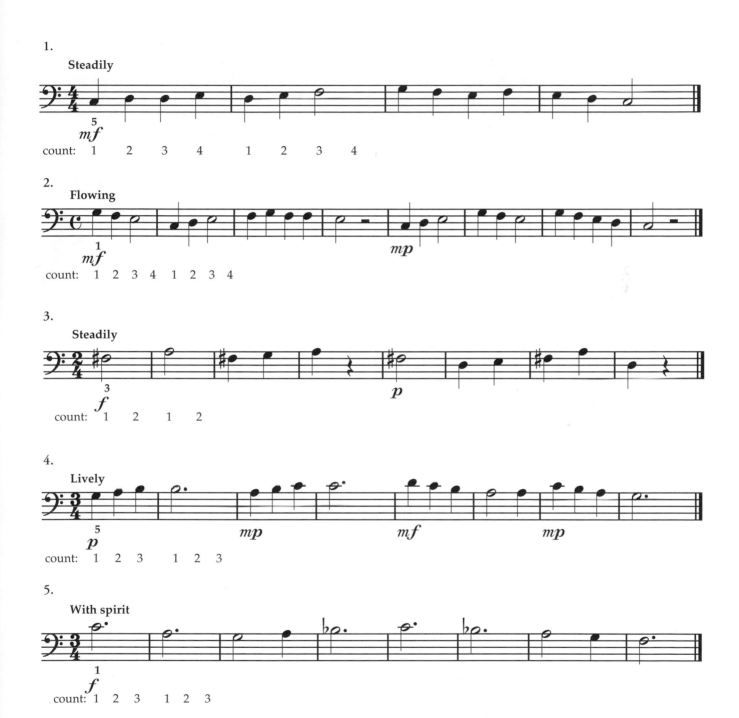

SLUR AND PHRASE MARKINGS

A **slur** or **phrase marking** is a curved line which appears above or below a group of notes. A short curved line is usually called a **slur marking***, and means that the notes within that curved line are to be played legato. A longer curved line (usually four measures in length) indicates **phrasing.**

A **phrase** is a musical sentence that is usually four or eight measures in length. The end of each phrase is a place of punctuation, and your fingers should be lifted off the keys so that there is a slight break. Be sure you do not interrupt the rhythmic flow of the music when you are phrasing.

Alternating Hands

Marching, Memories, and *Rock It!* use alternating hands—first one hand plays, then the other.

MARCHING

Student

E. M.

---

*Slurs are discussed further on page 99.

MARCHING

Accompaniment

Arranged by
Ken Iversen

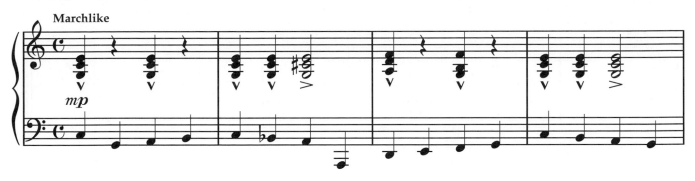

MEMORIES

Student

E. M.

MEMORIES

Accompaniment

E. M.

ROCK IT!

Student

E. M.

ROCK IT!

Accompaniment

Arranged by
Ken Iversen

With energy
Introduction

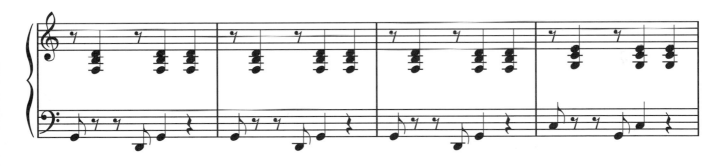

Melodies Divided between Two Hands

The melody is divided between the two hands. Let the starting tone and finger number be your guide in placing your hands in the correct positions.

1.

2.

Gently

Measure Numbers

The boxed number 5 identifies the fifth measure of the piece.

BOOGIE BEAT

Student

E. M.

BOOGIE BEAT

Accompaniment

E. M.

Driving

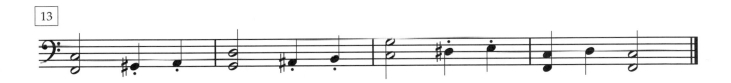

Five-Finger Notation

Love Somebody uses the five-finger pattern in G:

G MAJOR
FIVE-FINGER
PATTERN

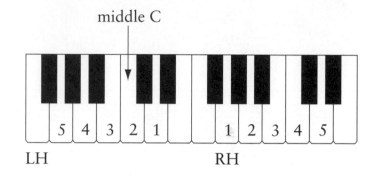

KEY SIGNATURE

Since *Love Somebody* uses the five-finger pattern constructed on G, we can say that it is written in the **key** of G. G is our tonic or **key note.**

The **key signature** appears after the clef signs and indicates the notes that should be played as sharps or flats throughout a piece—that is, the key signature helps to indicate the key of a piece.

Identifying Sharp Key Signatures

Major keys using sharp key signatures can be identified by taking the last sharp, in this case F♯, then moving up one half step higher to the next letter name, which would be G.

Note that although the F♯ is *not* used in the five-finger pattern of G, the F♯ must be written after the clef signs to indicate the key of G. All F's are to be played as F♯. It is necessary to use an F♯ in the key of G because with the introduction of the major scales on page 241, the five-finger pattern is extended to eight tones, and these tones must conform to a specific pattern of whole steps and half steps.

The G major scale is given below to illustrate where the F♯ is used.

G MAJOR
SCALE

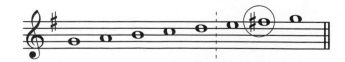

LOVE SOMEBODY

Student

Traditional

TRANSPOSITION

Now play this piece in the key of F major. Playing a piece in a different key (a different five-finger pattern) is called **transposition.** You are transposing this piece into the key of F major. Play it in the key of D major, also, and other keys of your choice.

LOVE SOMEBODY

Accompaniment

8va

EIGHTH NOTES AND EIGHTH RESTS

An **eighth note** (♪) receives one half of one beat if the meter signature has the quarter note receiving one beat.

An **eighth rest** (𝄾) represents a silence the same length as the value of the eighth note.

Two eighth notes are equal to one quarter note and should be played **evenly** in one beat. When two eighth notes are paired together, a **beam** is used.

beam

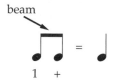

Practice counting the eighth notes like this:

Once you are able to feel the beat divided into two equal parts, count as follows:

Practice clapping and counting the rhythm that appears in *Feelin' Good*. After you have studied the rhythmic and melodic patterns, play it in the key in which it is written. What five-finger pattern is used?

Try playing this piece in various other keys, always starting with the fifth tone of each five-finger pattern.

FEELIN' GOOD

Student

E. M.

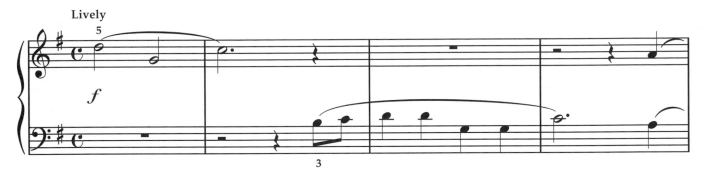

FEELIN' GOOD

Arranged by
Ken Iversen

Accompaniment

After you have studied the rhythmic and melodic patterns of this piece, play *Pagoda* as written and in other keys of your choice. For variety play this piece one octave higher than written.

PAGODA

Student

E.M.

Five-Finger Notation

After you have studied the rhythmic and melodic patterns in *Joyful Dance,* play it in the key of F major. The five-finger pattern follows:

F MAJOR
FIVE-FINGER
PATTERN

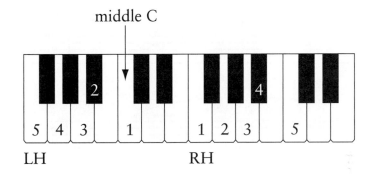

Play the piece in various other keys as well, always starting with the third finger of each hand.

JOYFUL DANCE

Student

E. M.

JOYFUL DANCE

Accompaniment

Arranged by
Ken Iversen

Tie

A **tie** is a curved line connecting two adjacent notes of the *same* pitch. The second note is *not sounded;* instead, it is held for the duration of its value. For example, the tied G below is held for the combined value of both notes, which is four beats in all.

WALTZING

Student   E. M.

WALTZING

Accompaniment

The whole rest (—) is used to indicate a full measure of silence in any meter, not just in ⁴⁄₄. In *Morning Has Broken* the value of the whole rest is three beats.

MORNING HAS BROKEN

Student

Gaelic
Arranged by E.M.

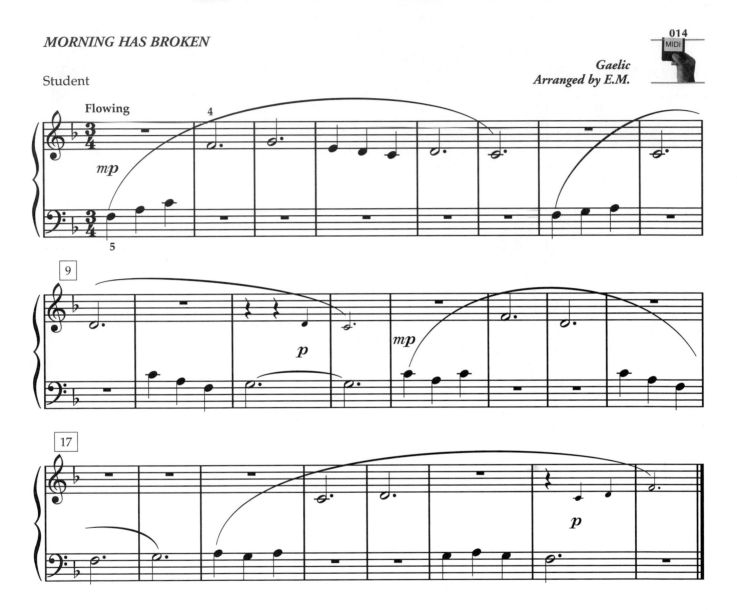

MORNING HAS BROKEN

Accompaniment

Gaelic
Arranged by E.M.

8va

Five-Finger Notation

Play *Little River* and *For the Beauty of the Earth* in the key of D, which has two sharps in the key signature. The five-finger pattern of D is shown below:

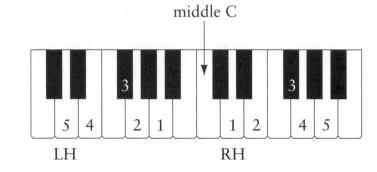

D Major
Five-Finger
Pattern

Ritardando (rit.)

Ritardando is a term indicating a gradual slowing of the tempo.

First play this piece as written. Then move both hands to the next D pattern one octave higher.

LITTLE RIVER

Student

German Folk Song

■ Transpose to F Major

LITTLE RIVER

Accompaniment

FOR THE BEAUTY OF THE EARTH

Conrad Kocher
Arranged by E.M.

FOR THE BEAUTY OF THE EARTH

Conrad Kocher
Arranged by E.M.

Accompaniment

DRONE BASS

A **drone bass** is an accompaniment that repeatedly uses the interval of a fifth. It is effective with many tunes. To construct a drone bass, take the lowest tone (tonic) and the highest tone of the five-finger pattern you are working in and sound them together with the left hand on the first beat of each measure, or as indicated in the music.

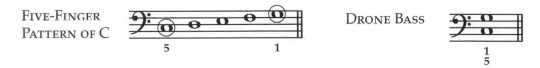

FIVE-FINGER PATTERN OF C   DRONE BASS

Highlander Tune and *French Canadian Round* use a drone bass accompaniment.

017
MIDI

HIGHLANDER TUNE

Student   *E.M.*

■ Transpose to G major

Ensemble Parts
Piano 1*

---

*The piano 1 part may also be played one octave higher than written.

Piano 2

Piano 3

Round

A **round** is a melody that is played with each new person (or group) starting the melody at specific times indicated.

French Canadian Round uses a drone bass in the left hand using the first and fifth tones of the five-finger pattern in F.

After you have studied and played this piece as written, play it as a round. The Piano 1 group begins and then the Piano 2 group will start when the first group has reached measure 3. This piece can be repeated as many times as desired.

FRENCH CANADIAN ROUND

Student

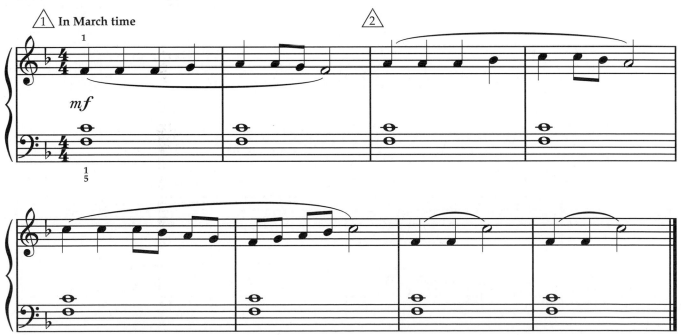

■ Transpose to D major

REPERTOIRE

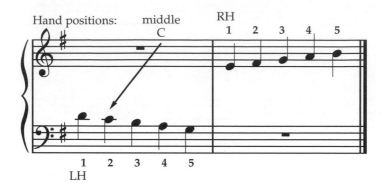

SURFING

Student

Lee Evans

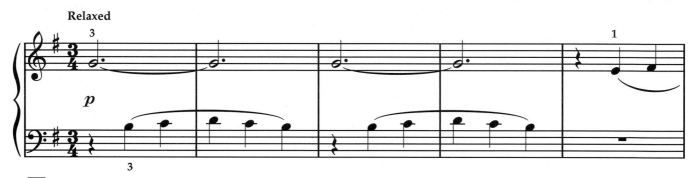

SURFING

Accompaniment

IMPROVISATION

Pentatonic Improvisation

Using the **pentatonic scale** (a five-tone scale built on the black keys only) is an excellent way to begin improvising because there will be no wrong notes! The songs listed below can be played with just the five black keys. Challenge yourself to figure out these tunes. (Note: the starting pitch is given in parentheses.)

Familiar Tunes to Play Using the Pentatonic Scale
   Amazing Grace (D♭)
   Arkansas Traveler (G♭)
   Auld Lang Syne (D♭)
   I'd Like to Teach the World to Sing (E♭)
   Nobody Knows the Trouble I've Seen (B♭)
   Swing Low, Sweet Chariot (B♭)
   Wayfaring Stranger (E♭)

Now, begin making up your own melodies, using black keys only, to the following accompaniments that are to be played by the instructor.

Instructor's Part

Improvising Melodies Using the Pentatonic Scale
Begin and end your melody on G♭.

PENTATONIC ACCOMPANIMENTS

Ken Iversen

Begin and end your melody on E♭.

Begin and end your melody on E♭.

Dorian Mode Improvisation

Now that you have worked with the black keys, try improvising melodies using only the white keys in the same manner. Again, all sounds will blend! The pattern of whole steps and half steps formed by the white keys from D to D is the scale of the **Dorian mode.**

Improvising Melodies Using the Dorian Mode

Begin and end your melody on D.

DORIAN ACCOMPANIMENT

Ken Iversen

12-Bar Blues Improvisation

Using the Pentatonic Scale

The **12-bar blues** form is so called because it always consists of twelve four-beat measures. Playing the black keys E♭, A♭, and B♭ with your left hand, as illustrated below, begin *Start of the Blues.* Do not stop or slow down when you change notes—keep the beat moving!

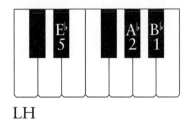

LH

START OF THE BLUES

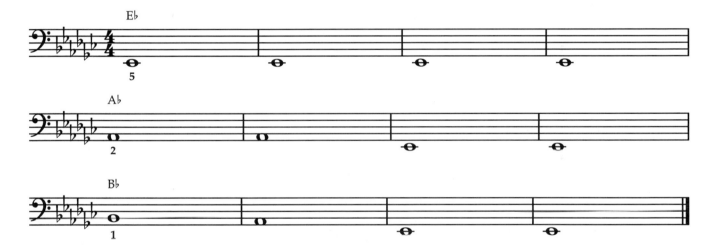

As soon as you have mastered this left-hand pattern, add the right hand and begin improvising on the black keys. Remember that it is impossible to play a wrong note! Let your right hand move freely on the black keys and *be sure to keep the beat moving.* If at first you have difficulty working with both hands, play various black-key patterns in quarter notes with the right hand until you feel comfortable enough to experiment with rhythmic patterns using other note values. Several rhythmic patterns are shown next to get you started. Try them and then add some of your own.

Using Dorian Mode

Following the same procedure described in the preceding paragraph, practice improvising blues in the Dorian mode to *Movin' on the White Key Blues*. Here is the left-hand pattern:

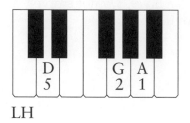

LH

MOVIN' ON THE WHITE KEY BLUES

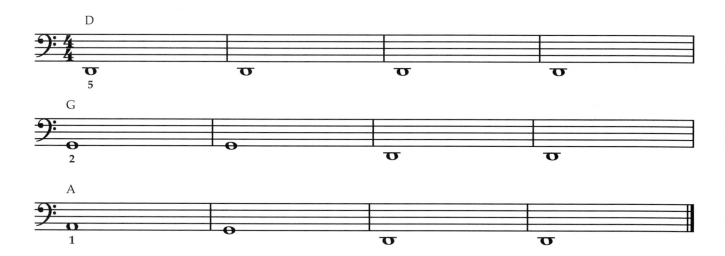

Major Five-Finger Pattern Improvisation

Improvise major five-finger pattern melodies using the rhythm patterns given on this page.

1. Improvise a melody using the right hand first, then the left hand, then with both hands. Be sure to end each example on the tonic. Occasional pitches have been provided to give you some help with the melody.
2. Improvise your own five-finger pattern melodies using other rhythms discussed in this unit.
3. Harmonize the improvised five-finger pattern melodies, using the rhythm patterns given. Then harmonize your own five-finger pattern melodies with new rhythms, using a drone-bass accompaniment.

1. Key of G

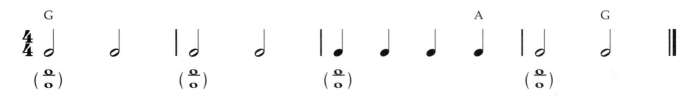

2.

3. Key of F

4.

5. Key of G♭

Improvisation with New Notations and Techniques

Some twentieth-century music uses **clusters**, which are sounds constructed of bunched seconds, such as all the tones of a five-finger pattern played simultaneously. Although clusters can be notated traditionally, a new notation consisting of stemmed, block-like figures is frequently used. The pitch of a cluster is determined by its position on the staff, as shown below:

blocked clusters
(played simultaneously)

broken clusters
(the notes are played in the direction of the arrow)

Sometimes composers use nonstandard sounds in their music and invent notations to suit their own purpose. For instance, the tapping of a spoon on a glass might be notated as ⌐ ⌐ or ⌐ ⌐, or a gradually slowing tempo, as ♩ ♩ ♩ ♩ ♩ ♩. Frequently, the composer will simply give verbal instructions within a specific measure, such as "strike a wooden board," "hum in a high register," and so forth.

Another sound that produces a special effect is the **glissando**, a sweeping sound that is used in both traditional and innovative pieces. This sound is produced by pulling one or more fingernails—usually the nail of the third finger—over the keys. The usual notation is ⌇⌇ *gliss.*

It's Up to You uses the notations we have just discussed. Observe that every measure is in ⁴⁄₄, and should be played in strict time, with no change of tempo. Play individual tones, harmonic intervals, clusters, and other sounds according to the written directions and rhythmic patterns provided. For example: ♩♩ means to play two half notes, while ♩ ♩ ♩ means to play a half-note cluster followed by two quarter-note clusters. Throughout, the exact pitches are up to you!

Following the directions given, improvise using the white keys only the first time you play the piece. Next, improvise with the black keys only. Work with the right or left hand only, then use alternating hands, and finally, use both hands together wherever possible. You might also play this as an improvisational ensemble piece.

IT'S UP TO YOU

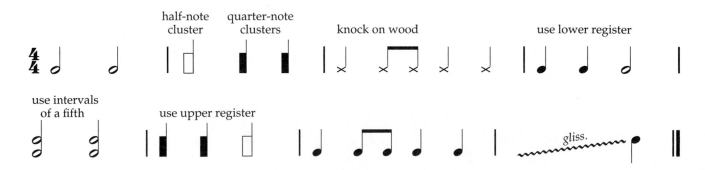

The composers of **aleatoric (chance)** music use the element of chance in creating a piece. For example, pitches and intervals may be determined by the numbers obtained from rolled dice. Aleatoric music also allows the performer to improvise freely or to select an arbitrary arrangement of patterns, as in *Taking a Chance.*

Play the numbered segments of *Taking a Chance* in any order you like. Remember to keep the beat moving! Improvise your own aleatoric segment in the two-measure blank (number 8). Use any of the contemporary techniques discussed so far.

Each time you play *Taking a Chance* it will sound like a different piece.

TAKING A CHANCE

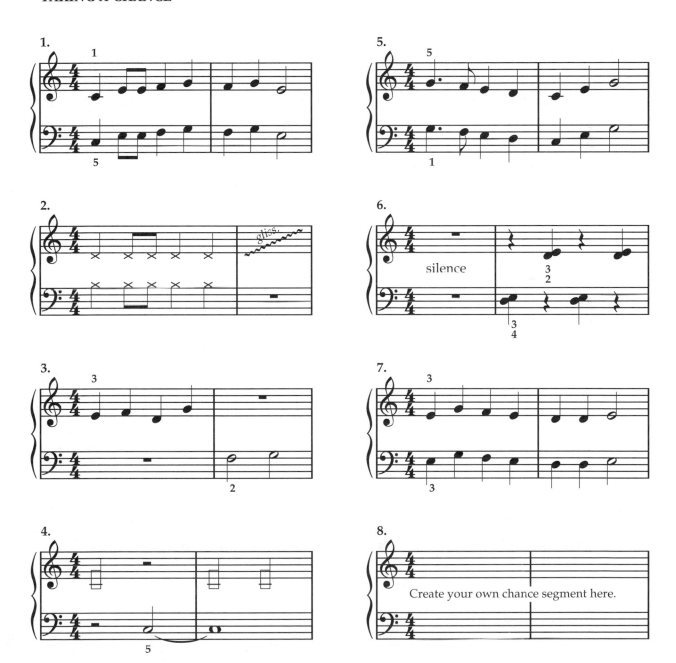

HARMONIZATION

Harmonize the following melodies using harmonic intervals of a fifth on the first beat of each measure marked with a short line (___). Use the notated example in the first measure as your guide. Write in the fifth for each measure where it is required. Notice that sometimes the left hand will be playing the fifth and at other times the right hand will be playing the fifth.

3.

4.

SIGHTREADING STUDIES

PRACTICE DIRECTIONS

For each of the following exercises, review the practice directions discussed earlier on page 26.

1. Clap the rhythm while counting the beat aloud before playing the exercise.
2. Place your hand in the correct five-finger position. Do not look down at the keys.
3. Study the interval patterns of the melody.
4. Do an abstract of the exercise. As you do so, say or sing aloud the letter names of the notes.
5. Play and count aloud.
6. Next, play and sing aloud the letter names of the notes. Do not stop or hesitate to find the notes. Remember to keep the beat moving!

Adding Drone-Bass Accompaniments

After you have completed the previous practice directions, transpose exercises of your choice to various other keys studied so far.

Then, harmonize Exercises 1 through 13 with a drone-bass accompaniment by taking the tonic and the interval of a fifth in the five-finger pattern you are working in and playing them together on the first beat of each measure.

Treble Clef Melodies for the Right Hand

1. Key of C

2.

3. Key of G

4. Key of F

5. Key of D

Bass Clef Melodies for the Left Hand

6. Key of C

7. Key of G

8. Key of F

9. Key of D

Five-Finger Pattern Studies in Major Keys
Determine what key each of the following examples is written in.

10.

11.

12.

With energy

13.

Lightly

TECHNICAL STUDIES

Practice examples 1, 2, and 3 in the various keys studied so far.

1. Parallel motion

2. Contrary motion

3. Melodic seconds

Play this pattern as written, starting on C. Using only white keys, shift the same pattern upward as you begin on D. Continue in new locations until the LH reaches middle C. Then work your way down an octave.

4.

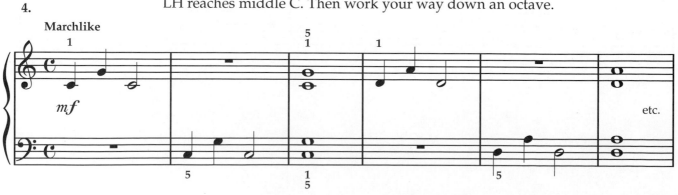

RHYTHMIC STUDIES

Tap and count the following rhythmic patterns with both hands as given. When clapping these patterns, start with a comfortable speed for the quarter pulse. Repeat the pattern at a slower tempo and then at a faster tempo. In addition, incorporate dynamic contrasts (f, p, mf, mp).

Then tap them out using various finger-number combinations. For example, Exercise 1 might be tapped out in the following manner:

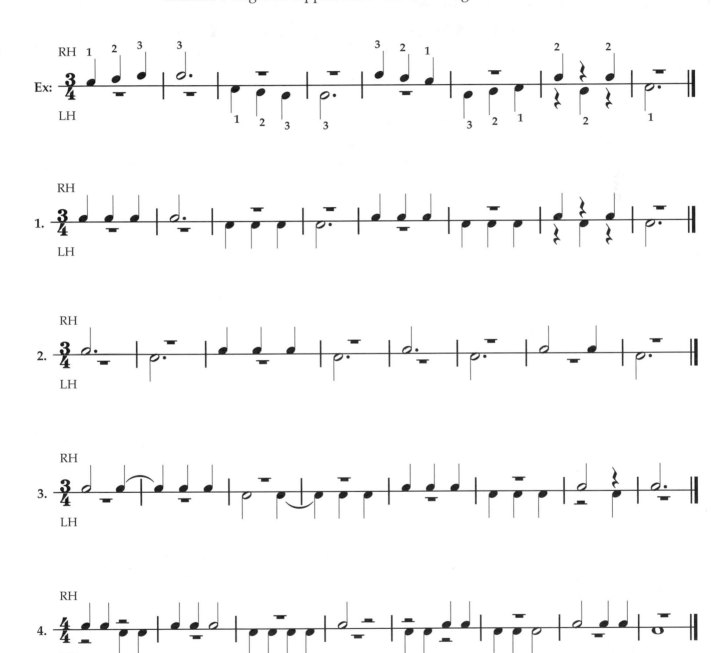

5.

6.
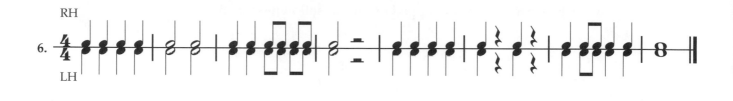

7.

8.

9.

10.

ENSEMBLE PIECES

Student-Teacher Duets

𝄆 𝄇 The **repeat bar** indicates that the piece should be repeated from the beginning or from wherever there is another repeat bar.

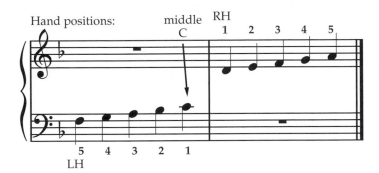

Hand positions:

LAND OF THE SILVER BIRCH

Canadian

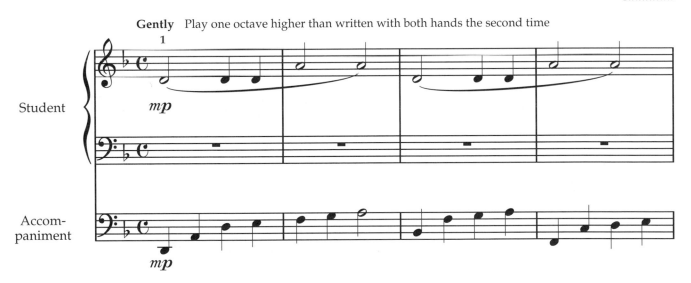

Gently   Play one octave higher than written with both hands the second time

Student

mp

Accom-paniment

mp

SUMMER BREEZES*

E. M.

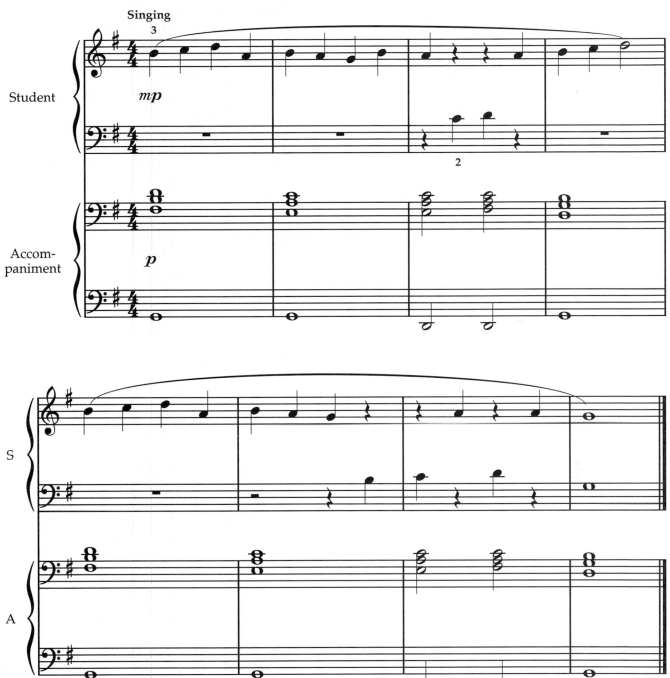

* The student part may be played one octave higher than written if so desired.

Da Capo al Fine

Da Capo al Fine means to return to the beginning of the piece and play to the measure where the word **Fine** (It., "end") appears.

LYRIC PIECE from The Children's Musical Friend, *Op. 87, No. 27*

Heinrich Wohlfahrt
(1797–1883)

Student

LYRIC PIECE *from* The Children's Musical Friend, *Op. 87, No. 27*

Heinrich Wohlfahrt
(1797–1883)

Accompaniment

Student Duets

ROCK FOR TWO

E.M.

FOLK SONG

French

TAG ALONG

E. M.

BLACK AND WHITE

E. M.

Piano 1: White-key cluster—use C-D-E played together.
Piano 2: Black-key cluster—use G♭-A♭-B♭ played together.

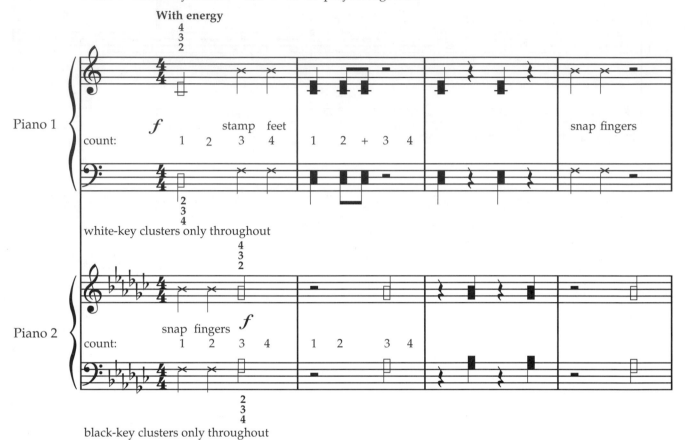

white-key clusters only throughout

black-key clusters only throughout

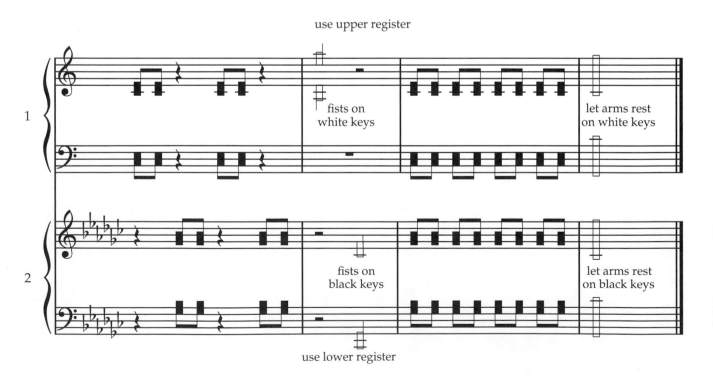

MORNING*

E. M.

* Two parts can be played at one piano if so desired.

WHISTLE DAUGHTER*

American

* Each part may be played in a higher or lower octave.

NAME   _____

DATE   _____

SCORE   _____

Short Answer

1. Write out the enharmonic names of the following pitches:

    1. G♭ _____   3. E♭ _____   5. C♭ _____

    2. C♯ _____   4. B♯ _____

2. Analyze the following intervals given. Indicate whether each interval is *harmonic* or *melodic* and then give the size of the interval.

____ ____   ____ ____   ____ ____   ____ ____   ____ ____

3. Name the checked pitches:

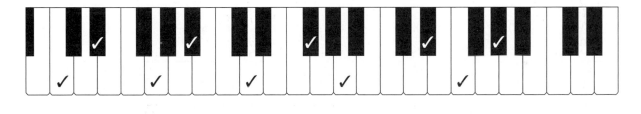

____ ____ ____   ____ ____ ____   ____ ____ ____   ____ ____

4. Write out the letter names for the following major five-finger patterns:

    1. G Major ___ ___ ___ ___ ___   4. F Major ___ ___ ___ ___ ___

    2. D Major ___ ___ ___ ___ ___   5. G♭ Major ___ ___ ___ ___ ___

    3. A Major ___ ___ ___ ___ ___

5. Build half steps upward from the note names given:

    1. E to _____   3. E♭ to _____   5. C to _____

    2. F♯ to _____   4. B to _____

6. Build whole steps up from the note names given:

    1. C to _____   3. E♭ to _____   5. E to _____

    2. F♯ to _____   4. B to _____

Construction

7. Create and write out 4 measures of rhythm for the following time signatures:

8. Construct harmonic intervals *up* from the notes given; next, write the letter names on the blanks below.

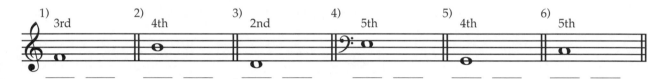

9. Construct harmonic intervals *down* from the notes given; next, write the letter names on the blanks below.

10. Name the following melodic intervals and write the letter names on the blanks below.

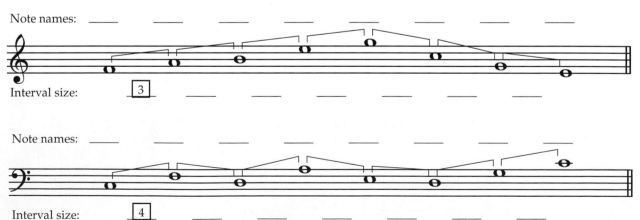

Matching

Write the numbers from Column A to correspond to the given answers in Column B.

COLUMN A	COLUMN B
1. natural sign (♮)	_____ rate of speed
2. interval	_____ common time
3. piano (*p*)	_____ basic pulsation
4. meter	_____ arrangement of note values
5. contrary motion	_____ ▬
6. tempo	_____ the distance from one note to another
7. ritardando	_____ moving in the same direction
8. half rest	_____ a gradual slowing down of the tempo
9. parallel motion	_____ three beats to a measure with the quarter note receiving 1 beat
10. 𝄴	_____ moving in the opposite direction
11. whole rest	_____ smoothly connected
12. cluster (▯)	_____ ▬
13. legato	_____ a group of bunched seconds sounded together at the same time
14. forte (*f*)	_____ raises a pitch one half step
15. sharp (♯)	_____ C to C♯
16. flat (♭)	_____ cancels a sharp or flat
17. rhythm	_____ lowers a pitch one half step
18. mezzo forte (*mf*)	_____ play loud
19. half step	_____ play soft
20. 3/4	_____ play moderately loud

The Five-Finger Pattern

PLAYING IN DIFFERENT REGISTERS

A **register guide**, like the one at the beginning of *Stepping Up in C* (below), will be used in Unit 2 to help you find the starting notes for both hands. It shows the location of middle C, the C an octave higher, and the C an octave lower.

Play the five-finger pattern up the keyboard in C, as shown below. Next, transpose the five-finger pattern to other keys of your choice.

STEPPING UP IN C

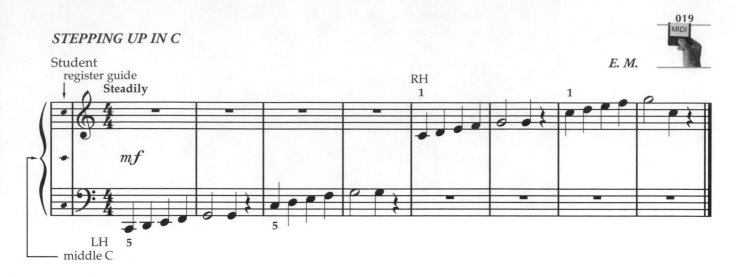

Student

register guide

E. M.

Accompaniment

Now play the five-finger pattern down the keyboard, following the same procedure.

STEPPING DOWN IN C

Student

E. M.

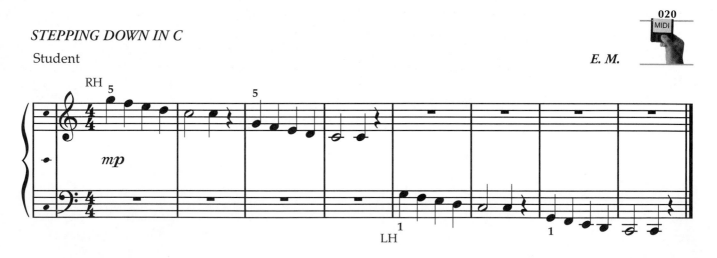

Accompaniment

Practice Strategies

Practice playing the following patterns in the various registers. First play the patterns in the key given and then transpose them to the keys of G and D major.

1.

3.

2.

4.

TEMPO MARKINGS

Tempo, as discussed earlier on page 25, is the rate of movement or speed. **Tempo markings** indicate how fast or slow the music is to be played. Several basic tempo markings that will be used for some of the pieces ahead are given below:

Allegro   fast; lively

Allegretto moderately fast

Moderato   moderately

Andante   at a walking pace; moving along

MORE DYNAMIC MARKINGS

ff fortissimo   very loud

pp pianissimo   very soft

Fermata (⌢)

A **fermata** (⌢) is used to sustain a note longer than the indicated time value.

Breezes Are Blowing is written in **Dorian mode** (as discussed earlier on page 56), which is made up of the pattern of whole steps and half steps formed by the white keys from D to D.

BREEZES ARE BLOWING

Luiseño Indian Rain Chant

 PRACTICE DIRECTIONS

1. Tap the rhythmic patterns of *Melody Study* with both hands.
2. Identify the direction of the melody by calling out (i.e., C-Up-Up-Up-Down-Down-Down, etc.) while tapping the rhythm patterns.
3. Play the piece as written.

MELODY STUDY (*No. 1 from* First Term at the Piano)

Béla Bartók (1881–1945)

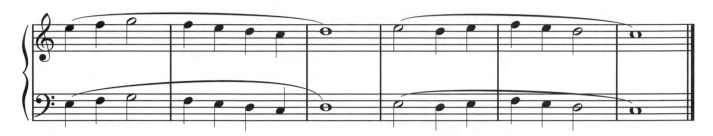

■ Transpose to other keys of your choice

The next piece uses the treble clef (𝄞) for both staves to avoid the use of a large number of leger lines. Why is the register guide in this piece different from the one previously used?

PERSIAN SCENE

E. M.

DOTTED QUARTER NOTES

A **dot** placed after a note increases its value by one-half:

A **dotted quarter note** is equal to a quarter note plus an eighth note.

♩. = 1½ beats (♩ plus ♪)

A **dotted quarter rest** (𝄾· or 𝄾𝄾) represents a silence of the same length as the value of a dotted quarter note.

Study the rhythmic pattern ♩. ♪♩ that appears below. Isolate this pattern and count as you clap:

♩.   ♪♩

1 + 2 + 3 +

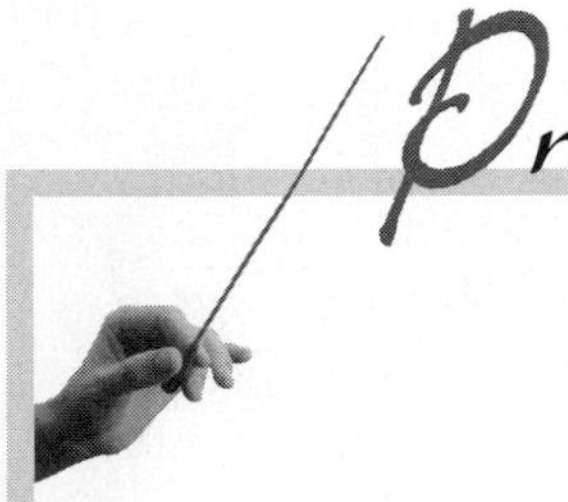

Practice Strategies

Clap or tap the following rhythm patterns which use dotted quarter note patterns.

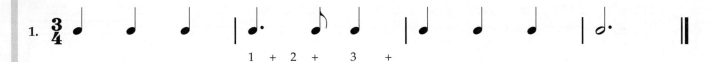

1.

1 + 2 + 3 +

Staccato

Staccato notes are marked with a dot above or below each note. They should be played very crisply and in a detached way. Staccato is the opposite of *legato* (smooth and connected).

Accent sign >

An **accent** (or) is a sign placed under or over a note to indicate stress or emphasis.

After you have studied the dotted quarter note rhythm patterns, play *Fiesta Time*. Note that the bass clef ($9\!:$) is used for both staves.

FIESTA TIME

Student   *E. M.*

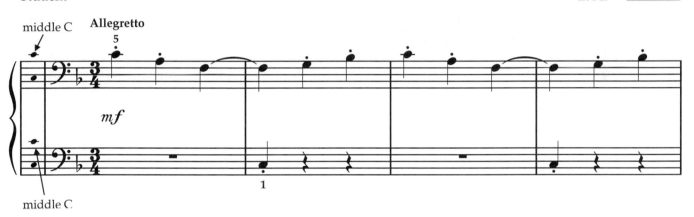

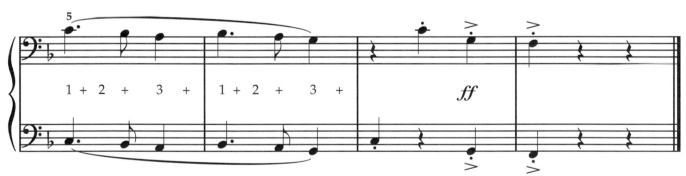

■ Transpose to G major

The B♭ in the key signature establishes the key of F major.

Damper Pedal

The **damper pedal**, which is the pedal to the right, is used to produce the blurred tonal effects needed to obtain the mood of the following piece.

Push the pedal down with the right foot, hold as indicated by the marking, and then release. (See pages 295–297 for a more thorough discussion of the damper pedal.)

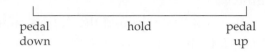

pedal   hold   pedal
down   up

Let *Evening Tide* sound smoothly connected (legato). As you play, do not look at the keys. At the end of each musical phrase, lift your hands at the same time you lift the damper pedal.

Now play the piece an octave higher than written, still alternating hands, and then an octave lower than written. Next, play the piece in different registers with the right hand an octave higher than written and the left hand an octave lower.

The F♯ and C♯ in the key signature establish the key of D major, although C♯ does not appear in this piece.

EVENING TIDE

E. M.

*Cross over left hand to play D.

ACCIDENTALS

Accidentals—sharps (♯), flats (♭), and naturals (♮)—are temporarily added to the body of a piece to alter the pitches. Unlike the sharps or flats in a key signature, these signs are cancelled by the bar lines. A natural sign is frequently used as a reminder in the measure following a temporary sharp or flat, as in the right-hand part of measure 2 in *Monday Blues*.

MONDAY BLUES

Student

E. M.

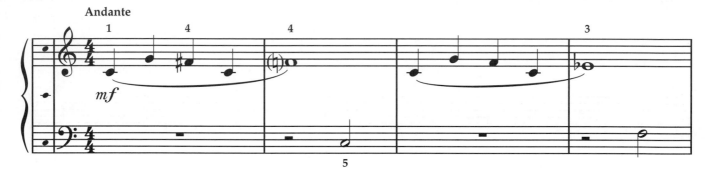

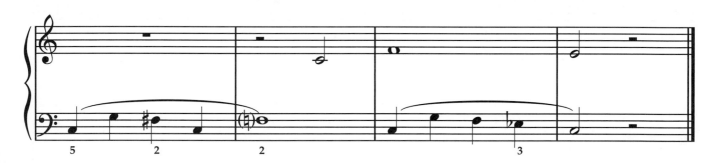

Accompaniment

Below, *Monday Blues* has been transposed to the key of F major, with the left-hand part moved to the lower register. Note the key signature of one flat.

E.M.

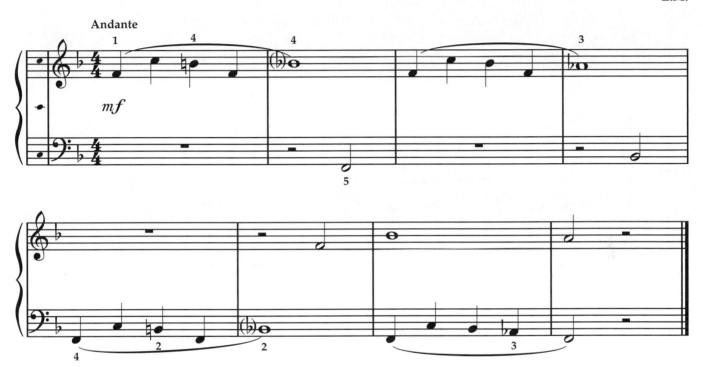

Upbeat and Downbeat

An **upbeat** begins with a beat or beats other than the first in the measure, as opposed to a **downbeat** (the first beat). When a piece begins with an upbeat, the missing beats in the first measure will be found at the end of the piece. Here the upbeat consists of one beat, so the last measure consists of three beats. The first complete measure is identified as measure one $\boxed{1}$.

ON THE TOWN

Student

E. M.

ON THE TOWN

Accompaniment

Ken Iversen

SLURS

A **slur** is a curved line above or below a combination of two or more notes to indicate that these notes are to be played legato. (Do not confuse this marking with the tie or curved phrase line.)

The *first* note of the slur usually *receives more emphasis than the others.*

The *last* note of the slur is usually *played more softly and is released a bit short of its full note value.* Think of two-syllable words like MOV-ing, WALK-ing, CLIMB-ing, to help you develop the dynamic shaping of two-note slurs.

↓ DROP
Weight on the key

↑ LIFT
Weight is released

Drop the wrist to play the first note of a slur.
Lift the wrist to play the last note of a slur.

Practice Strategies

Practice playing two-note slur combinations of the five-finger patterns ascending and descending, first with hands separately and then with hands together. Next, try practicing three-note slur combinations in the same manner.

For example:

Two-Note Slurs

Three-Note Slurs

Practice playing the various slur combinations before playing *Casey Jones*.

CASEY JONES

American

■ Transpose to F major

Sforzando (sfz)

Sforzando (*sfz*) is a dynamic marking that means to play strongly accented.

Remember that accidentals are carried out throughout the measure and cancelled by the bar line or the use of a natural sign (♮).

OLE!

E. M.

PARALLEL MOTION

In **parallel motion**, both hands move in the same direction.

The left hand in the piece *Stompin!* is playing a harmony to the right-hand melody. (See especially measures 5 and 7.)

STOMPIN!

Student

E.M.

■ Transpose to G and F

STOMPIN!

Accompaniment

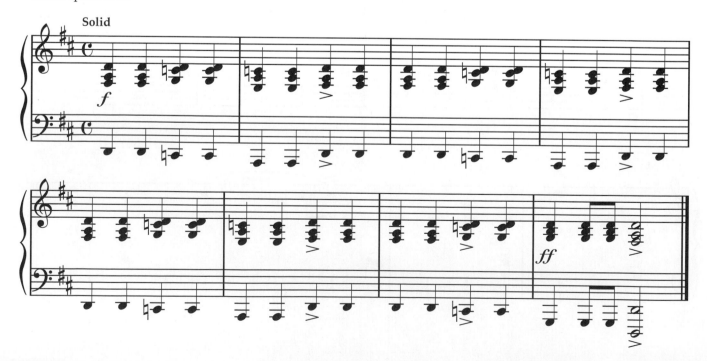

$\frac{6}{8}$ TIME

6 6 beats to the measure

8 the eighth note ($\eighthnote$) receives the beat

The note values in $\frac{6}{8}$ =

Notes			**Rests**	
$\eighthnote$ eighth note	= 1 beat		γ	= 1 beat
$\quarternote$ quarter note	= 2 beats		$\restquarter$	= 2 beats
$\quarternote\cdot$ dotted quarter note	= 3 beats		$\restquarter\cdot$ or γ $\restquarter$	= 3 beats
$\halfnote\cdot$ dotted half note	= 6 beats		$\restquarter\cdot$ $\restquarter\cdot$ or ‒·	= 6 beats

$\frac{6}{8}$ Example:

1 2 3 4 5 6   1 2 3 4 5 6   1 2 3 4 5 6   1 2 3 4 5 6

Practice Strategies

Tap and count aloud the note values for the patterns that follow. Notice that there is an accent (>) on the first and fourth beats in every pattern, except the last measure in example 1.

When a piece in $\frac{6}{8}$ is played quickly, it is easier to count *two* beats to a measure rather than six, with the dotted quarter note receiving one beat. Once you are familiar with these rhythmic patterns, try tapping and counting aloud the patterns with two beats to the measure. Accent the first and second beats in every pattern.

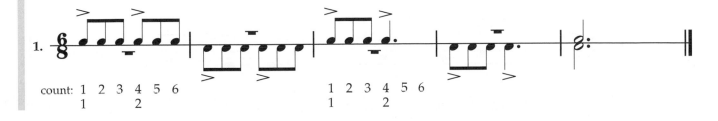

count: 1 2 3 4 5 6   1 2 3 4 5 6
     1   2   1   2

TWO STUDIES IN $\frac{6}{8}$ TIME

Study 1   Moderato

Study 2   Moderato

---

*Play *f* the first time through and *p* the second time.

ALLEGRETTO

Antonio Diabelli (1781–1858)

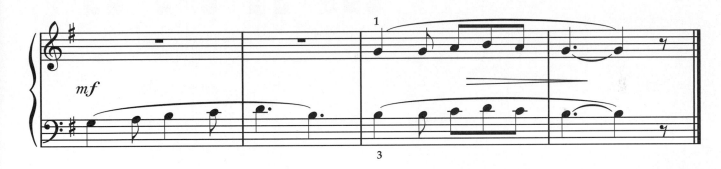

FLEMISH FOLK SONG

Five-Finger Notation

First play the *Warm-Up Study in Gb Major*. Then study the rhythmic and melodic patterns in *The Donkey*. Play this piece in the key of Gb major, the five-finger pattern of which follows:

Gb MAJOR
FIVE-FINGER
PATTERN

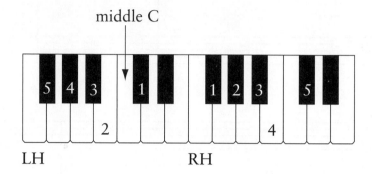

IDENTIFYING FLAT KEY SIGNATURES

Major flat key signatures are identified by taking the name of the next to the last flat (always the second flat to the left).

WARM-UP STUDY IN G♭ MAJOR

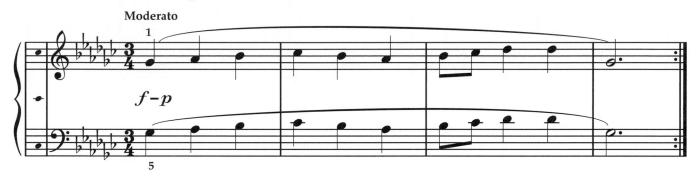

Sequence

A **sequence** is a pattern of tones that is repeated at a higher or lower pitch.

Measures 5–6 of the following piece have the same tonal pattern as measures 1–2, but are played at a higher pitch. The six flats in the key signature establish the key of G♭.

THE DONKEY

Student

American

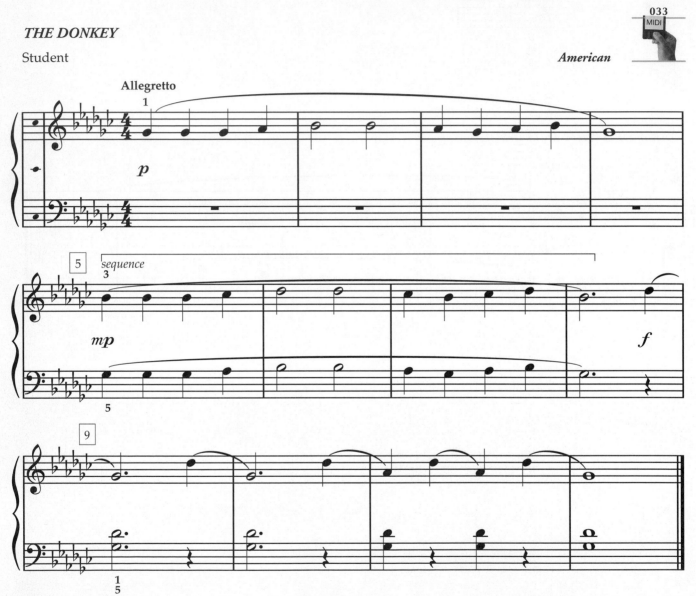

- Play this piece as a round, with each person (or group) starting four measures after the preceding person (or group).

- Transpose to G major. (Just change the key signature to F♯. The actual reading of the notes on the staff will remain the same.)

THE DONKEY

Accompaniment

American

Five-Finger Notation

The key of A major has three sharps in the key signature. Construct the five-finger pattern of A, as shown below:

A MAJOR
FIVE-FINGER
PATTERN

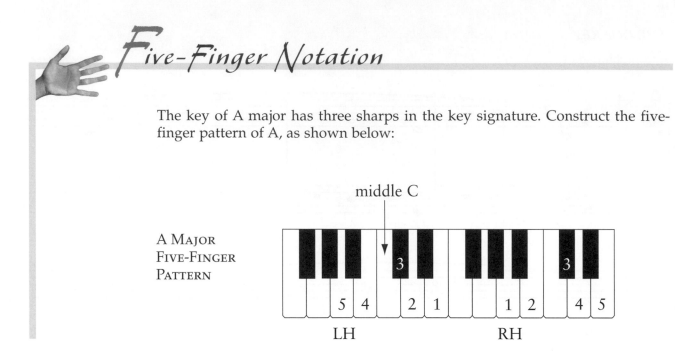

Study the melodic and rhythmic patterns before playing *Two Études in A Major.* An *étude* is a technical study.

TWO ÉTUDES IN A MAJOR

Study 1   Allegretto

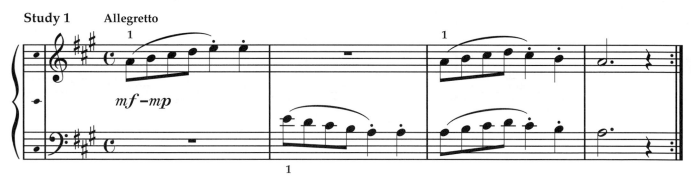

Study 2   Andante

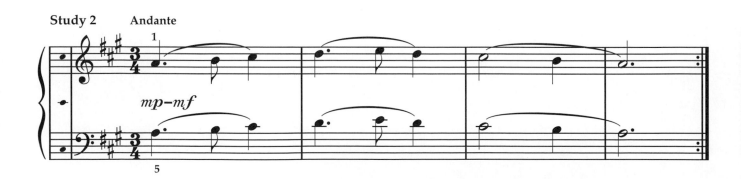

CHANGE OF DYNAMICS

crescendo (cresc.) or <img_1> means to gradually play louder

diminuendo (*dim.*) or means to gradually play softer

A Sonata Theme uses seconds, fifths, and parallel motion to harmonize the melody.

A SONATA THEME

Wolfgang Amadeus Mozart (1756–1791)

Five-Finger Notation

Reading Study in E Major, Follow Me, and *Wheels* are in the key of E major, which has four sharps in the key signature. Here is the five-finger pattern of E.

E Major
Five-Finger
Pattern

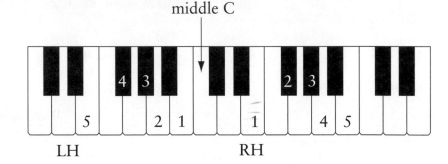

READING STUDY IN E MAJOR

FOLLOW ME

Piano 1

E. M.

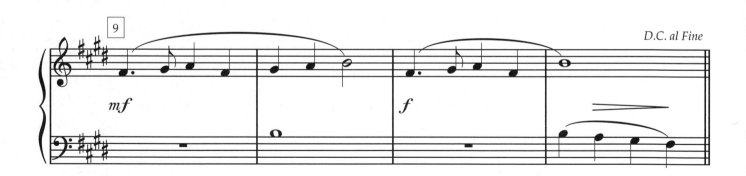

FOLLOW ME

Piano 2

FOLLOW ME

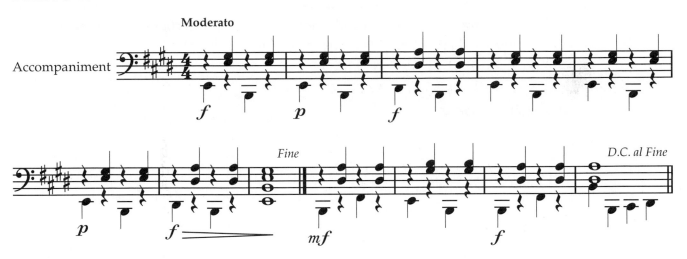

Accompaniment

Moderato

WHEELS

E. M.

Allegro

CONTRARY MOTION

In **contrary motion** the hands move in opposite directions. Study the direction of the note patterns in the *Studies in Contrary Motion*.

STUDIES IN CONTRARY MOTION

Study 1 **Andante**

Study 2 **Allegretto**

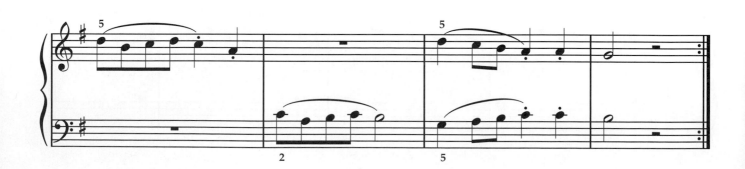

Calypso Beat and *Mysterious Corridors* use contrary motion.

8va----------┐

When **8ᵛᵃ** appears *above* a note or chord, play it an octave higher than written.

    When the octave sign **8ᵛᵃ** appears *below* a note or chord, play it an octave lower than written.

MYSTERIOUS CORRIDORS

Student

E. M.

MYSTERIOUS CORRIDORS

Accompaniment

MAJOR TRIADS

A **triad** consists of three tones—the **root,** so called because it is the tone on which the triad is constructed; the *third;* and the *fifth.* A triad is also called a **chord.**

   Major triads are formed by taking the first (root), third, and fifth tones of the major five-finger patterns and sounding them together.

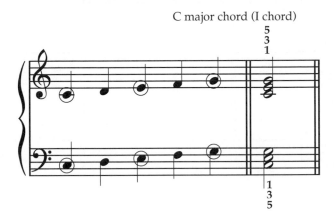

FIVE-FINGER STUDIES AND TRIADS IN MAJOR

Practice the following major five-finger patterns and the major triads formed from them in the keys shown. You will be moving up in half steps, or *chromatically,* as you start each five-finger pattern followed by the major triad. Remember to use the whole step, whole step, half step, whole step formula in building each of the major five-finger patterns.

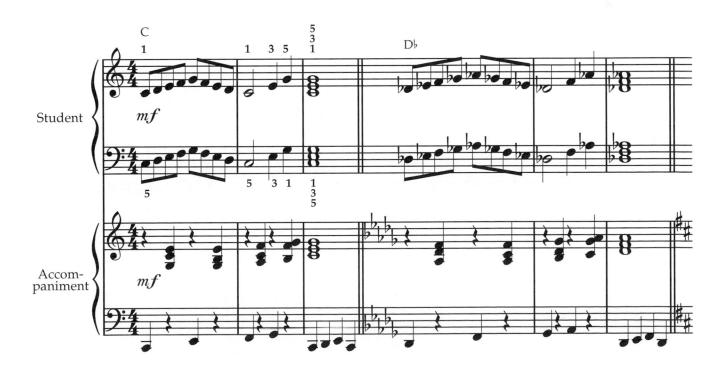

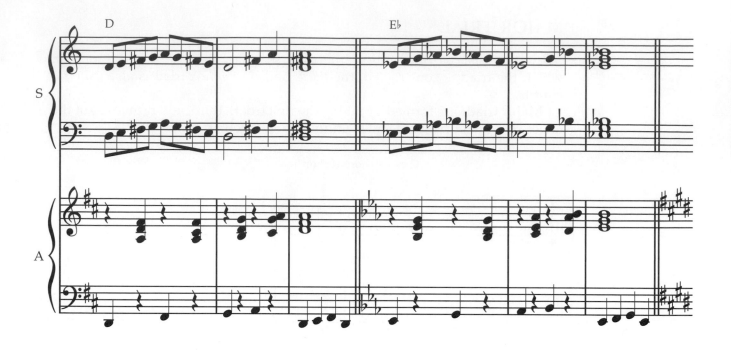

Major Triad Groups

Another way of learning the major triads and their spellings is to categorize them in like groups as follows.

The chord group of C, F, and G triads *uses only the white keys.*

C

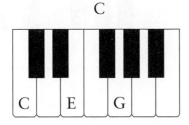

F

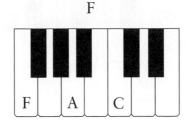

G

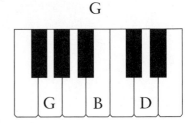

Practice this three-chord grouping and the others below, first with the right hand, then with the left, and then with both hands. Learn to develop a "feel" for each chord and the movement from one chord to the next. Look for tones that repeat—common tones—to help you when moving from one chord to another.

The chord group of D, E, and A *uses only white keys in the open fifth with the third a sharped black key.*

D

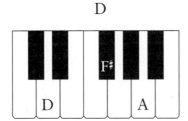

E

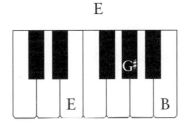

A

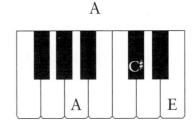

The chord group of D♭ (C♯), E♭, and A♭ *uses only black keys in the open fifth with the third a white key.*

D♭

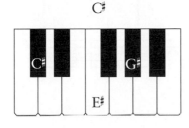

E♭

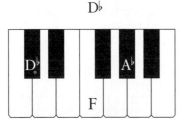

A♭

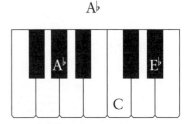

C♯

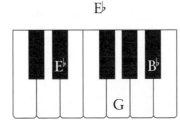

The G♭ (F♯) triad *uses only black keys.*

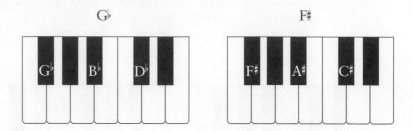

The B and B♭ major triads use the following arrangements:

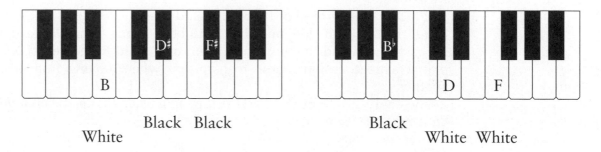

Practice Strategies

Triads without their thirds are called **open fifths.** Playing open fifths in half-step progressions is good preparation for playing major and later the minor triads. Using both hands, construct open fifths starting on C and play them both upward and downward as illustrated next.

Notice that if the lower tone of the fifth is a white key, the upper tone will also be a white key. If the lower tone is black, the upper tone will also be black. The only two exceptions are the fifths B♭-F (black-white) and B-F♯ (white-black).

Open Fifths

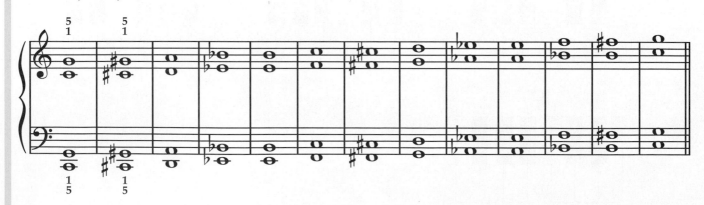

Play the following major triads with each hand separately, then with both hands, first upward, then downward.

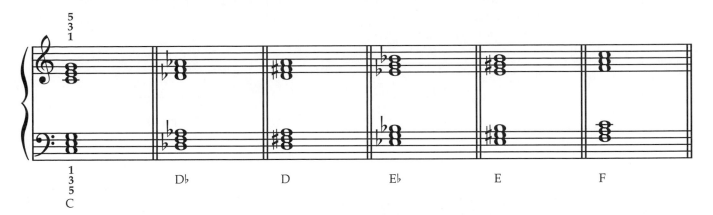

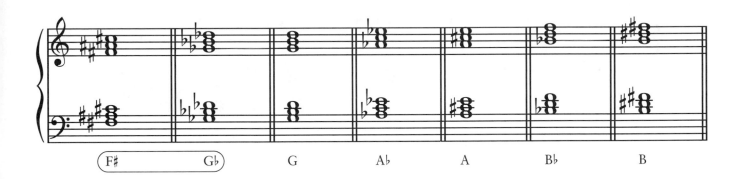

Practice playing major triads, one at a time, in various registers, as well. For example:

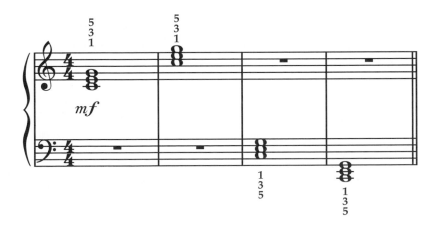

THE MINOR FIVE-FINGER PATTERN

The **minor five-finger pattern** (also called a **minor pentachord** or **minor pentascale**) can be constructed on any of the twelve tones. The minor five-finger pattern is constructed as follows:

Tonic: → 1   2   3   4   5

WHOLE STEP   HALF STEP   WHOLE STEP   WHOLE STEP

Five-Finger Notation

Here is the five-finger pattern in D minor:

D MINOR
FIVE-FINGER
PATTERN

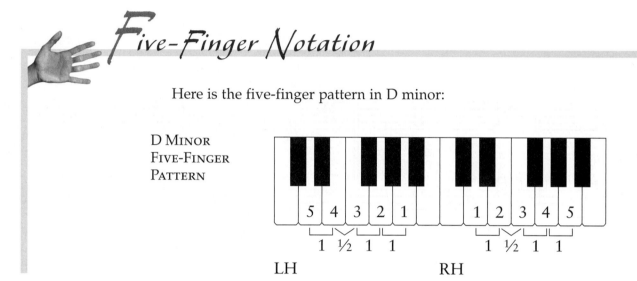

An easy way to play the minor five-finger pattern is to begin with the major five-finger pattern and lower the third tone one half step:

Practice Strategies

Play other five-finger melodies such as *Love Somebody* (page 37) and *Ode to Joy* (page 17) in minor by lowering the third tone one half step. Can you hear the difference between major and minor?

Play measures 1, 2, 4, 5, and 6 of *Erie Canal* staccato (detached) where shown and the rest of the piece legato (smooth and connected).

ERIE CANAL

W. Allen

Play *Zum Gali Gali* in E minor.

ZUM GALI GALI

Israeli

Imitation and Inversion

Imitation is the repetition of a musical idea in another voice. In **inversion,** a musical idea is presented in contrary motion to its original form.

Play *Imitation and Inversion* also as a duet with each player doubling the treble or bass clef with both hands.

IMITATION AND INVERSION

Béla Bartók
(1881–1945)

MINOR TRIADS

Minor triads are formed by taking the major triad and lowering the third (the middle note) one half step.

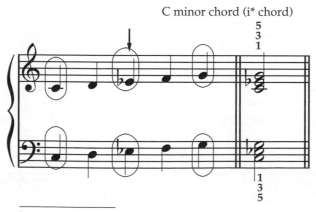

*The small roman numeral denotes a minor chord.

FIVE-FINGER STUDIES AND TRIADS IN MAJOR AND MINOR

Practice all major and minor five-finger patterns along with all major and minor triads as shown.

Arranged by Ken Iversen

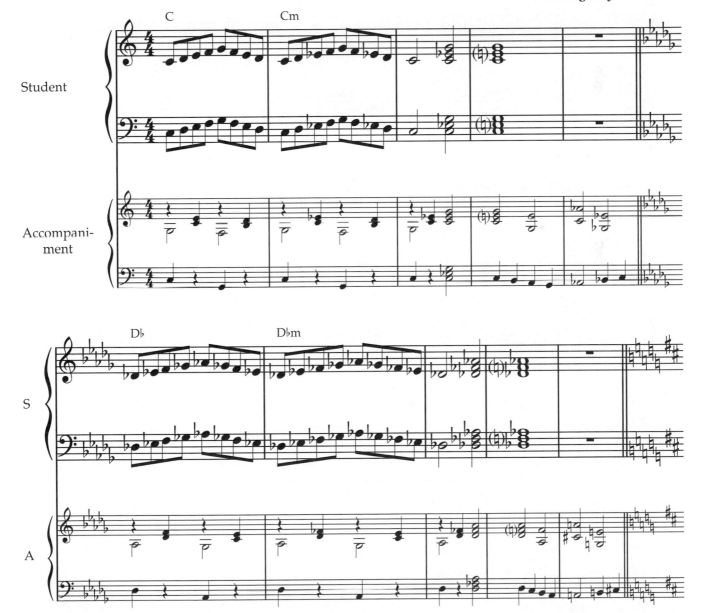

Student

Accompani-
ment

S

A

* The small "m" stands for minor.

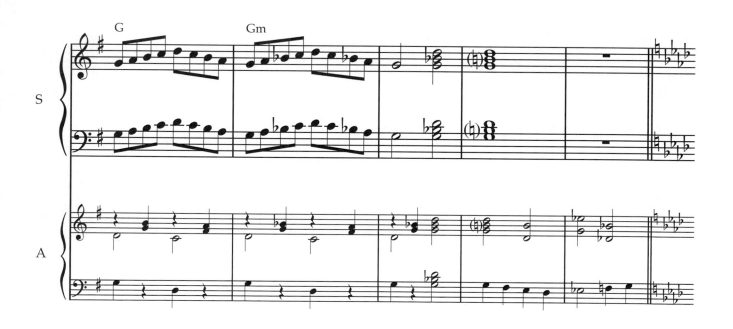

Practice Strategies

Play the major-minor-major progression below chromatically upward and downward starting with C. Practice playing these chords in various registers.

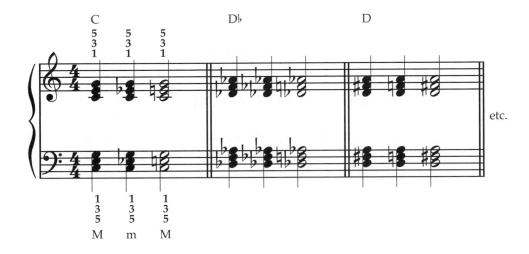

Next, play the minor triads with each hand separately, then with both hands. Practice playing minor triads, one at a time, in various registers, as well. The * denotes a double flat, which lowers a tone two half steps, or the equivalent of one whole step.

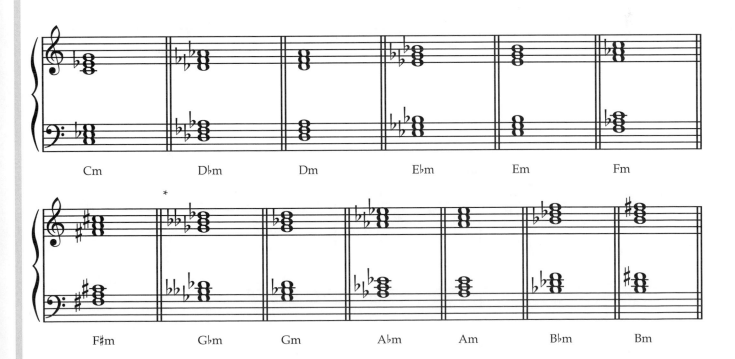

MORE TEMPO MARKINGS

Vivace   quickly; spirited

Andantino somewhat faster than Andante

Lento   slow

Largo   slow; broad

a tempo

a tempo means return to the original tempo

PIECES USING MAJOR AND MINOR TRIADS

Aaron's Song uses open fifths and major and minor triads melodically throughout. First study the triads, assigning the proper letter names (GM, Em, etc.) to the triads that appear in the preparatory exercise below. Next, identify and block (play as a chord or open fifth) the triad patterns used every two measures in the piece. Finally, play the piece as written.

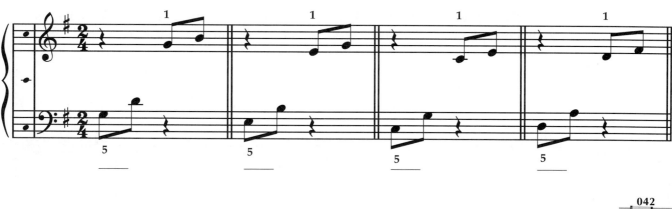

AARON'S SONG

Student

Aaron Peirick

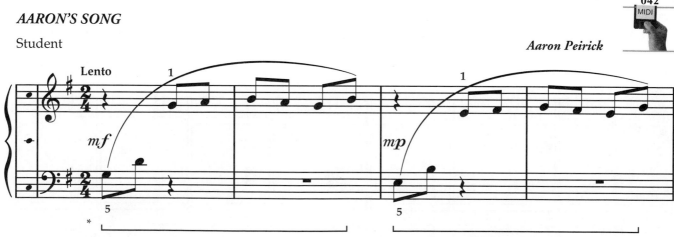

---

* The use of the damper pedal is optional throughout.

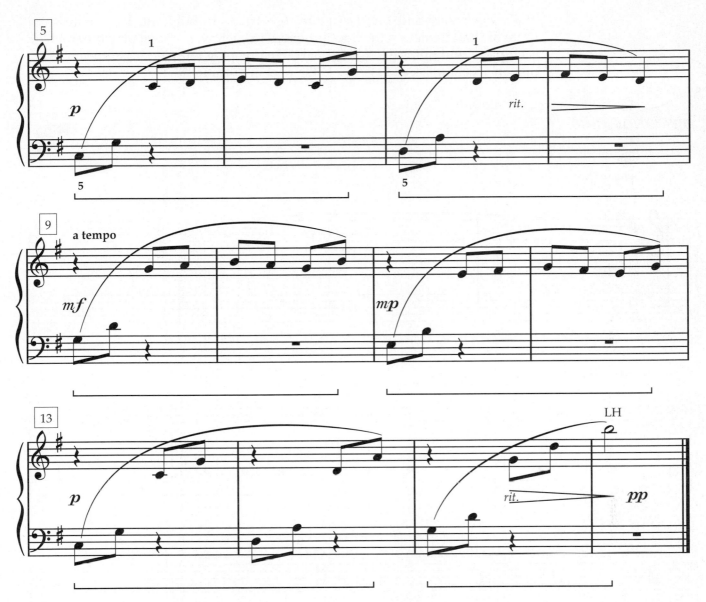

The accompaniment may be played one octave higher than written. The accompaniment can also be played by another instrument or group of instruments, or sung.

Accompaniment

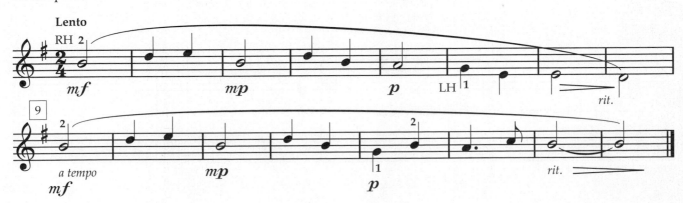

Pyramids Afar and *Mostly Upward* use triads throughout. First, name and write in triad names on the lines provided in each piece. Then play the triads in each piece without the left-hand part. Finally, play the pieces as written. Note that an accent mark can also look like ∧ as in measure 7.

PYRAMIDS AFAR

E. M.

MOSTLY UPWARD

E. M.

THE DOMINANT SEVENTH CHORD

The **V⁷** or **dominant seventh chord** is constructed by building a major triad on the *fifth* degree (tone) of the five-finger pattern in all keys and then adding a minor third.

Five-Finger Notation

FIVE-FINGER PATTERN IN C

V⁷ (Root Position)

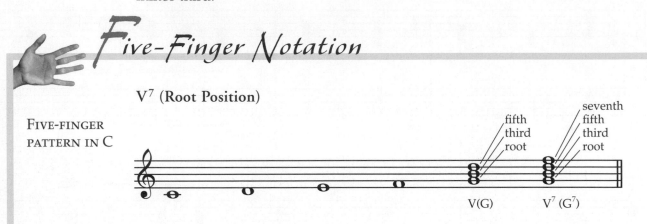

The *V* chord has a root, third, and fifth; the *V⁷* chord has a root, third, fifth, and seventh.

The roman numeral V represents the fifth degree, the root on which the triad is constructed. The arabic numeral 7, to the right of the V, represents the interval of a seventh between the root and the highest tone of the chord. Since the root is used as the lowest tone of the chord, we say that the chord is in **root position.**

Root position

The V⁷ chord also derives its letter name from its root. Thus, in the key of C, as above, the V⁷ chord is called a G⁷ chord; in the key of G, V⁷ is called D⁷; and in D, V⁷ is called A⁷.

V⁶₅ Inversion

First inversion

An easier way to play the V⁷ chord is to rearrange, or **invert,** the chord so that a tone other than the root is used as the lowest tone. When the third of the chord is used as the lowest tone, we say that the chord is in **first inversion*** and we call it **V⁶₅**. Note that the root of the chord now appears as the top tone and the rest of the tones have been inverted:

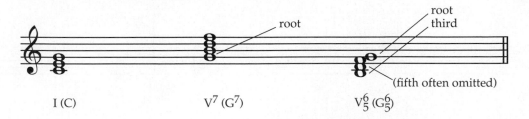

---

* Chords and their inversions are discussed further on pages 317–322.

The numbers represent the intervals formed between the lowest tone and the ones above. In V_5^6 in C, the 6 represents the sixth from B to G, and the 5 represents the fifth from B to F:

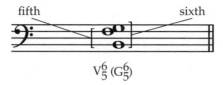

$V_5^6 (G_5^6)$

Note that V_5^6 forms its letter name (G_5^6 above) from the fifth degree, the root, just as V^7 does.

The **V_5^6 chord** for all keys is constructed by sounding the *4th* and *5th* tones of the five-finger pattern together with the tone *a half step down* from the first tone (or *tonic*).

Five-Finger Notation

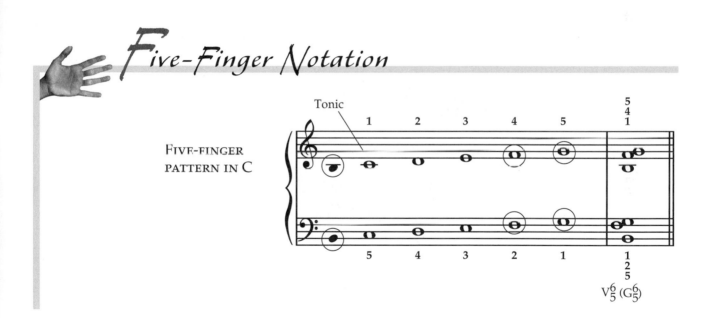

FIVE-FINGER PATTERN IN C

An easy way to move from the I (tonic) chord to the V_5^6 chord in any given key is to remember the following steps:

1. The *top* note remains *the same*.
2. The *middle* note moves *up* a *half step*.
3. The *bottom* note moves *down* a *half step*.

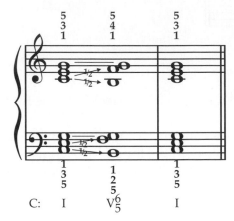

C: I V_5^6 I

When playing combinations of I and V_5^6, remember that the same V_5^6 chord is used in both major and minor, as illustrated below:

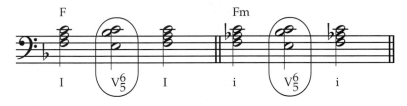

I V_5^6 I   i V_5^6 i

Playing the V_5^6 instead of the V^7 in root position at this point allows more ease in playing the chord progressions involving dominant seventh chords.

Practice Strategies

I–V_5^6–I Chord Progressions

1. Practice playing I and V_5^6 chords with the left hand in major and minor in all keys, as shown.
2. Give the root (or letter name) of each chord as you play it.
3. Remember not to look at the keys.
4. Try to develop a feel for the I–V_5^6–I progression and anticipate the changing of chords.

1.

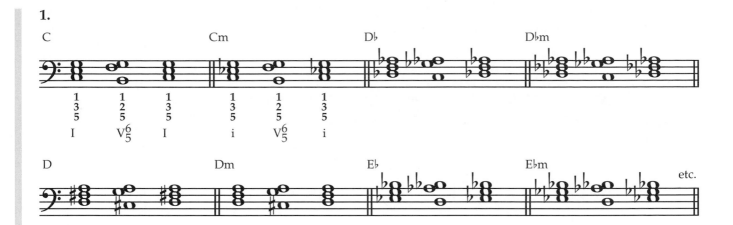

Another way of practicing the I–V$_5^6$–I chord progression is to play the chords with the right hand while the left hand plays the root (or letter name) of each chord as shown below:

2.

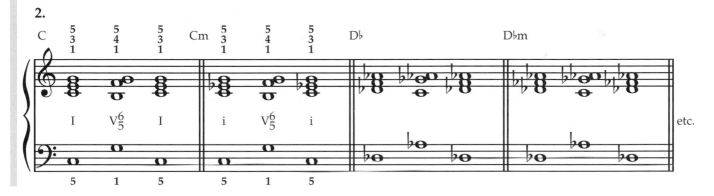

BLOCK-CHORD ACCOMPANIMENT WITH I AND V$_5^6$

PRACTICE DIRECTIONS

1. Identify the key of each of the following pieces by checking the key signature. In addition, look at the lowest note at the end of the piece; it will usually be the tonic, or key note.
2. Study the rhythmic and melodic patterns of each piece, then play the I–V$_5^6$–I progression several times before trying two hands together.
3. Transpose these pieces to other keys.
4. Try playing these pieces in selected minor keys of your choice.

    To play the five-finger pattern in minor, remember to *lower the third tone* of the major five-finger pattern *one half step.* Then take the major I chord and make it minor by *lowering the third (or middle tone) one half step,* as well.

AUSTRIAN FOLK SONG

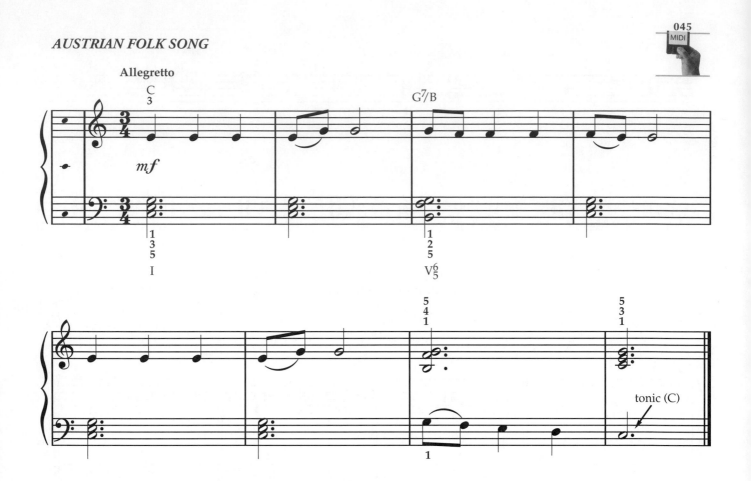

MUSIC CHORD SYMBOLS

Music chord symbols are often given as follows:

G^7 = chord name   the letter *before the slash* indicates the chord being played

/B = bottom note   the bottom letter appearing *after the slash* indicates the lowest note

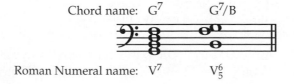

Chord name: G^7 G^7/B

Roman Numeral name: V^7 V^6_5

BELLS OF LONDON

* Gently roll the chords as marked.

CHILEAN FOLK SONG

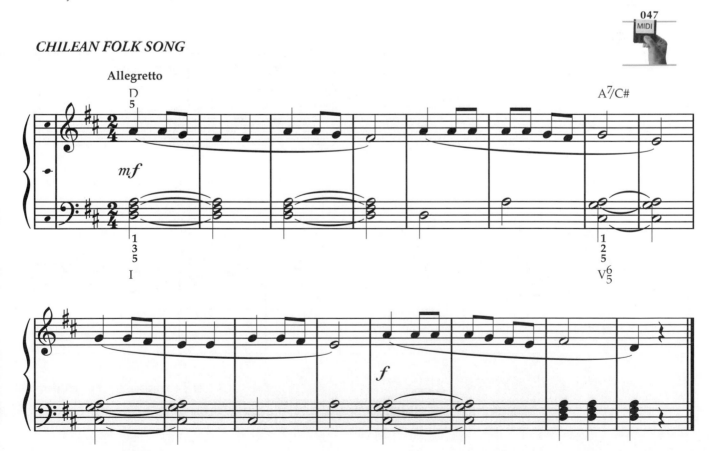

The key of E♭ major has three flats in the key signature. The five-finger pattern of E♭ major is shown below:

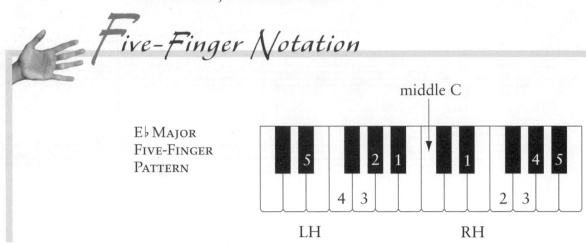

Five-Finger Notation

E♭ MAJOR
FIVE-FINGER
PATTERN

STUDIES IN E♭ MAJOR

Study 1   Moderato

■ Transpose to D major

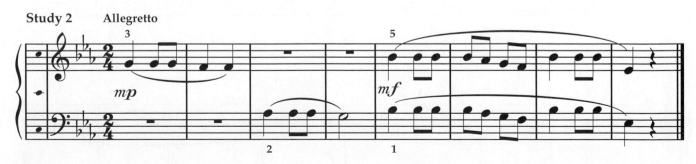

Study 2   Allegretto

■ Transpose to C major

Study the left-hand I–V$^6_5$–I chord progression in E♭ major before playing *English Folk Song*.

ENGLISH FOLK SONG

Student

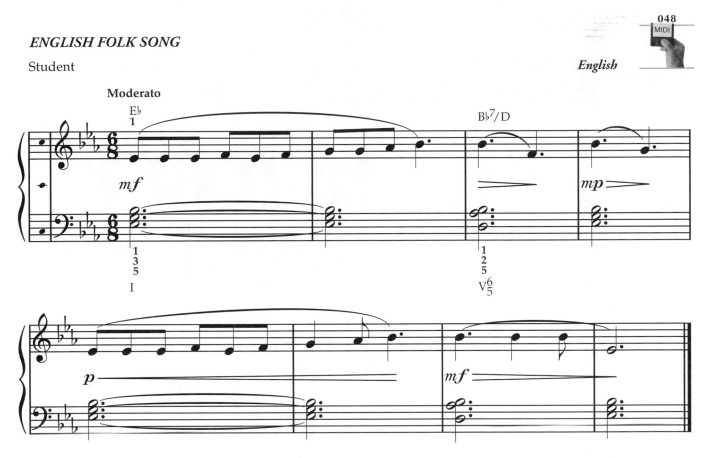

ENGLISH FOLK SONG

Arranged by Ken Iversen

Accompaniment

The key of A♭ major has four flats in the key signature. Here is the five-finger pattern:

Five-Finger Notation

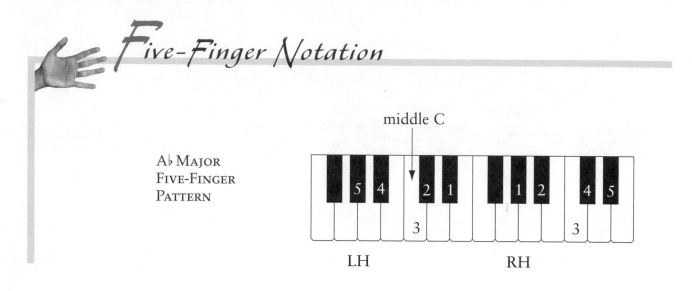

A♭ MAJOR
FIVE-FINGER
PATTERN

middle C

ÉTUDES IN A♭ MAJOR

Study 1   Andante

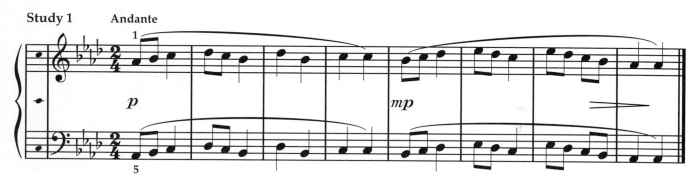

Study 2

Allegretto

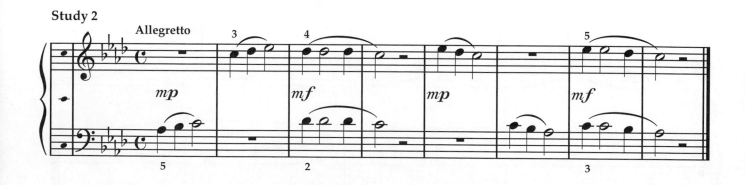

GERMAN FOLK SONG

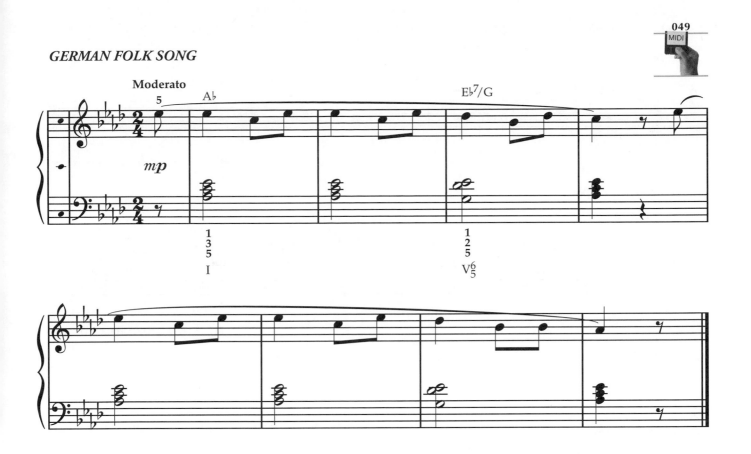

FIVE-FINGER MELODIES WITH LETTER-NAME CHORD SYMBOLS FOR I AND V$_5^6$ CHORD ACCOMPANIMENTS

Play the following melodies which use letter-name chord symbols for the I and V$_5^6$ chord harmonizations.

1. FOLK SONG

German

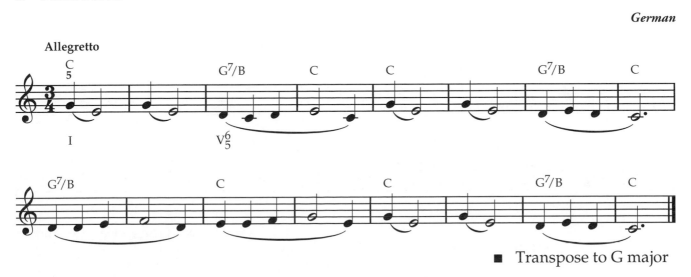

■ Transpose to G major

2. *SOUTH AMERICAN FOLK SONG*

■ Transpose to D major

3. *GERMAN TUNE*

■ Transpose to F major

4. *SWEDISH FOLK SONG*

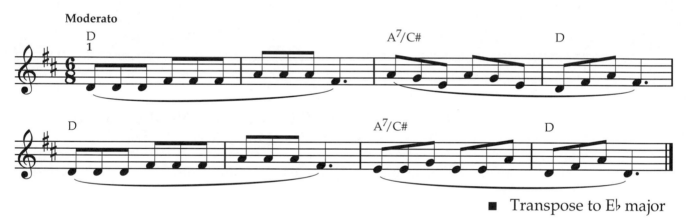

■ Transpose to E♭ major

5. *HEY LIDEE*

American

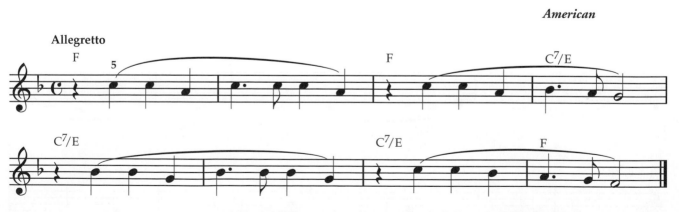

■ Transpose to A major

THE SUBDOMINANT CHORD

The root-position **IV** or **subdominant chord** is constructed by building a major triad on the 4th degree of the five-finger pattern in all keys.

Root Position: The IV$^6_4$ Inversion

Five-Finger Notation

FIVE-FINGER
PATTERN IN C
MAJOR

IV(F)

By inverting the IV triad and putting the *fifth* of the chord on the bottom, you will have an easier way to move between the I and IV chords. Note that the root of the IV$^6_4$ chord now appears as the middle tone.

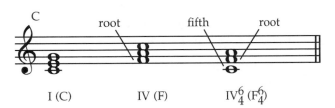

C   root   fifth   root

I (C)   IV (F)   IV$^6_4$ (F$^6_4$)

As with V^7 and V$^6_5$, the arabic numbers $^6_4$ represent the intervals formed between the lowest tone and the ones above. In IV$^6_4$ in C, the 6 represents the sixth from C to A, and the 4 represents the fourth from C to F.

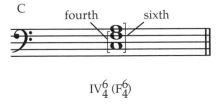

C   fourth   sixth

IV$^6_4$ (F$^6_4$)

The IV$_4^6$ chord for all keys is constructed by sounding the *first* and *fourth* tones of the five-finger pattern together with the *sixth* tone, which is a *whole step up* from the fifth tone of the five-finger pattern.

Five-Finger Notation

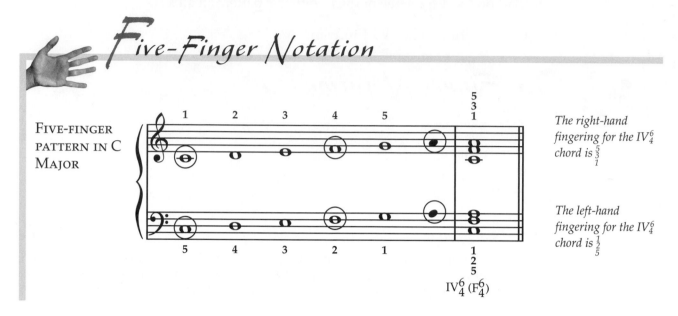

FIVE-FINGER PATTERN IN C MAJOR

IV$_4^6$ (F$_4^6$)

The right-hand fingering for the IV$_4^6$ chord is $\frac{5}{3}$ $_1$

The left-hand fingering for the IV$_4^6$ chord is $\frac{1}{2}$ $_5$

An easy way to move from the I (tonic) chord to the IV$_4^6$ chord in any given key is to remember the following steps:

1. The *top* note moves *up* a *whole step*.
2. The *middle* note moves *up* a *half step*.
3. The *bottom* note remains *the same*.

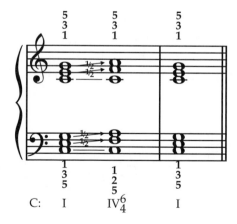

C: I   IV$_4^6$ I

The IV$_4^6$ chord derives its *letter name* from the root, which is the 4th tone of the five-finger pattern.

For example: in the key of C, the IV$_4^6$ chord is called an F$_4^6$ chord.
in the key of G, the IV$_4^6$ chord is a C$_4^6$ chord.
in the key of D, the IV$_4^6$ chord is a G$_4^6$ chord.

Practice Strategies

Practice playing the chord progression I–IV$_4^6$–I–V$_5^6$–I with the left hand in all major keys, as shown next.

I–IV$_4^6$–I–V$_5^6$–I

Chord Progressions

1. Use the fifth tone of the five-finger pattern as the first tone (or *tonic*) of each subsequent chord progression.
2. Remember not to look at the keys.
3. Try to develop a feel for the progression and anticipate the changing of chords.

After you have mastered the progression in major keys, try playing the i–iv$_4^6$–i–V$_5^6$–i progression in various minor keys of your choice. (See the progressions on pages 388–389.) Remember that the i chord in minor has its *third* tone lowered a half step, the iv$_4^6$ chord has its *sixth* tone lowered a half step, but the V$_5^6$ chord remains unchanged.

MAJOR KEYS

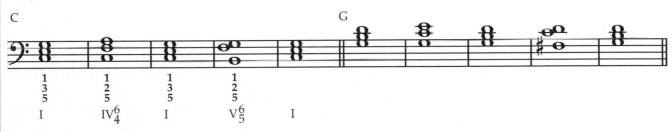

minor key example

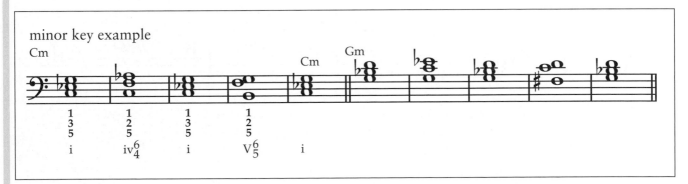

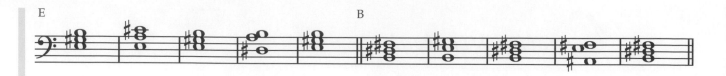

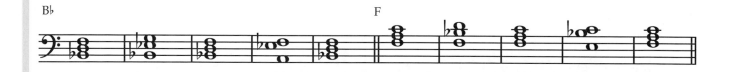

Another way of practicing the I–IV$_4^6$–I–V$_5^6$–I chord progression is to play the chords with the right hand while the left hand plays the root (or letter name) of each chord as shown below:

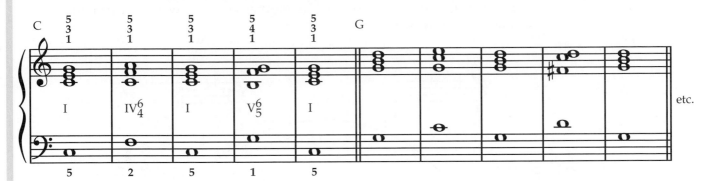

After you feel secure playing the harmonic progression in major keys, play the i–iv$_4^6$–i–V$_5^6$–i progression in various minor keys following the format above.

CADENCES

A **cadence** is a musical punctuation used at the end of a phrase. It marks a close in the melody or harmony.

Authentic Cadence

A phrase that ends with a dominant (V) [or a dominant seventh in root or inverted position (V^7 or V$_5^6$)] to tonic (I) chord progression closes with an **authentic cadence.**

Authentic Cadences

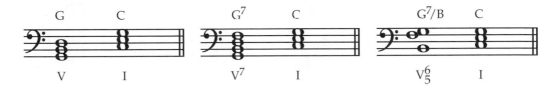

Plagal Cadence

A phrase that ends with a subdominant (IV) in root position or in one of its inverted positions (like IV$_4^6$) to tonic (I) chord progression closes with a **plagal cadence.** Sometimes the plagal cadence is nicknamed the "Amen" cadence because it often appears at the end of church hymns.

Plagal Cadences

THE CIRCLE OF FIFTHS AND MAJOR KEY SIGNATURES

When you used the fifth tone of the five-finger pattern in one key to form the first tone of the five-finger pattern in another key, you were constructing what is called the **circle of fifths.**

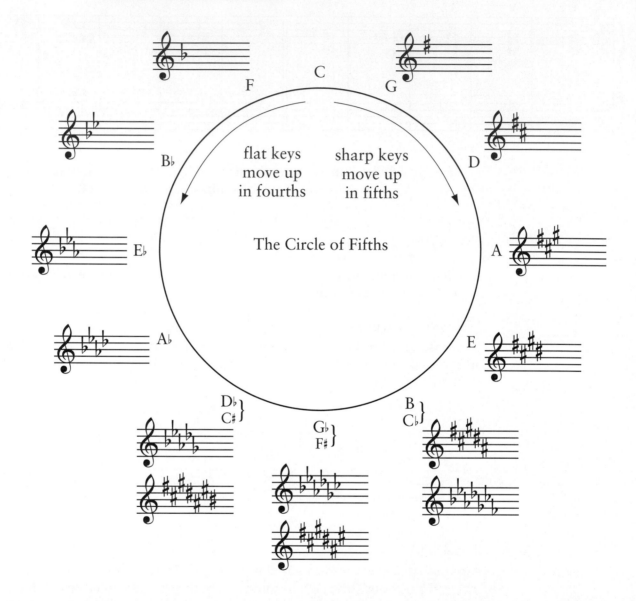

The circle of fifths is a convenient tool for memorizing key signatures. Read it clockwise for the **sharp keys.** Starting from C and moving by fifths, each new key adds one more sharp to the key signature.

Read it counterclockwise for the **flat keys.** Starting from C and moving by fourths, each new key adds one more flat. Note the enharmonic keys at 5:00, 6:00, and 7:00.

Remember that sharp key signatures in major keys are identified by taking the last sharp, then moving up one half step higher to the next letter name.

Remember that flat key signatures in major keys are identified by taking the name of the next-to-the-last flat (always the 2nd flat to the left).

Learn the key signatures of every major key as quickly as possible, either by their order in the circle of fifths, or by remembering this rule of thumb: *the number of sharps and flats in two keys with the same letter names will always add up to seven*. For example:

keys	sharps/flats		total
C, C♯	7	0	7
C, C♭	0	7	7
G, G♭	1	6	7
D, D♭	2	5	7
A, A♭	3	4	7
E, E♭	4	3	7
etc.			

Remember also that the order of flats is the reverse of the order of sharps in their key signatures.

sharp keys: F♯ C♯ G♯ D♯ A♯ E♯ B♯

flat keys: B♭ E♭ A♭ D♭ G♭ C♭ F♭

PIECES WITH I–IV$_4^6$–V$_5^6$ ACCOMPANIMENTS

BANKS OF THE OHIO

American

■ Transpose to F major

BEAUTIFUL BROWN EYES

Traditional

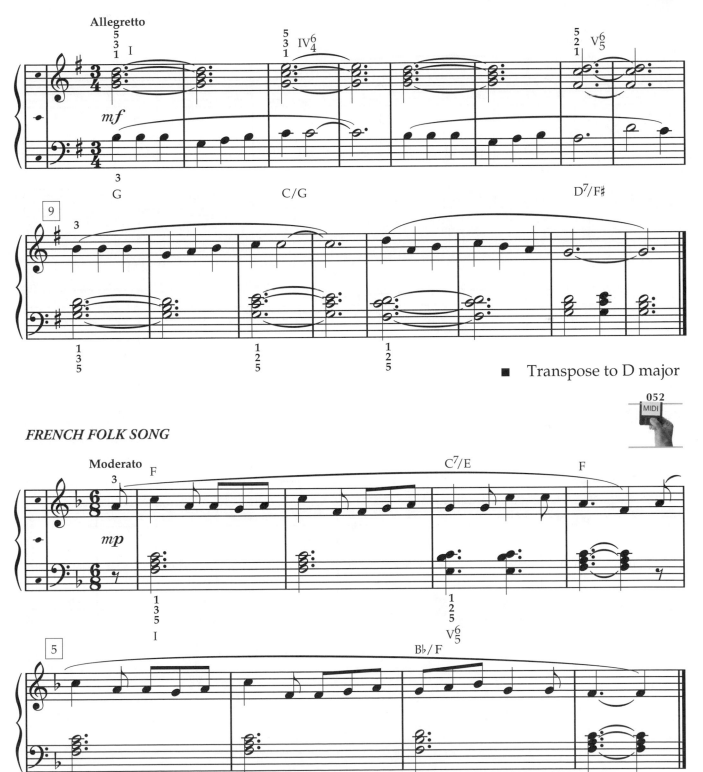

■ Transpose to D major

FRENCH FOLK SONG

■ Transpose to A major

JINGLE BELLS

J. S. Pierpont

Allegretto

Jin - gle bells, jin - gle bells, jin - gle all the way, Oh, what fun it

is to ride in a one-horse o - pen sleigh. ____ Jin - gle bells, jin - gle bells,

jin - gle all the way, Oh, what fun it is to ride in a one-horse o - pen sleigh.

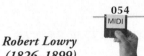

SHALL WE GATHER AT THE RIVER

Student

Robert Lowry
(1826–1899)

SHALL WE GATHER AT THE RIVER

Accompaniment

WHEN THE SAINTS GO MARCHIN' IN

Student

Traditional

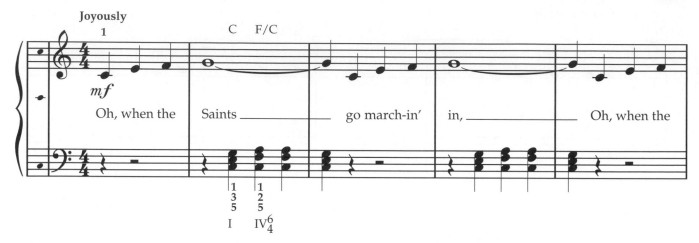

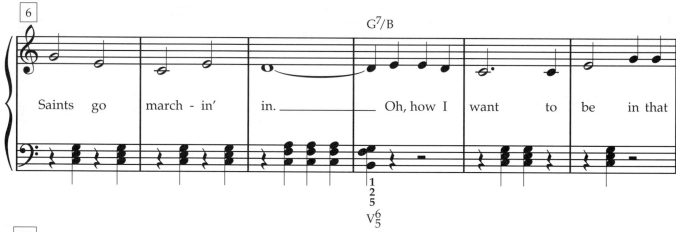

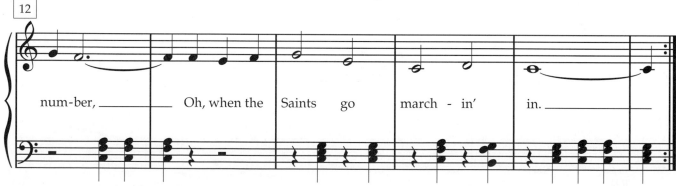

WHEN THE SAINTS GO MARCHIN' IN

Arranged by
Ken Iversen

Accompaniment

Composite Meter

Festive Dance is written in **composite meter,** which is a combination of two different meters. Here $\frac{3}{4}$ and $\frac{2}{4}$ are combined to produce $\frac{5}{4}$. Before playing the piece, tap out some of the rhythmic patterns in $\frac{5}{4}$ as given in the *Practice Strategies* section.

Practice Strategies

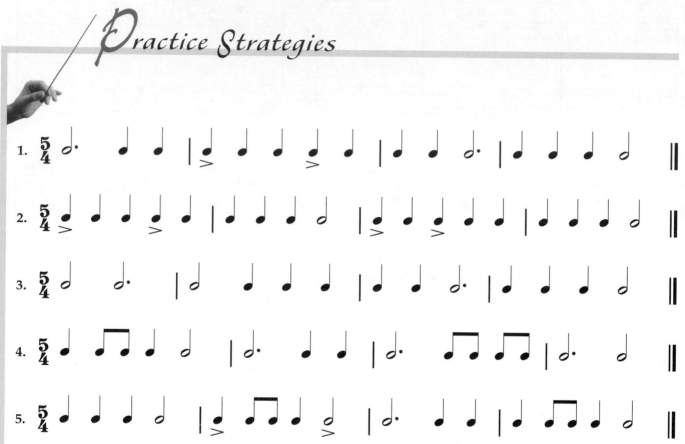

How many of the rhythms given above can you find in *Festive Dance*?

FESTIVE DANCE

Student

E.M.

056
MIDI

FESTIVE DANCE

Accompaniment

Allegro

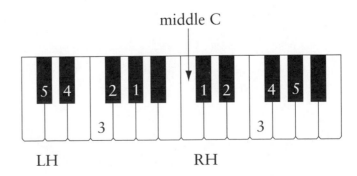

Five-Finger Notation

Two Studies and *Gentle Rain* are in the key of D♭ major. Here is the five-finger pattern:

middle C

D♭ MAJOR
FIVE-FINGER
PATTERN

5 4 2 1 3 1 2 4 5 3

LH   RH

TWO STUDIES

Study 1

■ Transpose to E major

Study 2

■ Transpose to D major

GENTLE RAIN

Student   *E.M.*

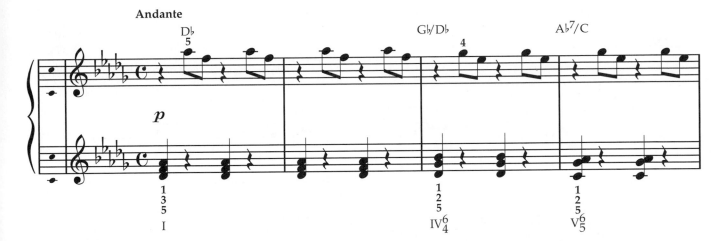

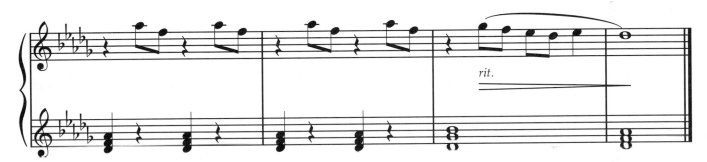

■ Transpose to C major

GENTLE RAIN

Accompaniment

Tenuto $\bar{p}$

A **tenuto** is a short horizontal line ($\bar{p}$) above or below a note. It means that the note should be played for its full value.

MELODY *from* Op. 39

Dmitri Kabalevsky (1904–1987)

■ Transpose to D♭ major

Calisthenic Studies and *This Land Is Your Land* are in the key of B♭ major; here is the five-finger pattern:

Five-Finger Notation

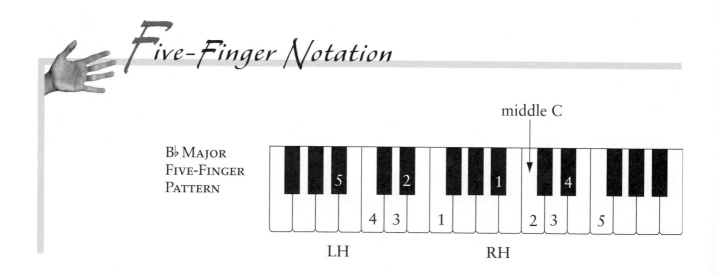

CALISTHENIC STUDIES

Study 1   **Allegretto**

Study 2   **Allegro**

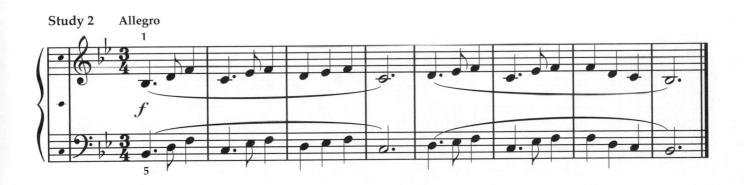

THIS LAND IS YOUR LAND

Words and music by
Woody Guthrie (1912–1967)
adapted E. M.

Student

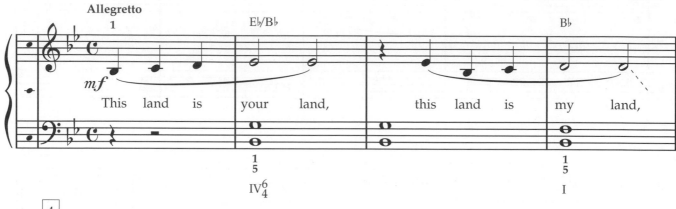

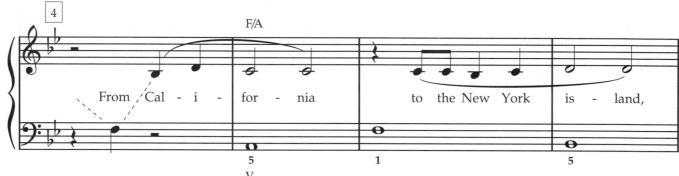

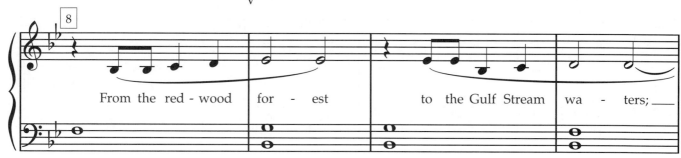

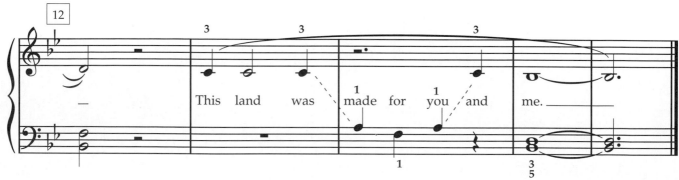

Ludlow, 1956, N. Y.—1988 renew

THIS LAND IS YOUR LAND

Accompaniment

Arranged by
Ken Iversen

Studies and *Zulu Farewell Song* are in the key of B major; here is the five-finger pattern:

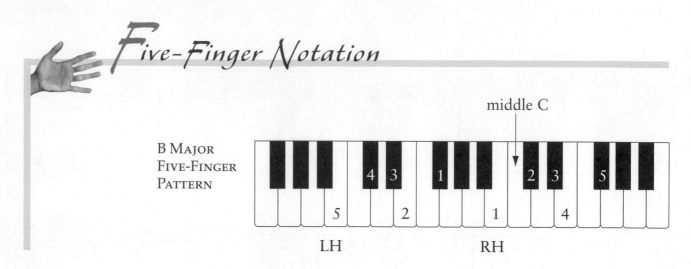

Five-Finger Notation

B MAJOR
FIVE-FINGER
PATTERN

middle C

LH   RH

STUDIES IN B MAJOR

Study 1   Moderato

Study 2   Andante

Zulu Farewell Song uses harmonic intervals of a fifth and sixth in the left-hand accompaniment.

ZULU FAREWELL SONG

Student

E. M.

ZULU FAREWELL SONG

Accompaniment

Arranged by
Ken Iversen

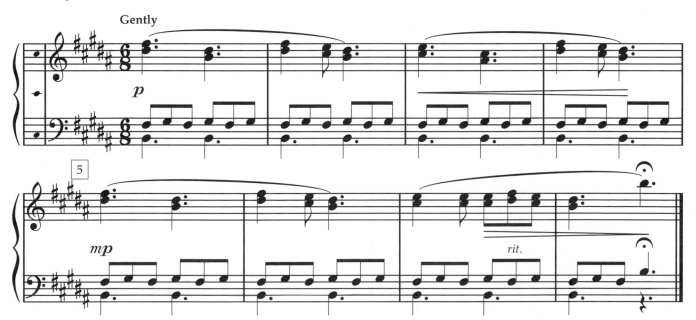

FIVE-FINGER MELODIES WITH LETTER-NAME CHORD SYMBOLS FOR I, IV$_4^6$, AND V$_5^6$ CHORD ACCOMPANIMENTS

Play the following five-finger melodies which use letter-name chord symbols for the I, IV$_4^6$, and V$_5^6$ chord harmonizations.

CHRISTMAS DAY IS COME

Traditional Irish Carol

Christ-mas Day is come, _ Let us now re - joice,

Let us all re - joice, _ Christ - mas _ Day is come.

ALLELUIA

Traditional

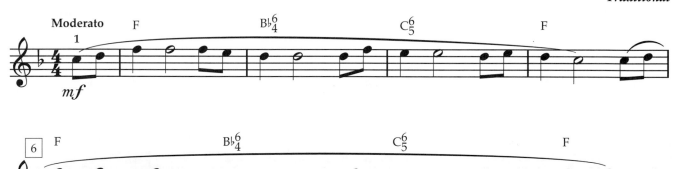

GIT ALONG, LITTLE DOGIES *(excerpt)*

Cowboy Song

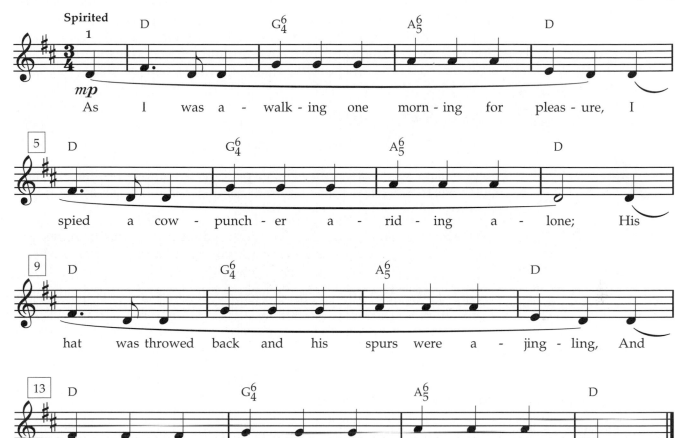

As I was a - walk-ing one morn-ing for pleas-ure, I

spied a cow - punch - er a - rid - ing a - lone; His

hat was throwed back and his spurs were a - jing - ling, And

as he ap - proached he was sing - ing his song.

DRINK TO ME ONLY WITH THINE EYES *(excerpt)*

Traditional

CHANGING FIVE-FINGER POSITIONS

Changing five-finger positions involves moving from one five-finger position to another. This means shifting the entire hand to a new position.

Except for the examples in the improvisation section of this unit, all hand-position shifts will be indicated by a circle around the fingerings involved.

Practice Strategies

Practice playing a series of five-finger patterns in various positions. The objective is to move from one pattern to another without any hesitation in the beat.

For example: Start with the five-finger pattern of C major, moving upward and downward with both hands; start next with F major, and so on.

Practice the hand-position shifts shown next before playing *Study*. Use the same procedure for the pieces that follow.

USING MORE THAN A SINGLE FIVE-FINGER POSITION

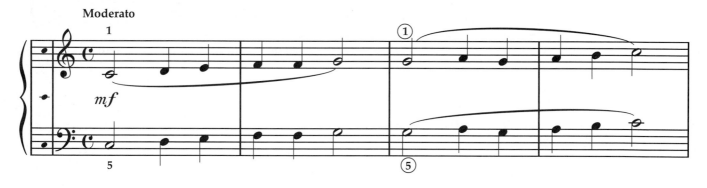

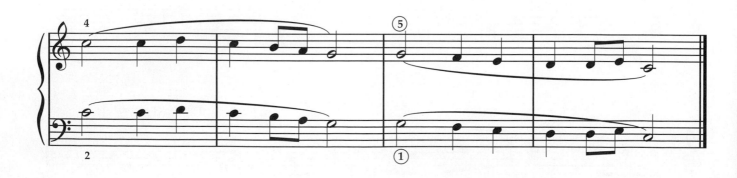

Study begins in the five-finger pattern of G, shifts to the five-finger pattern of D, and then returns to the original pattern of G.

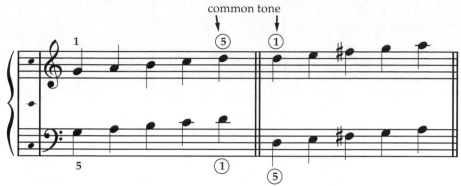

PRACTICE DIRECTIONS

1. In measure 9, use the D in the right hand as the *common tone* to shift to the five-finger pattern of D. Only a fingering change will be required.

2. In the left hand, make the shift to the D pattern by moving the fifth finger from G *down* to D. Your hands will be playing two octaves apart.

3. Do not look down at the keys when making the change and be sure to keep the beat moving—don't slow down! Use the same procedure when returning to the original position of G.

STUDY

061
MIDI

Béla Bartók
(1881–1945)

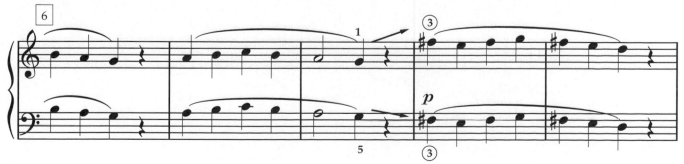

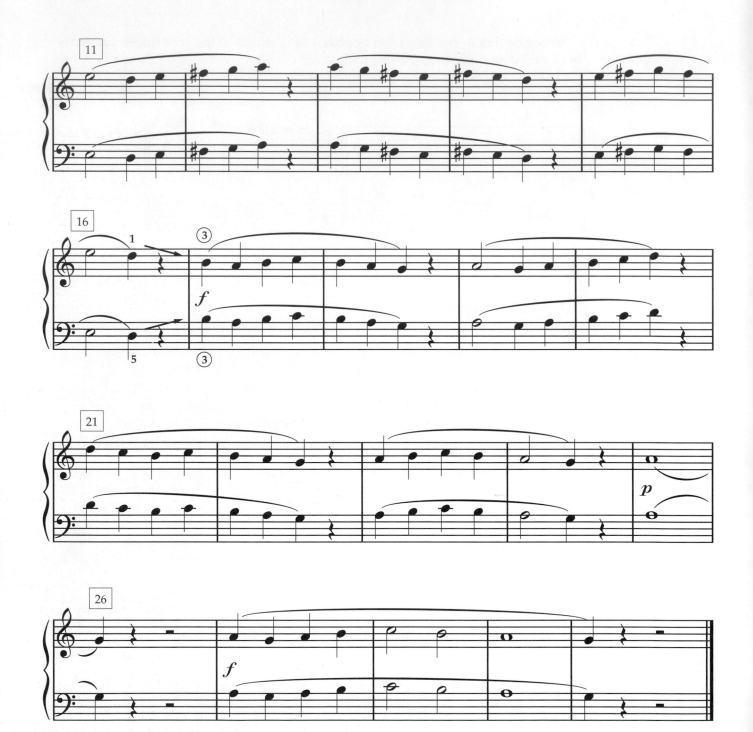

Practice the left-hand position shift before playing *Belly-Button Blues*.

BELLY-BUTTON BLUES

E. M.

Practice this hand-position shift before playing *Steamroller Rock*:

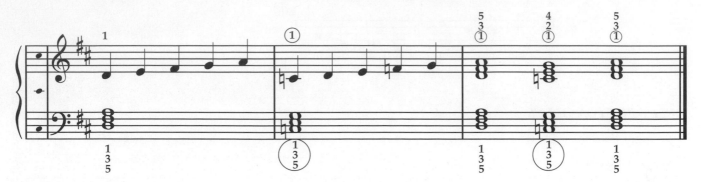

STEAMROLLER ROCK

E. M.

Practice these three hand-position shifts before playing *Time-Clock Blues*. Remember to look ahead of the notes you are playing to prepare for the hand-position changes.

TIME-CLOCK BLUES

E. M.

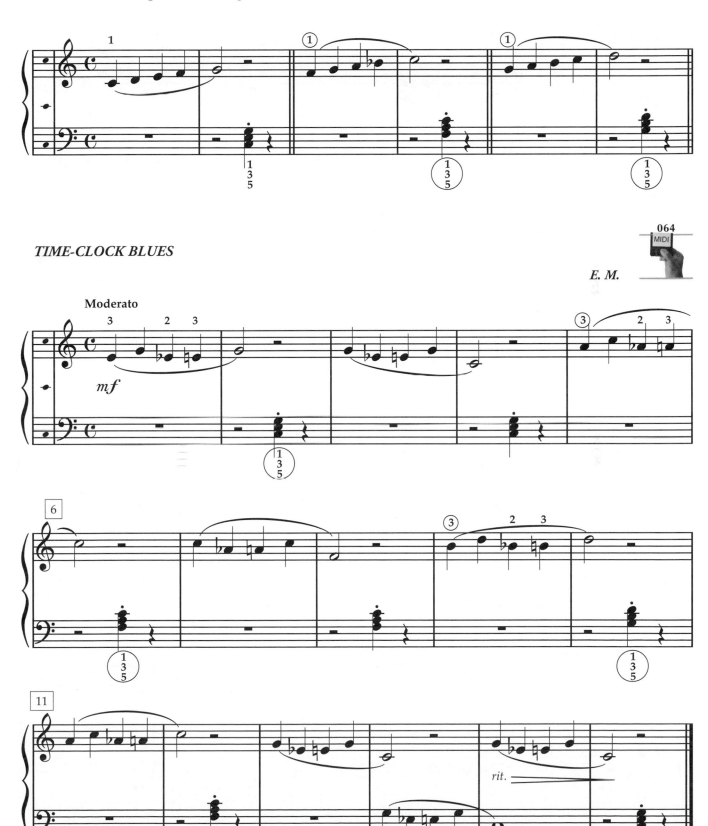

Practice the hand-position shifts in each hand before playing *Round-the-Corner Boogie.*

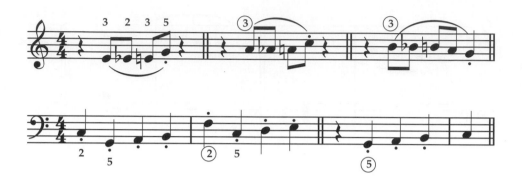

ROUND-THE-CORNER BOOGIE

E.M.

REPERTOIRE

Scherzando

Scherzando is a tempo marking that means to play in a joking manner, playfully.

A LITTLE JOKE

Dmitri Kabalevsky
(1904–1987)

IMPROVISATION

Pentatonic Improvisation

Use the five black keys (the pentatonic scale) to improvise various melodies with the right hand, and use the left hand to play an accompaniment in fifths. The four sets of fifths that can be played on the black keys are shown below:

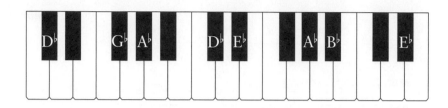

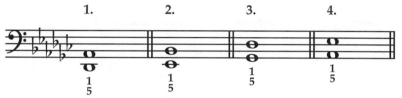

PRACTICE DIRECTIONS

1. For an "Eastern" sound, play sustained open fifths in the accompaniment, as illustrated in *Japanese Gardens*.

2. Then play this piece in different registers—for example, with the right hand one and two octaves higher than written.

3. Finally, make up your own melody to the accompaniment.

4. For *Japanese Gardens*, place the right-hand thumb on G♭ and the rest of the fingers on the corresponding black keys:

JAPANESE GARDENS

E. M.

PRACTICE DIRECTIONS

1. For a drumming sound, play a fifth (for example, E♭ and B♭) in the lower register on every beat in $\frac{4}{4}$ meter, as in *Little River Call*.
2. With the right hand, begin playing various melodies on the black keys. Play *Little River Call* to give yourself some ideas.
3. Then begin to improvise your own melodies.
4. For *Little River Call*, place the right-hand thumb on D♭, and the rest of the fingers on the corresponding black keys:

LITTLE RIVER CALL

E. M.

Improvise your own accompaniment (single notes, fifths, etc.) on the black keys to the pentatonic melody that appears next. Play the melody and accompaniment in different registers.

SAPPORO SUNSET

E. M.

12-Bar Blues Improvisation

1. Before playing *Starting the Blues,* practice the major chords of C, F, and G with your left hand, as shown below. You will have to move the left hand out of position to build these three chords.
2. Start by playing the tones of C, F, and G with the little finger of your left hand until you can play them easily without looking down at the keys. Work to develop a feel for the distances, or intervals, between the tones.
3. Next, review and play the chords in the same manner, first as whole notes on the first beat of each measure, and then in the quarter-note figures as written.

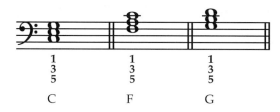

12-Bar Blues Chord Pattern

Starting the Blues, like any 12-bar blues, can be played in any major key, using the chords I, IV, and V. The left hand will always follow this pattern:

I	I	I	I
IV	IV	I	I
V	IV	I	I

STARTING THE BLUES

C (I)

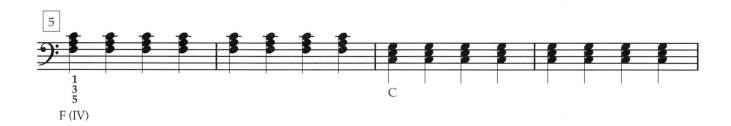

F (IV)   C

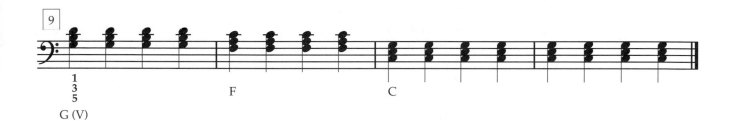

G (V)   F   C

Playing the major chords of C, F, and G in the left hand, improvise a right-hand melody using the tones in the chord you are playing.

For example, with the C chord, the right hand would play a melody with the tones C, E, G; with the F chord, a melody with the tones F, A, C; and so on. Here is a simple example:

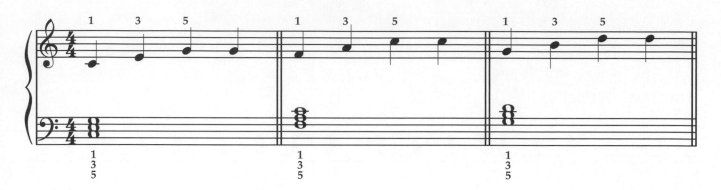

Numerous blues melodies can be improvised by changing the note combinations and using a variety of rhythm patterns. Here are just a few ways of playing the same melody with four different rhythm patterns:

Melodies can be improvised not only with the tones in the chord you are playing, but also with all the tones of the *five-finger pattern* for that chord. For instance, in *Walkin' Through Blues* the C-chord melody tones use the five-finger pattern of C, the F-chord melody tones use the five-finger pattern of F (making it necessary to play B♭), and the G-chord melody tones use the five-finger pattern of G. Just remember to match the five-finger pattern to the chord you are playing. In other words, think of the left-hand chord as the key you are playing in when improvising the right-hand melody combinations.

Also improvise different rhythm patterns to the left hand such as:

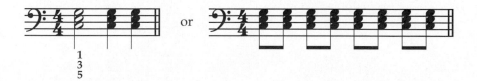

WALKIN' THROUGH BLUES

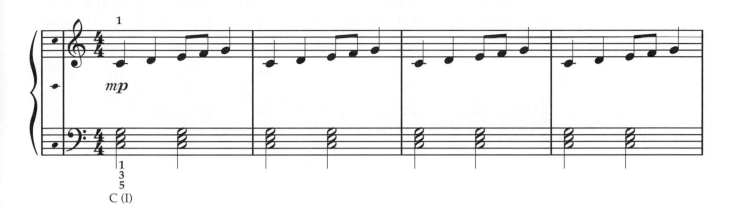

Blue Note

Now include what is called the **blue note**. With the right hand, construct the C major chord. Next, lower the third a half step from E to E♭ to form a C minor chord. The lowered third, E♭ in this case, becomes the so-called blue note.

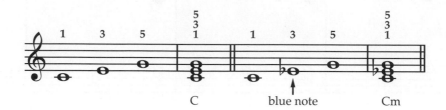

You will be using the three tones of the major chord and also the blue note in *Blue-Note Blues.* Before playing the piece, practice the individual chord patterns as illustrated. Use the second finger of the right hand to play the blue note.

BLUE-NOTE BLUES

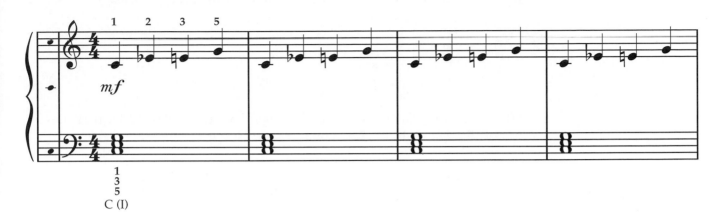

Next, reverse the parts so that the right hand plays the chords, one octave higher, and the left hand plays the melody, one octave lower.

Next, for added harmonic color, improvise melodies to an accompaniment of open fifths that move downward chromatically in several places:

After you are familiar with the downward pattern, play fifths that move chromatically *upward* to the fifths on C, F, and G:

Finally, make up your own combinations of fifths moving both downward and upward chromatically to the fifths on C, F, and G, similar to those used in *Blues Beat*.

BLUES BEAT

The following accompaniment effectively provides the strong, recurring rhythms characteristic of rock music. It uses a broken major triad and a lowered third (blue note):

After practicing this accompaniment pattern, play *Rockin' Blues.* Then, using the same pattern, improvise your own melodies.

ROCKIN' BLUES

The following chart illustrates the I, IV, and V chords in every major key. Use this chart to help you improvise your own 12-bar blues and transpose them to various keys.

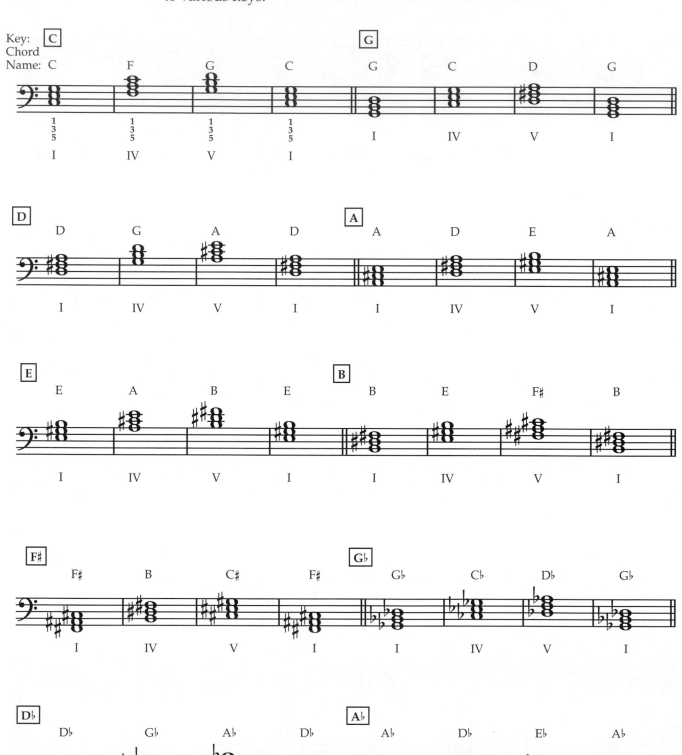

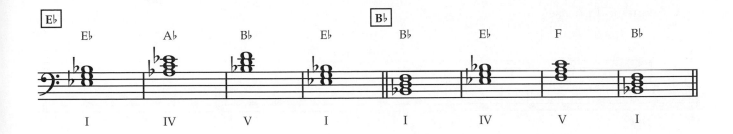

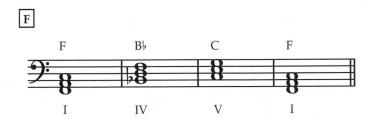

CREATIVE MUSIC AND HARMONIZATION

The following examples of phrase pairs are designed to help you create music of your own. Each example consists of two matching phrases, each four measures in length. After you have studied and played them, try improvising a matching phrase 2 to the three incomplete examples on pages 196–197.

1. Parallel phrases

In phrase 2 of the first example, measures 5 and 6 are **parallel** to the first two measures of phrase 1; that is, they repeat those measures. Measure 7 uses a change of rhythm and moves stepwise toward the tonic or key note in measure 8 with a 2–4–3–2 pattern.

2. Inverted phrases

In phrase 2 of the second example, measures 5 and 6 repeat the first two measures, but they **invert** (reverse) the order of D-F♯-A to read A-F♯-D and E-G-A to read A-G-E. The rhythmic structure of phrase 2 is identical to that of phrase 1. Measure 7 prepares to move to the tonic with a 5–4–2–3 pattern.

3. Sequential phrases

In phrase 2 of the third example, measures 5 and 6 appear in **sequence** to measures 1 and 2; that is, the same melodic pattern is repeated at a different pitch. As in the first example, measure 7 introduces a change of rhythm (dotted quarter and eighth). Frequent use of the I-chord tones (F, A, C) gives a strong sense of key. As in the other two examples, measure 8 ends on the tonic.

Using parallelism, inversion, or sequence, write a phrase that matches each of the three following phrases.

3.

Improvise matching phrases to the five-finger melody given below. Select your best phrase and write it down for both hands to play. Transpose it to other keys. Play with the right hand an octave higher, then with the left hand an octave lower. Finally, play with both hands in different registers at the same time.

4.

I and V$_5^6$ Chords in Major

Harmonize the following melodies with a I or V$_5^6$ chord on the first beat of each measure. The correct chord will be the one with some of its tones represented in the melody. Before creating the chord, look at the notes of each measure, especially strong beat notes, and plan a chord that will fit those notes before your ear tells you something is wrong. Write in the chord for each measure.

5.

6.

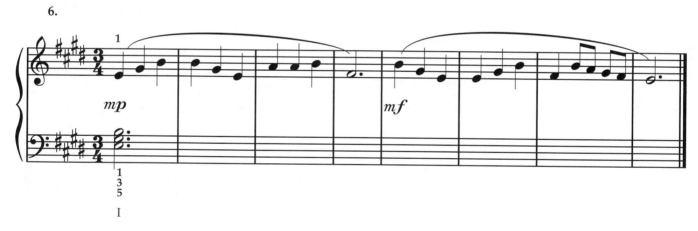

Write a matching phrase for the one given and harmonize using I and V$_5^6$ chords.

7.

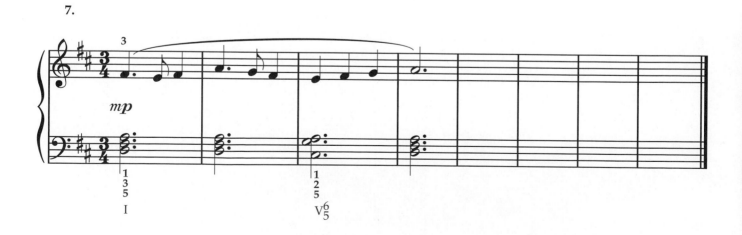

Add a matching phrase to the one below, using a single-note accompaniment in the left hand. Single tones can substitute for complete chords.

8.

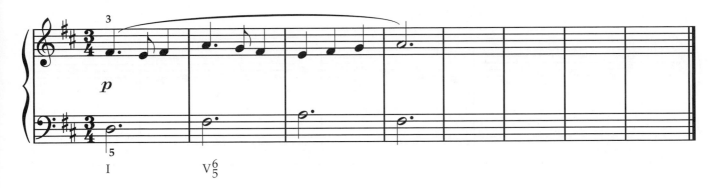

i and V$^6_5$ Chords in Minor

Harmonize the following melody in minor with a i or V$^6_5$ chord on the first beat of each measure. Note that two chords are needed in measure 8.

9.

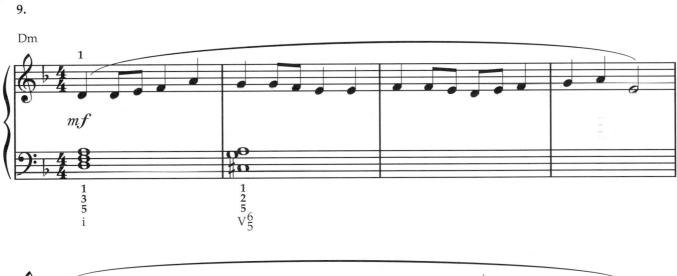

Improvise matching phrases to the one given, harmonizing the minor melodies with i and V$^6_5$ chords. Then select one melody to write down, along with the harmonization.

10.

I, IV$^6_4$, and V$^6_5$ Chords in Major

Complete the harmonization for the examples below, using I, IV$^6_4$, and V$^6_5$ chords.

11.

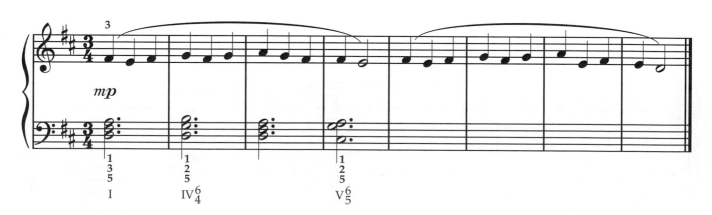

12.

Improvise matching phrases to the one below, using I, IV$_4^6$, and V$_5^6$ chords for the harmonization. Then select one melody to write down, along with the harmonization.

13.

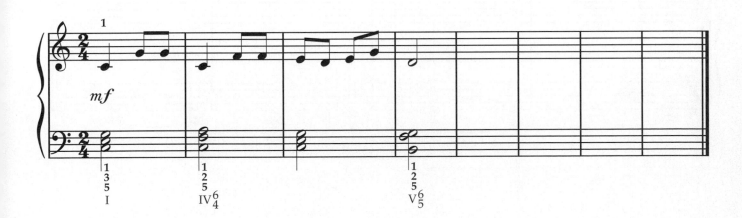

Write a melody that blends with the left-hand accompaniment below:

14.

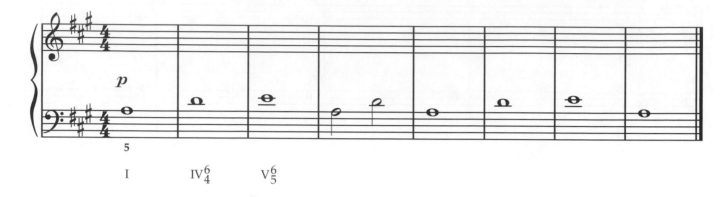

Improvising in Various Styles

Improvise melodies in the Dorian mode (the seven white keys from D to D) to the left-hand accompaniment of open fifths.

15.

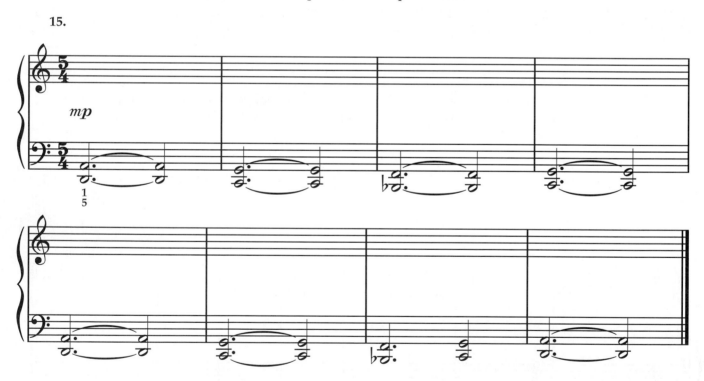

Improvise various open fifths melodically and harmonically in both hands in a style similar to the one provided below. Explore a wide range of high and low sounds, shifting between different sections of the keyboard.

16.

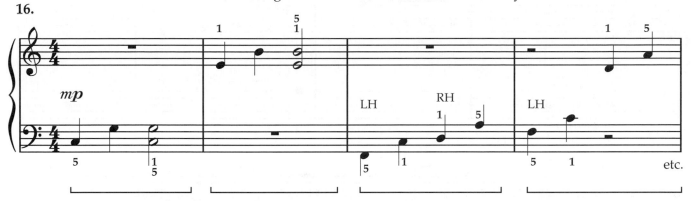

SIGHTREADING STUDIES

PRACTICE DIRECTIONS

1. Determine the key of the study.
2. Observe the meter signature, then tap out the rhythmic pattern, counting aloud as you do so.
3. Study the melodic and harmonic patterns.
4. Place hands in the correct position. Once you begin playing, do not stop or hesitate to find the notes. Keep the beat moving!
5. Play the notes while keeping your eyes on the printed page.

Melodies with Various Rhythmic Patterns

1. Key of D

2. Key of Dm

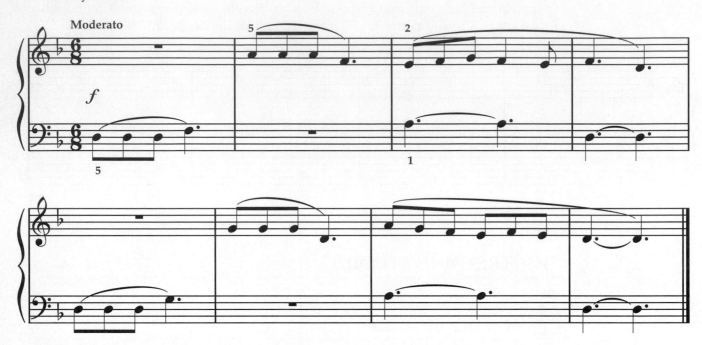

Different Registers and Register Changes

3. Key of _____

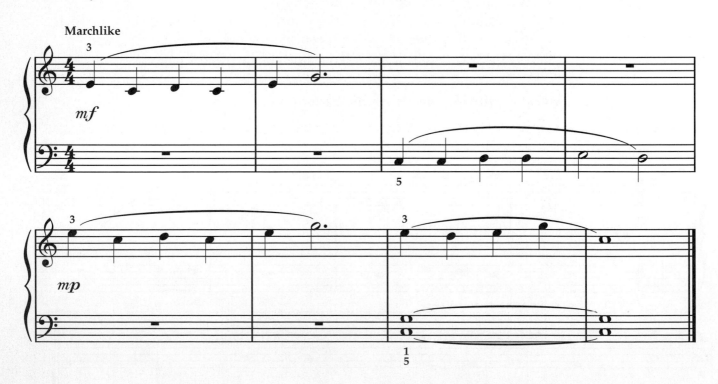

4. Key of Gm

5. Key of _____

Slurred Notes

6. Key of _____

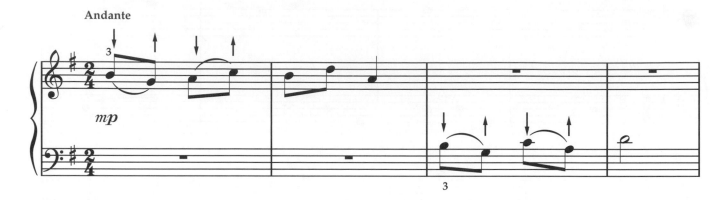

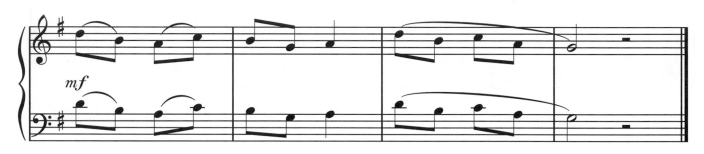

7. Key of _____

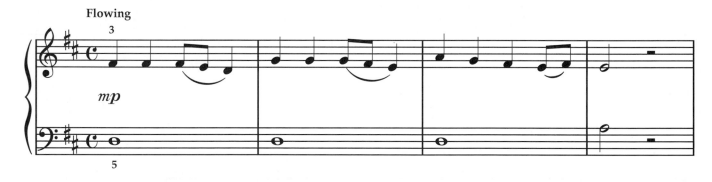

Staccato Notes

8. Key of D♭

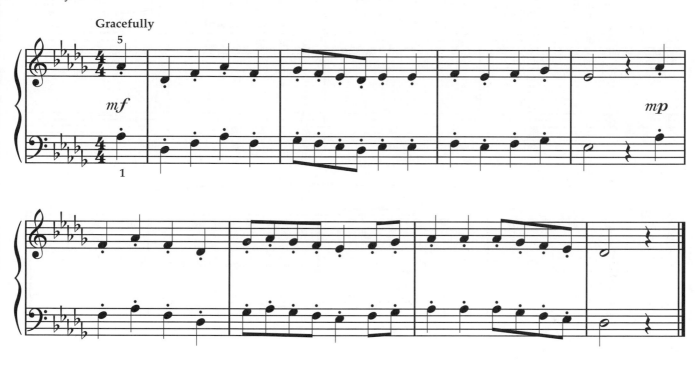

Parallel and Contrary Motion

9. Key of B♭

10. Key of E

Melody with Accompaniment in Fifths

11. Key of Em

I and V$^6_5$ Chords

12. Key of _____

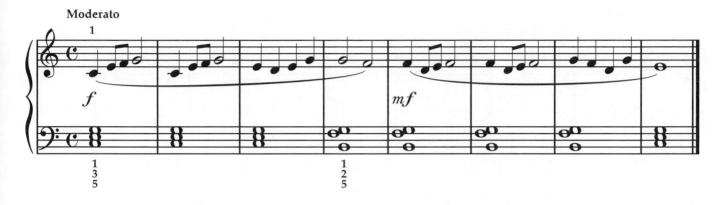

13. Key of Cm

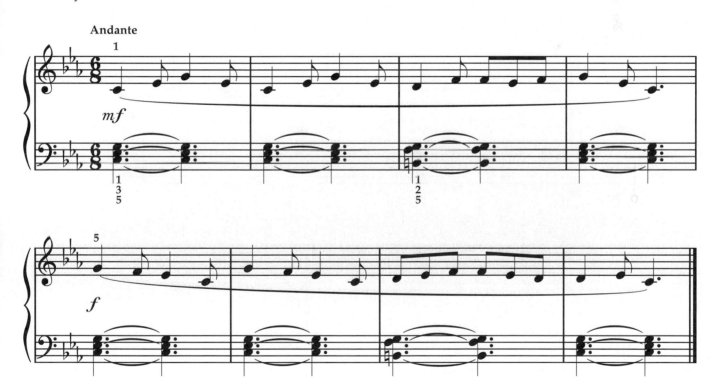

I, IV$^6_4$, and V$^6_5$ Chords

14. Key of _____

15. Key of E♭

Change of Five-Finger Position

16. Key of _____

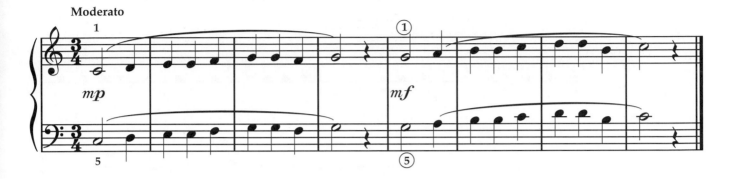

17. Key of C

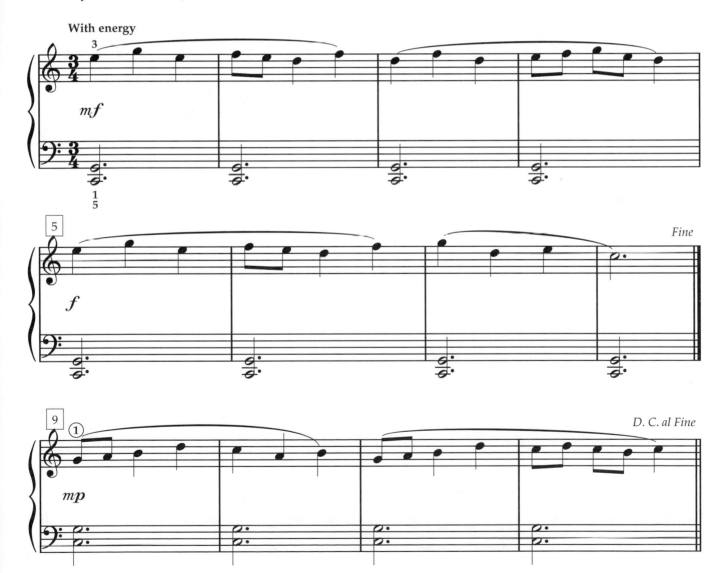

RHYTHMIC STUDIES

Tap and count the following rhythmic exercises with both hands, or work with different objects (i.e., pencils, spoons, hitting against bottles) to obtain different timbral choices.

TECHNICAL STUDIES

1. Contrary motion

Practice this exercise in various keys of your own choice.

2. Fingerbuilders

Practice this exercise in various tempos using different dynamic levels.

3. Coordination Exercises

a.

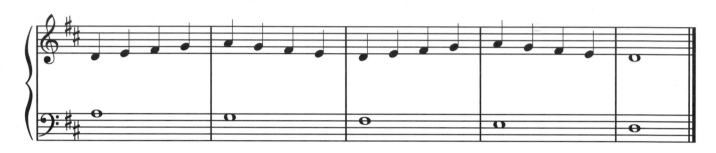

b.

In a **canon**, one melodic line/voice imitates another.

c.

CANON

E. M.

ENSEMBLE PIECES

Student-Teacher Duets

Dal Segno al Fine (*D.S. al Fine*) means to repeat from the sign 𝄋 to **Fine**.

RAZZLE DAZZLE

Student

Lee Evans

RAZZLE DAZZLE

Accompaniment

Lee Evans

First and Second Endings

La cinquantine has a **first ending** and a **second ending** indicated by the marks shown below.

After playing the piece through the first ending, go back to the beginning and play the piece again, this time skipping the first ending and going directly to the second ending.

LA CINQUANTINE*

Gabriel Marie (1852–1958)
Arranged by Faber and Faber

Student

*The student part may be played one octave higher than written if so desired.

LA CINQUANTINE

Accompaniment

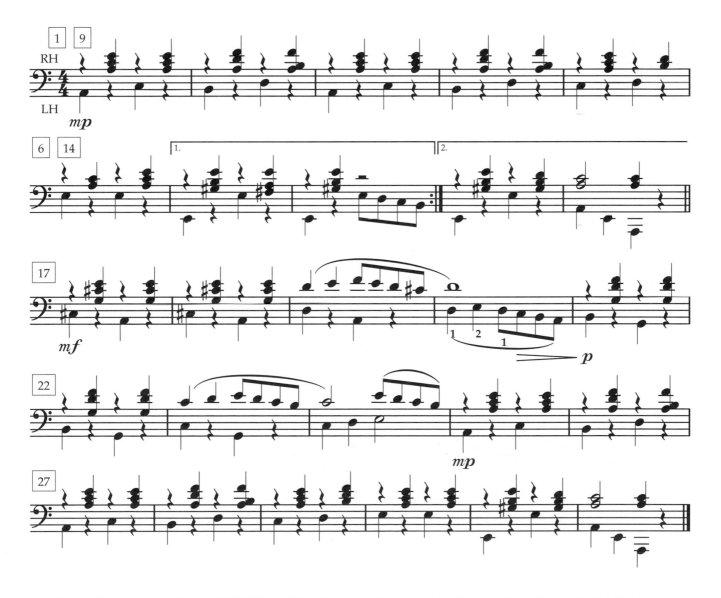

BALLAD*

Student

Dennis Alexander

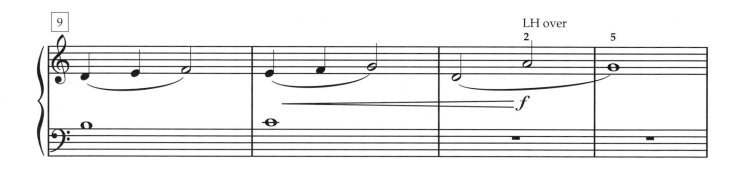

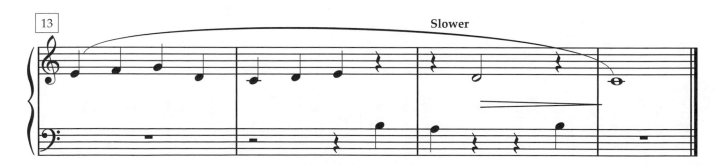

*The student plays one octave higher than written when playing at one piano.

BALLAD

Accompaniment

Dennis Alexander

MERRY-GO-ROUND *from* Twelve Duets on Five Notes, *No. 3*

Arthur Foote
(1853–1937)

Student

Allegro   Both hands one octave higher than written throughout if played at one piano

MERRY-GO-ROUND *from* Twelve Duets on Five Notes, *No. 3*

Arthur Foote
(1853–1937)

Accompaniment

Student Ensemble Pieces

SPRING *from* The Four Seasons

Antonio Vivaldi (1678–1741)
Arranged by Ken Iversen

CANON

(1653–1706)
Arranged by Ken Iversen

Accompaniment

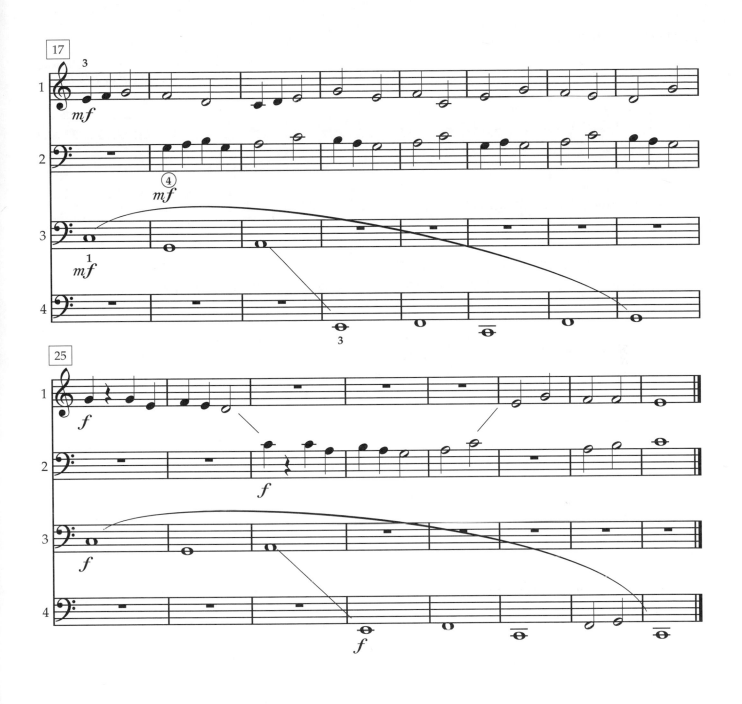

AMAZING GRACE

Traditional
Arranged by Ken Iversen

ALOUETTE*

French
Arranged by E.M.

* Piano 3 is optional. The Piano 1 and 2 parts may be played at one piano if the Piano 1 part is played an octave higher than written and the Piano 2 part an octave lower than written.

NAME _____

DATE _____

SCORE _____

Short Answer

1. Name the major key for each of the key signatures given:

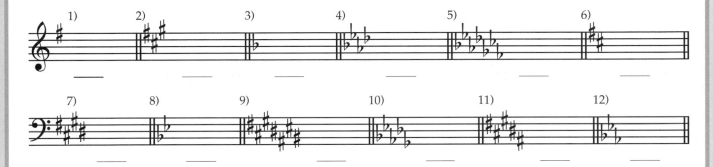

2. Identify the quality (major or minor) of the triads below. Use the upper-case letter to signify major (i.e., D for D major) and the upper-case letter followed by a small m to signify minor (i.e., Dm for D minor).

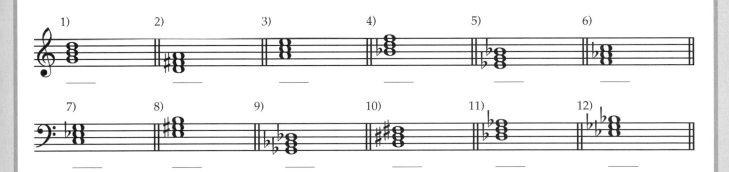

Construction

3. Finish the following rhythm patterns in the meter signatures given using only *one* note to complete each measure.

4. Build each of the major and minor five-finger patterns on the keyboards provided below. In doing so, be sure to remember to use five different letter names.

1. C major

2. C minor

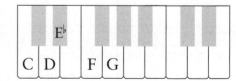

3. D♭ major (C♯ major)

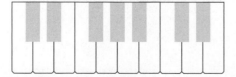

4. C♯ minor

5. D major

6. D minor

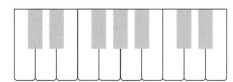

7. E♭ major

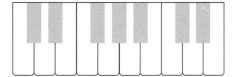

8. E♭ minor

9. E major

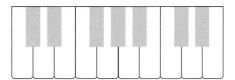

10. E minor

11. F major

12. F minor

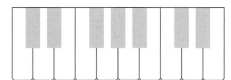

13. F♯ major (G♭ major)

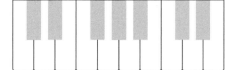

14. F♯ minor

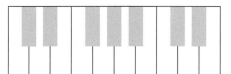

15. G major

16. G minor

17. A♭ major

18. A♭ minor (G♯ minor)

19. A major

20. A minor

21. B♭ major

22. B♭ minor (A♯ minor)

23. B major (C♭ major)

24. B minor

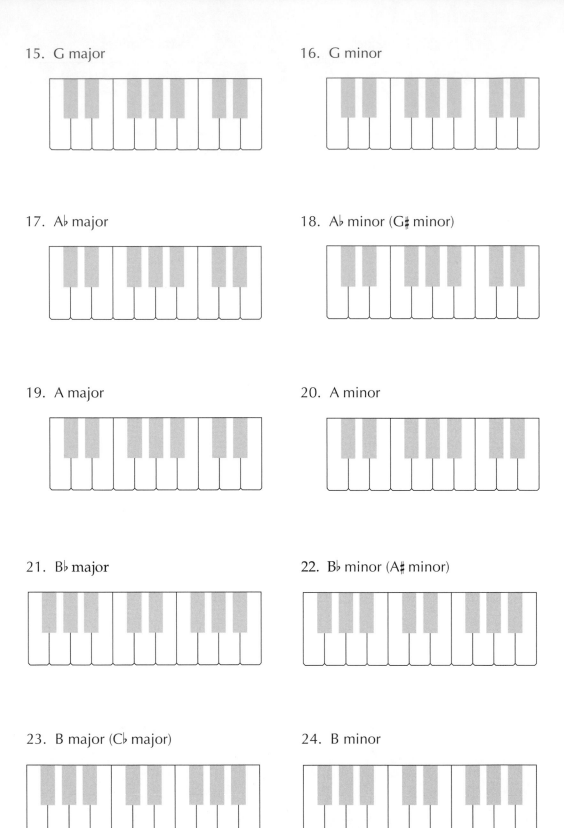

Matching

Write the numbers from Column A to correspond to the given answers in Column B.

COLUMN A	COLUMN B
1. upbeat	_____ a root, third, and fifth
2. *Fine*	_____ begins on the first beat
3. Allegro	_____ play strongly accented
4. crescendo	_____ play very loud
5. ♩ ˙	_____ play in a detached manner
6. fortissimo (*ff*)	_____ note-for-note imitation of one melody line by another
7. downbeat	_____ begins with a beat other than the first in the measure
8. sforzando (*sfz*)	_____ hold longer than the indicated time value
9. sequence	_____ the eighth note receiving 1 beat
10. Andante	_____ ⎣____⎦
11. $\frac{6}{8}$	_____ play an octave higher or lower than written
12. accidentals	_____ gradually becoming louder
13. pianissimo (*pp*)	_____ a combination of two meters
14. triad	_____ play quickly
15. damper pedal	_____ play very soft
16. *8va* - - - - ⌐	_____ play at a walking pace
17. composite meter	_____ finish or "end"
18. canon	_____ a pattern of tones repeated at a higher or lower pitch
19. fermata (⌢)	_____ gradually becoming softer
20. diminuendo	_____ sharps, flats, and naturals temporarily added

Pieces with Easy Accompaniments

MAJOR SCALES

This unit introduces pieces that go beyond the five-finger pattern—that is, pieces with an extended range—along with a variety of easy accompaniments to play and improvise.

Most melodies and chords are based on some kind of scale system. A **scale** (from the Italian word *scala*, ladder) is a step-by-step series of tones in a specific pattern. In most scales, this pattern is a combination of whole steps and half steps.

In the **major scale**, the pattern consists of eight tones with half steps between tones 3 and 4 and between 7 and 8, and with whole steps between the other tones.

For example, in the C major scale, the half steps occur between E and F and between B and C.

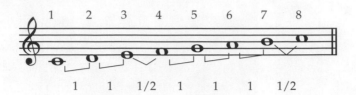

In all other major scales, it is necessary to use one or more black keys (accidentals) to preserve the pattern of whole steps and half steps.

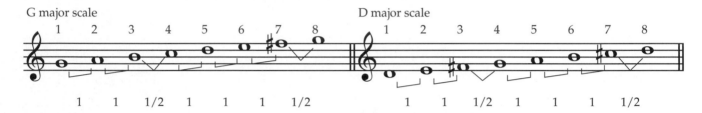

MAJOR SCALES IN TETRACHORD POSITION

The major scale may be divided into two **tetrachords,** each tetrachord consisting of *two whole steps and one half step.* A whole step separates the two tetrachords.

C MAJOR
SCALE IN
TETRACHORDS

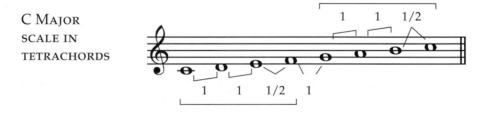

The two tetrachords are divided into a *lower position* tetrachord, played by the left hand, and an *upper position* tetrachord, played by the right hand. An easy way to start playing the major scales is by using four fingers (no thumbs) in each hand as the tetrachord position.

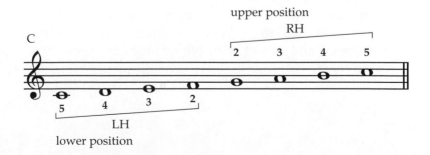

The major scales in tetrachord position and their key signatures are shown next. Begin practicing the major scales using sharp keys in tetrachord positions starting with C major and continuing in the circle of fifths* through C♯ major. Notice that the upper tetrachord of the C major scale, G–A–B–C, becomes the lower tetrachord of the G major scale. This progression of the upper tetrachord becoming the lower tetrachord of the next scale in the circle of fifths is continued throughout the major scales. Each new scale retains the sharp or sharps of the previous scale and adds one new sharp to the *seventh* degree.

Sharp keys

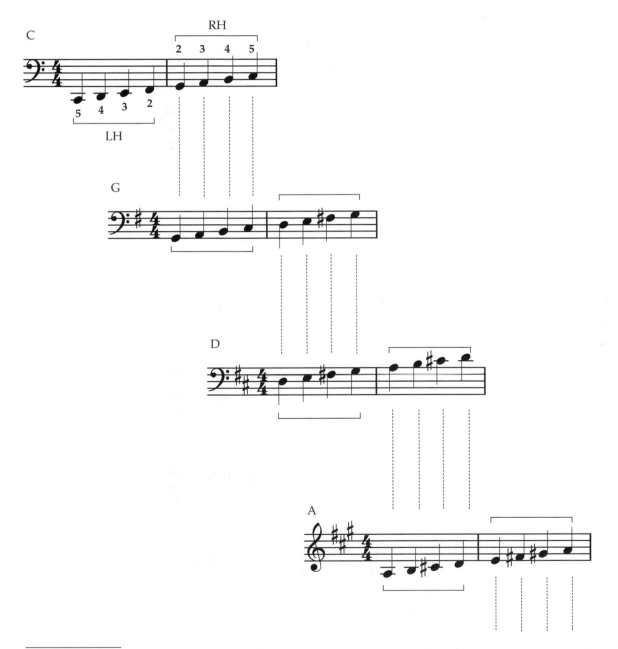

* Refer to the circle of fifths on page 156.

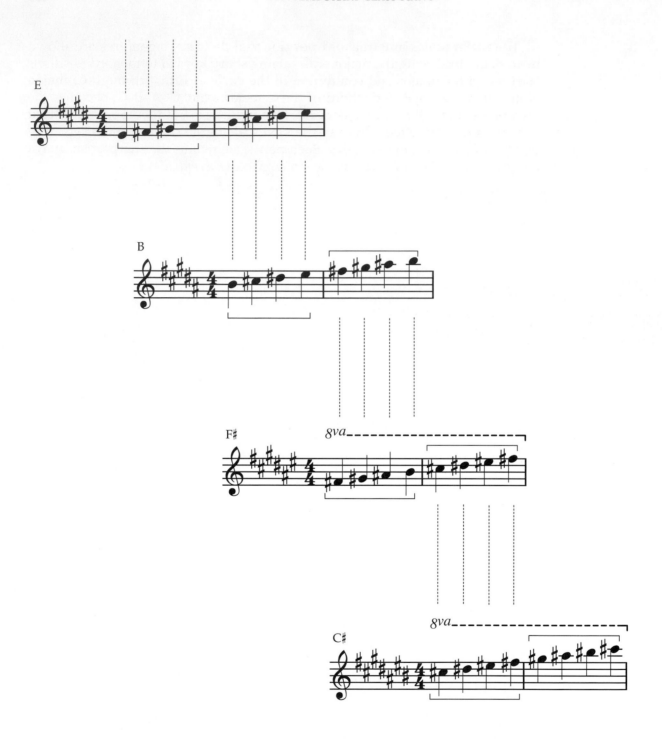

Next, begin practicing the major scales using flat keys in tetrachord position starting with C♭ major and continuing in the circle of fifths through C major. Notice that, similar to scales using sharp keys, the upper tetrachord of the C♭ major scale, G♭–A♭–B♭–C♭, becomes the lower tetrachord of the G♭ major scale. This procedure is continued from one major scale to the next. Each new scale retains the flat or flats of the previous scale and adds one new flat (when starting with C major and moving to C♭ major in the circle of fifths) to the *fourth* degree.

Flat keys

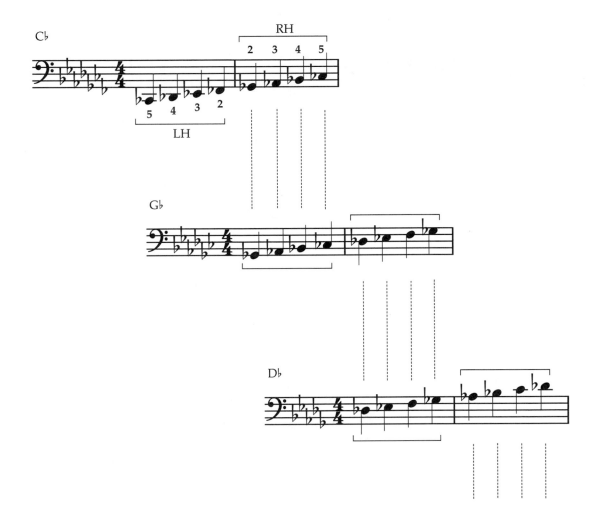

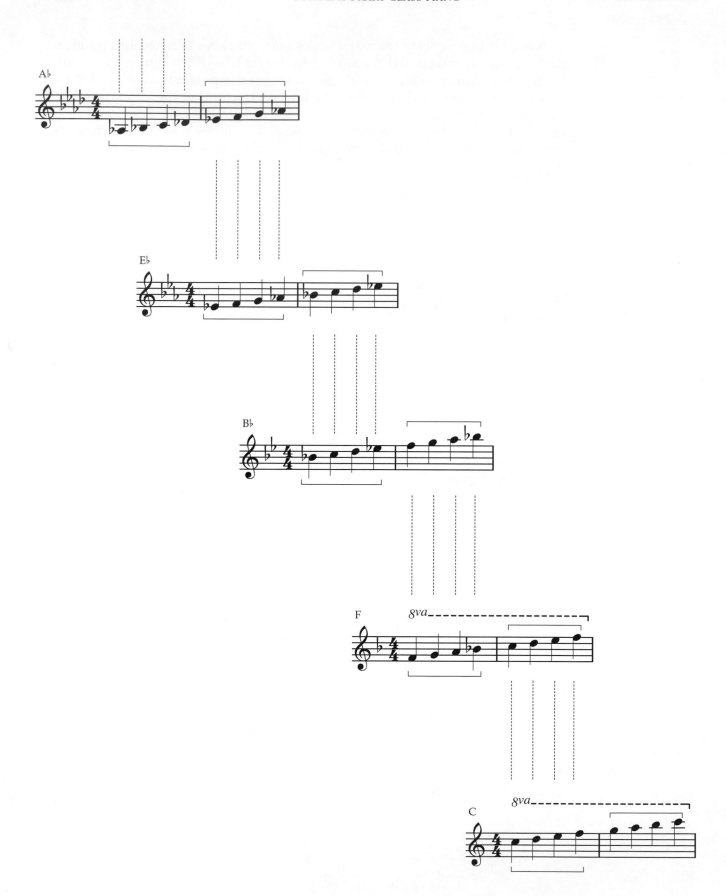

MAJOR SCALES WITH FINGERINGS FOR BOTH HANDS TOGETHER

The major scales with fingerings for both hands together and their key signatures are shown next.

- Each *sharp scale* begins on the fifth degree of the preceding scale (the clockwise order of the circle of fifths).
- Each *flat scale* begins on the fourth degree of the preceding scale (the counterclockwise order of the circle of fifths).

Practice Strategies

Practice playing the following warm-up scale preparation exercises:

- Next, practice playing these scales, first with hands separately, then with hands together.
- Be sure to observe the fingerings provided. The five-finger pattern of any key is taken from the first five tones of the corresponding scale. Only the fingerings differ.
- The places where both hands use the same finger numbers in the scales are bracketed to help you learn the correct fingerings more quickly. The keyboard diagrams give the location of scale tones and also help you to visualize the entire scale pattern at once.

Major Scales and Fingerings*

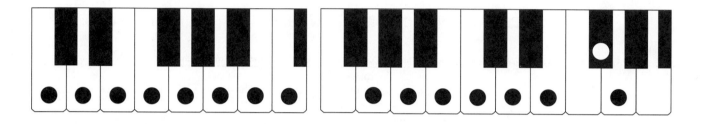

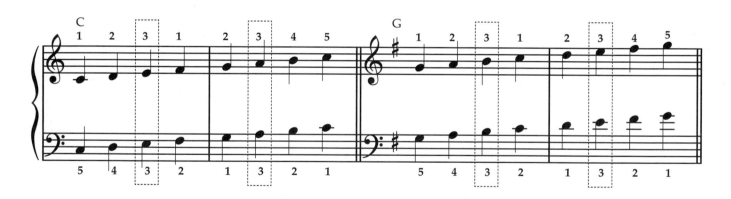

---

* Major scales and their fingerings in two octaves are given in Appendix B, on pages 528–531.

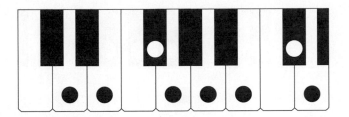

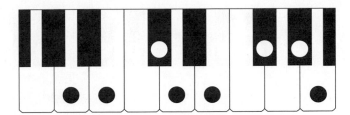

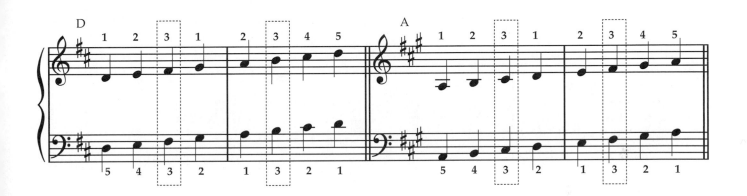

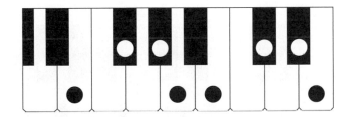

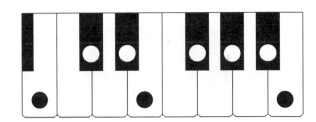

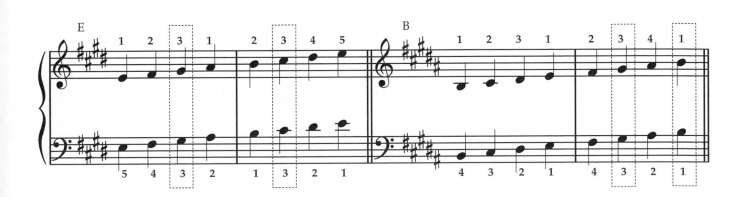

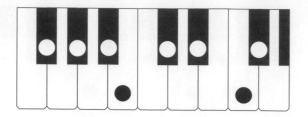

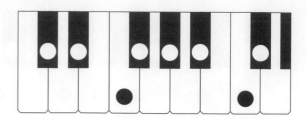

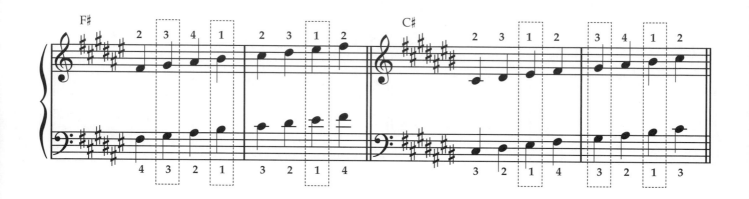

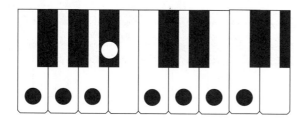

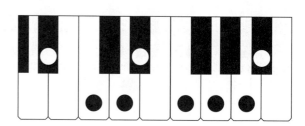

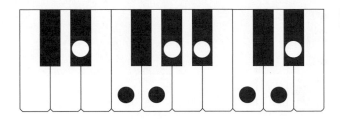

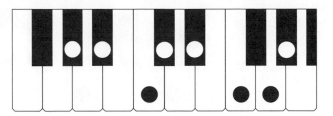

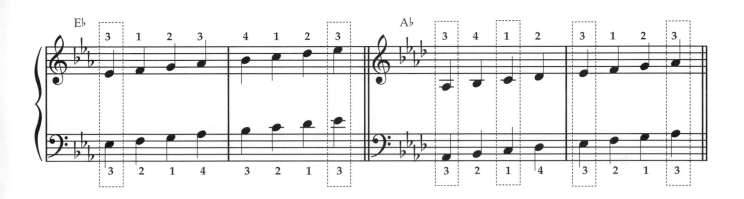

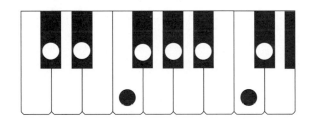

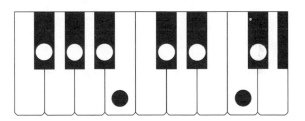

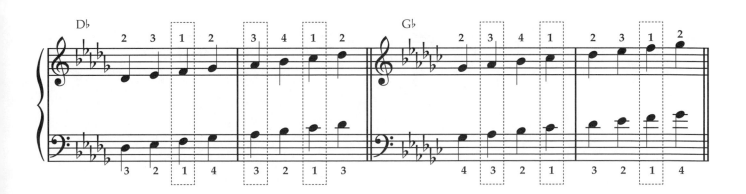

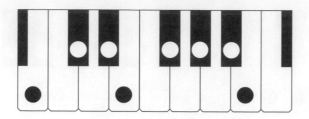

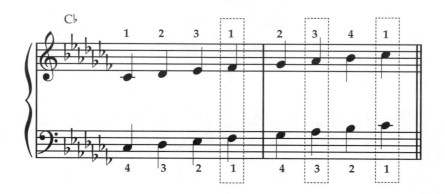

SCALE STUDIES IN CLUSTERS

The major scales can be practiced in clusters to learn the scale patterns and their specific fingerings more easily. Using one hand at a time, block scales as illustrated below, moving from one group to the next in a continuous motion.

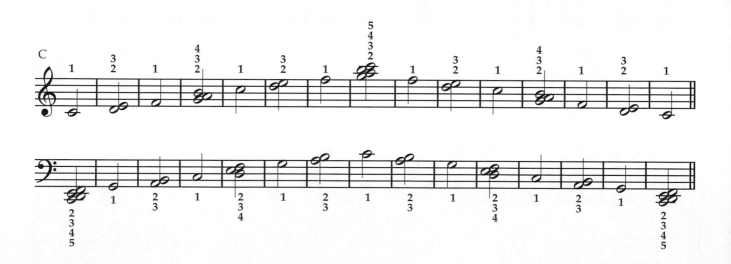

The black-key scales—B (C♭), C♯ (D♭), and F♯ (G♭)—can be learned more readily when they are blocked. The black-key scales that follow should be practiced both ascending and descending, first with hands separately, and then with hands together.

Note that each hand uses the same fingering:

group of two black keys	RH	2-3
	LH	3-2
group of three black keys	RH	2-3-4
	LH	4-3-2

The white keys primarily use the thumb of each hand.

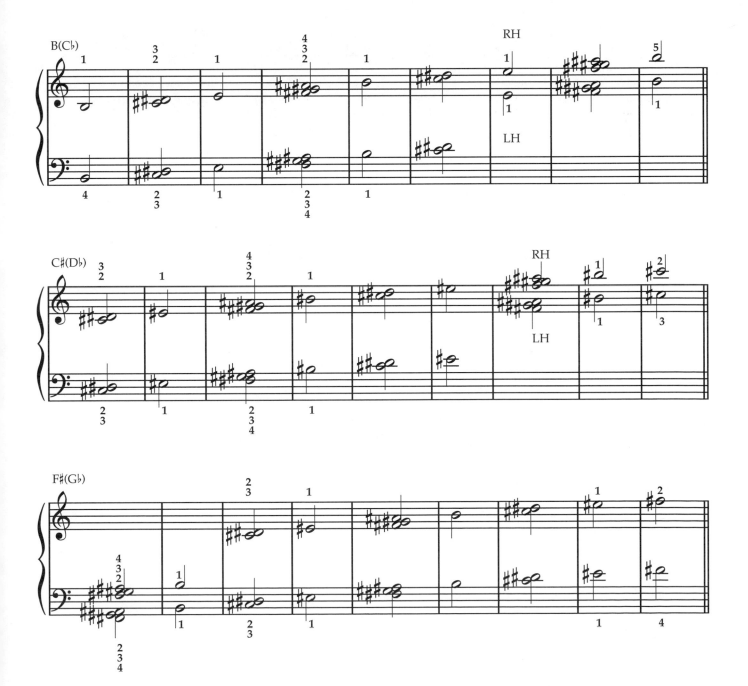

TRIADS ON MAJOR-SCALE DEGREES

Triads, like other chords, can be constructed on every degree (tone) of the scale of any key, taking into account the sharps or flats in the key signature for that key.

- Triads constructed on the first, fourth, and fifth degrees are **major**.
- Triads constructed on the second, third, and sixth degrees are **minor**.
- The triad constructed on the seventh tone is **diminished** (see page 328).

Study the triads constructed on the two scales that follow.

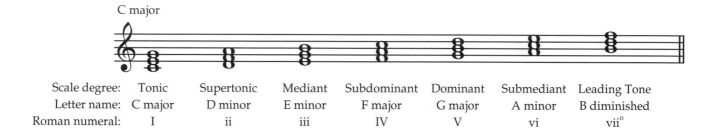

Scale degree:	Tonic	Supertonic	Mediant	Subdominant	Dominant	Submediant	Leading Tone
Letter name:	C major	D minor	E minor	F major	G major	A minor	B diminished
Roman numeral:	I	ii	iii	IV	V	vi	vii°

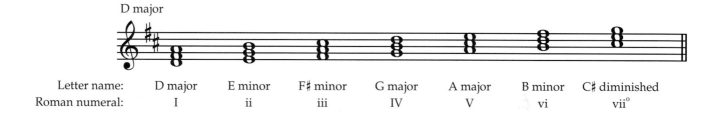

Letter name:	D major	E minor	F♯ minor	G major	A major	B minor	C♯ diminished
Roman numeral:	I	ii	iii	IV	V	vi	vii°

Each triad can be identified by its scale-degree name, its letter-name chord symbol, or the Roman numeral traditionally used to designate the scale degree.

- Uppercase Roman numerals are used for major triads.
- Lowercase Roman numerals are used for minor triads.

To identify triads and other chords by scale-degree names or Roman numerals, you must know the key of a piece.

For example, if asked to play a dominant (V) chord, you would play a G major triad in the key of C, and an A major triad in the key of D.

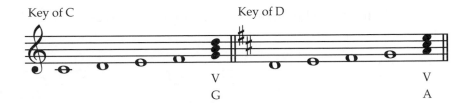

Practice Strategies

Play triads on each scale degree in the keys of C, F, and G. As you play the chord, give the scale degree and identify the chord by letter name.

INTERVALS OF A SIXTH, SEVENTH, AND EIGHTH (OCTAVE)

Intervals of a sixth, seventh, and eighth (octave) require an expansion or stretch of the hands.

Practice Strategies

Practice playing the following intervals, which are given both melodically and harmonically in the key of C. First, practice hands separately, and then with both hands.

■ Transpose to D and F major

EXTENDING THE FIVE-FINGER POSITION

Melodies that extend beyond the five-finger position have certain fingering changes that differ from the fingerings of the five-finger position. Most of these changes will be one of the following four types:

1. **Extension:** The fingers extend outside the five-finger position.

2. **Substitution:** The fingers are changed on the repeat of the same tone or tones.

3. **Crossing:** The finger or fingers cross over or under another finger or fingers.

4. **Contraction:** The fingers are contracted (brought closer together) within the five-finger position.

The Strawberry Roan shows examples of contraction and extension of fingerings. In measure 12, contraction occurs in the right hand when the fourth finger moves to F so that the first three fingers are available to play the lower notes of the melody.

THE STRAWBERRY ROAN

Student

Cowboy Song

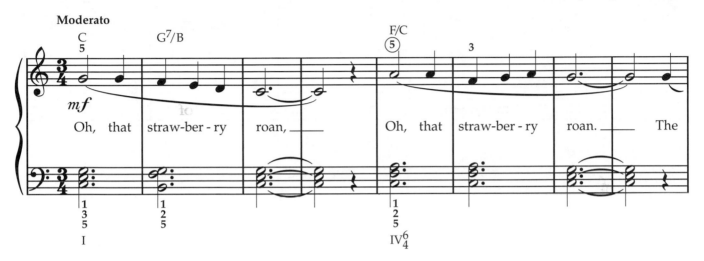

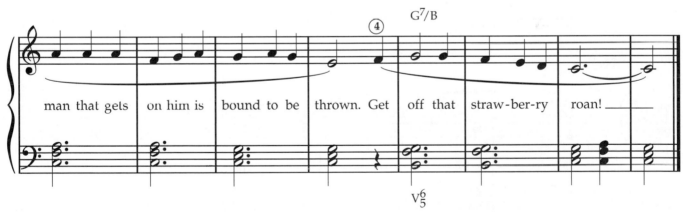

■ Transpose to D and E major

Simple Gifts, Michael, Row the Boat Ashore, and Kum Ba Ya use extended fingering in the melody.

SIMPLE GIFTS

Student

Shaker Hymn

■ Transpose to F major

MICHAEL, ROW THE BOAT ASHORE

Student

Spiritual

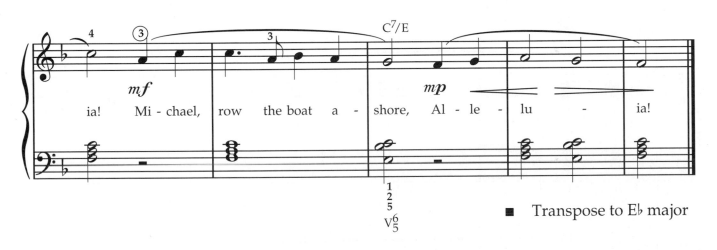

■ Transpose to E♭ major

Alla breve 𝄵

Alla breve is a meter signature that indicates cut time ($\frac{2}{2}$). Count **one** for each half note.

KUM BA YA

Student

Traditional

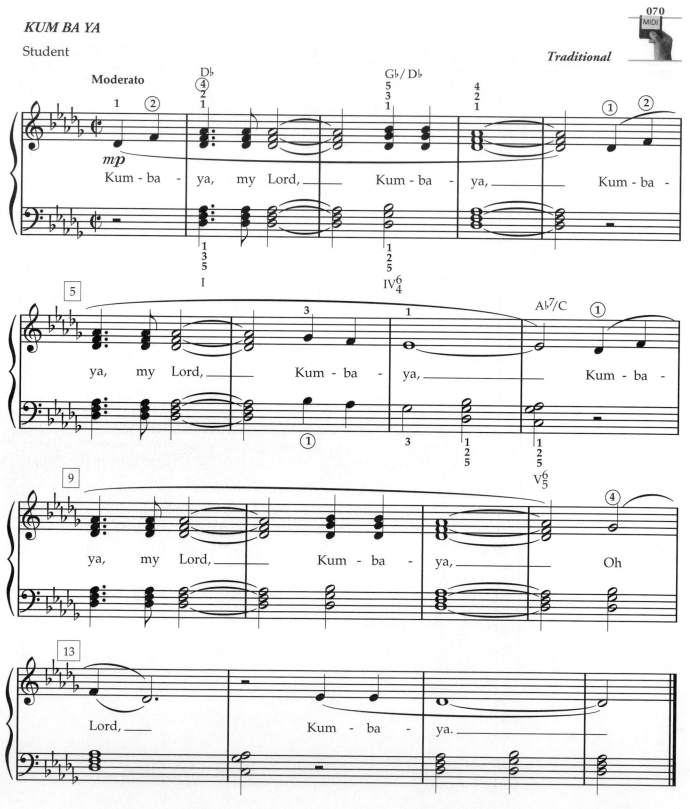

■ Transpose to D major

It Came upon the Midnight Clear uses fingering substitution in measure 3 with the third finger replacing the fourth finger on C so that the last two fingers are available to play the upper notes of the melody.

IT CAME UPON THE MIDNIGHT CLEAR

Richard S. Willis

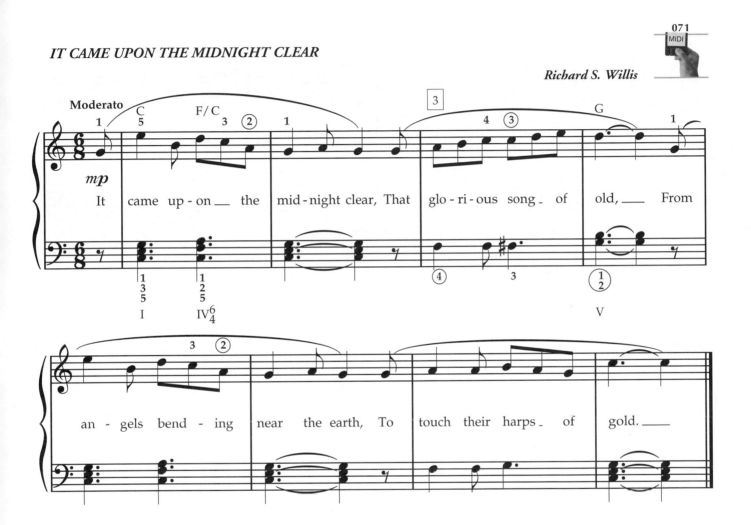

What kind of fingering is used in measure 6 of the melody?

MARY ANN

Calypso Song

Why does *Obsiwana* begin with the second finger starting the melody? What kind of fingering is used in measure 3 of the melody?

OBSIWANA

Ghanaian Folk Song

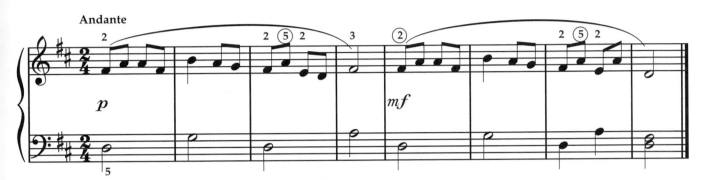

■ Transpose to D♭ major

SIXTEENTH NOTES AND SIXTEENTH RESTS

Four sixteenth notes are equal to one quarter note.

1 quarter note.

count: 1   +   2   +

One sixteenth note by itself is written with two flags. Groups of sixteenth notes are often joined with a double beam.

A sixteenth rest (𝄿) represents a silence of the same length as the value of a sixteenth note.

Practice Strategies

Tap and count the following rhythmic exercises which use sixteenth notes with both hands as given.

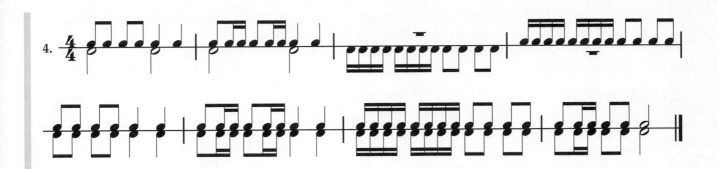

4. $\frac{4}{4}$

Keep in the Middle of the Road and Galway Piper use sixteenth notes in the melody.

Examples of extension are used in measures 4 and 8.

KEEP IN THE MIDDLE OF THE ROAD

African-American Spiritual

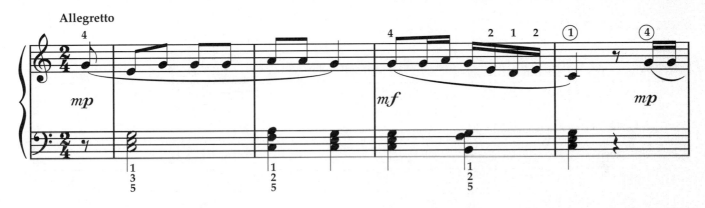

Allegretto

■ Transpose to F major

In measures 3, 5, and 7, examples of fingers crossing occur in the right-hand part between the thumb and the second finger.

Remember not to look down at the keys when making finger changes.

THE GALWAY PIPER

Irish

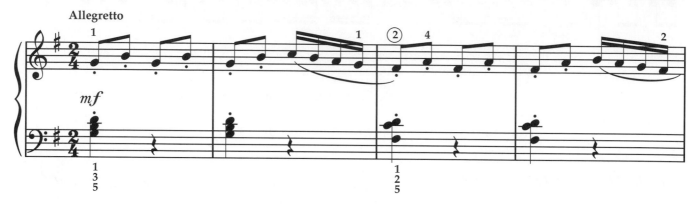

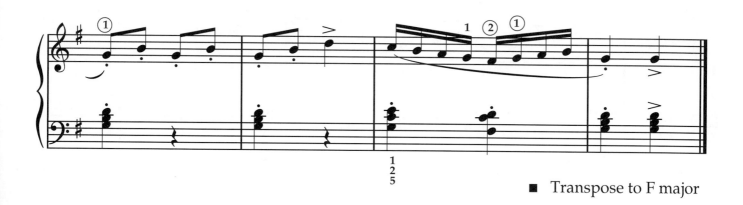

■ Transpose to F major

THE DOTTED EIGHTH NOTE

The dotted eighth note will have the same value as an eighth note tied to a sixteenth note.

A dotted eighth note will frequently be followed by a sixteenth note.

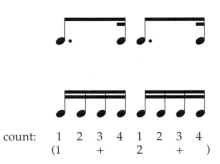

count: 1   +   2   +   ah

Another way of practicing this dotted-note rhythm is to count a fast four for the sixteenth-note groupings, with the sixteenth note occurring on four.

count: 1   2   3   4   1   2   3   4
        (1   +   2   +   )

Practice Strategies

Tap and count the following rhythmic exercises which use the dotted eighth note followed by a sixteenth note with both hands as given.

1.

2.

3.

Oh! Susanna uses the dotted eighth note followed by a sixteenth note. You will also find examples of extended fingering in the piece.

OH! SUSANNA

Stephen Foster (1826–1864)

Transpose to F major

Round and Round (a round, as its name suggests) uses crossing, extension, and substitutions.

ROUND AND ROUND

John Hilton (1599–1657)

Examples of fingers crossing over and under are found in *Scale Study* and *A Little Scale*.

SCALE STUDY

Carl Czerny (1791–1857)

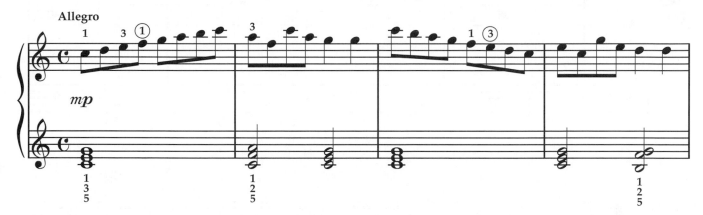

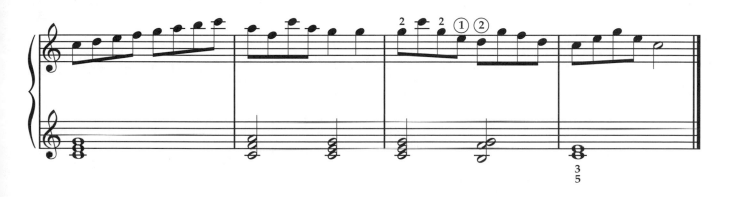

A LITTLE SCALE

Daniel Gottlob Türk (1750–1813)

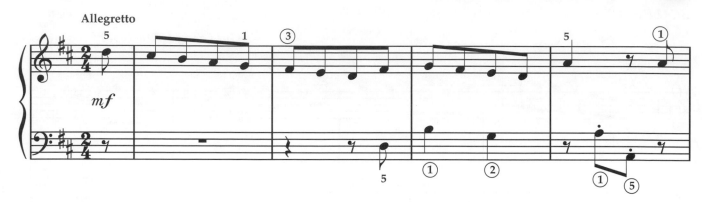

MUSICAL FORMS: AB AND ABA

The word *form* refers to the architecture or structure of music. Two of the most common forms used in songs are **two-part song form** (sometimes referred to as **binary** or **AB form**) and **three-part song form** (sometimes referred to as **ternary** or **ABA form**).

Two-part song form (AB form) is illustrated in *Mexican Hat Dance*.

Section A	A—phrase 1
	A′—variation of phrase 1
	A and A′ repeated
Section B	B—contrasting phrase (introduces new material)
	B′—variation of contrasting phrase
	B and B′ repeated

MEXICAN HAT DANCE

Traditional

Three-part song form (ABA form) is illustrated in *Irish Washerwoman*.

A—phrase 1

A′—repeat of phrase 1 with some alteration

B—contrasting phrase (introduces new material)

A—phrase 1 (Da Capo section)

A′—repeat of phrase 1 with some alteration (Da Capo section)

Con Moto

Con moto is a tempo marking that means to play quickly, "with motion."

IRISH WASHERWOMAN

Irish

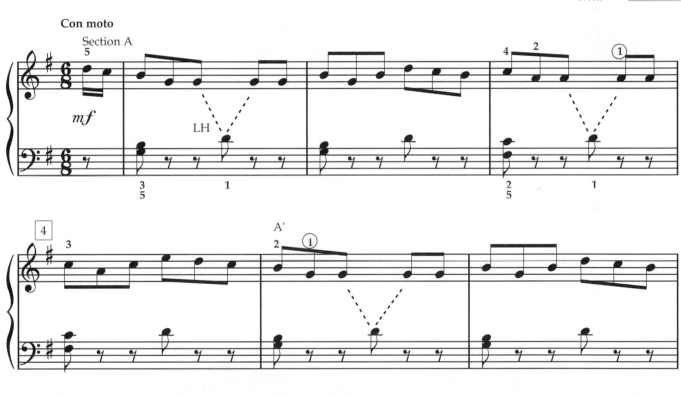

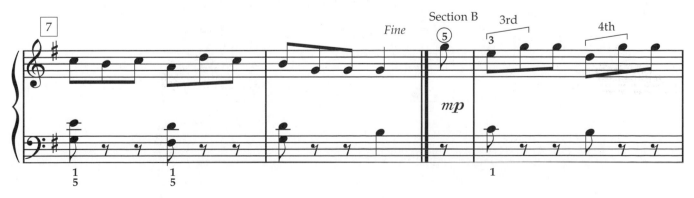

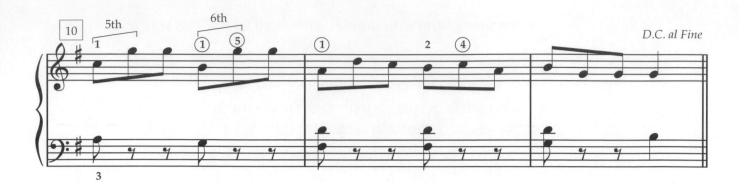

MELODIES WITH LETTER-NAME CHORD SYMBOLS FOR I, IV$^6_4$, AND V$^6_5$ CHORDS

Play the following melodies which use letter-name chord symbols for the I, IV$^6_4$, and V$^6_5$ chord harmonizations.

WHEN I COME BACK

German

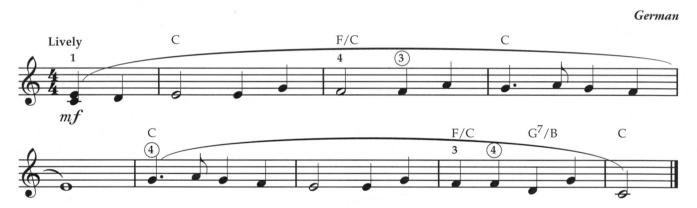

LA CUCARACHA

Mexican

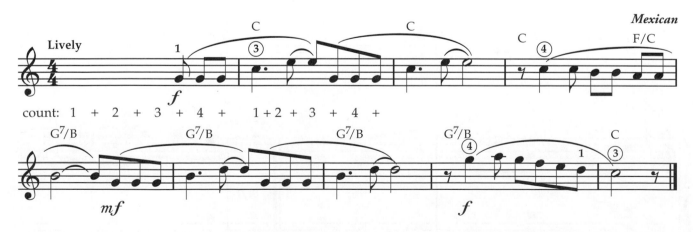

ROCK OF AGES

Thomas Hastings (1784–1872)

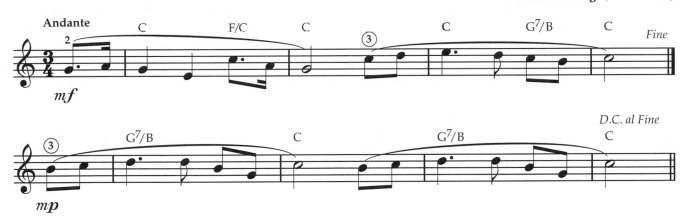

A CHRISTMAS CAROL

Bohemian

In the next piece, the right- and left-hand parts overlap. Let the left hand play an incomplete chord (the root and third) while the right hand takes the fifth for the melody.

NOBODY KNOWS THE TROUBLE I'VE SEEN

Spiritual

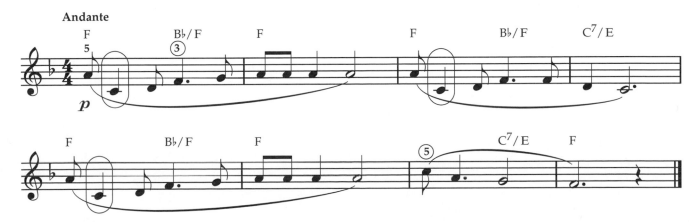

BROKEN-CHORD ACCOMPANIMENT PATTERNS

Practice the following broken-chord accompaniment patterns and substitute them in some of the pieces on pages 280–284. The patterns use I, IV$_4^6$, and V$_5^6$ chords and are in a variety of meters. For simplicity, all are notated in the key of F. Transpose to other keys as necessary.

First, the basic pattern is shown in block-chord form:

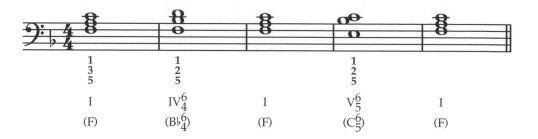

$\frac{2}{4}$ Pattern

$\frac{3}{4}$ Patterns

$\frac{4}{4}$ Patterns

$\frac{6}{8}$ Patterns

Play *Frankie and Johnny* with a block-chord accompaniment as given.

FRANKIE AND JOHNNY

Traditional

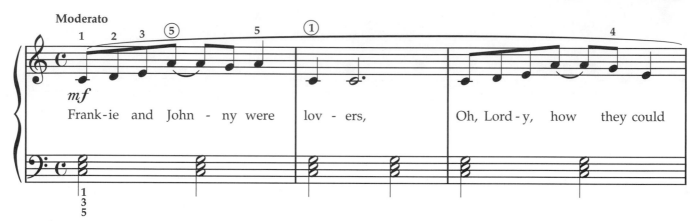

Next, play the same melody using a broken-chord pattern in the accompaniment.

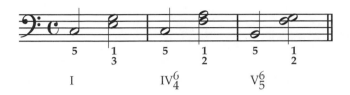

I   IV$^6_4$ V$^6_5$

FRANKIE AND JOHNNY

Traditional

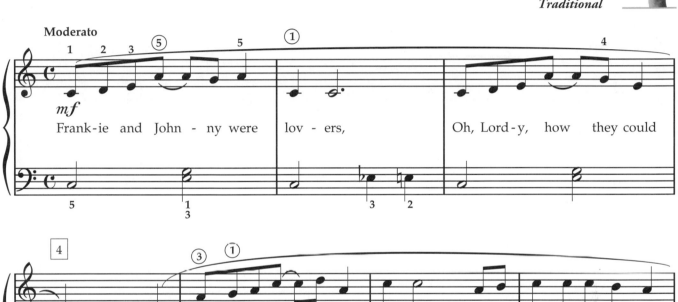

Moderato

mf

Frank-ie and John - ny were lov - ers, Oh, Lord-y, how they could

love. They swore to be true to each oth - er, just as true as the stars a -

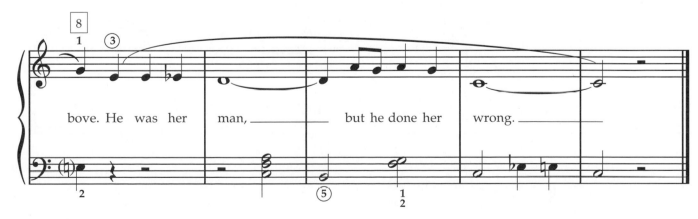

bove. He was her man,_____ but he done her wrong._____

Practice the broken-chord accompaniment in *Vive la Compagnie* before playing the piece as written.

I   IV$_4^6$ V$_5^6$

VIVE LA COMPAGNIE

French

WALTZ PATTERN

The next two pieces, *Du, du liegst mir im Herzen* and *My Hat, It Has Three Corners*, use the **waltz pattern,** a broken-chord accompaniment in which the first beat is stressed and the second and third beats are played staccato. Think of playing *down* on the key for beat one, and playing *up* on the keys for the other two beats (oom-pah-pah).

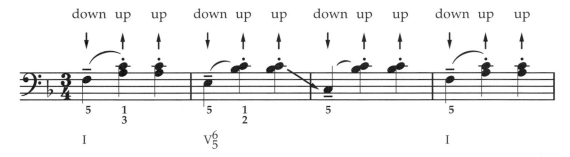

The small arrow in the left-hand part of measure 6 in *Du, du liegst mir im Herzen* indicates a jump down to the note C.

DU, DU LIEGST MIR IM HERZEN

German

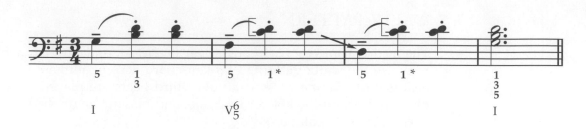

* Take both notes with the left-hand thumb

MY HAT, IT HAS THREE CORNERS

German

ARPEGGIO ACCOMPANIMENT PATTERNS

An **arpeggio** is a chord in which every note is played separately, one after the other. Practice the following arpeggio patterns in the same way as described on page 278 for broken-chord patterns.

Play some of the earlier pieces studied as well as some of the melodies in Unit 5, using various arpeggio accompaniments as given on the following page.

2/4 Patterns

In *On Top of Old Smoky,* the left-hand accompaniment is made up of arpeggio figures based on the I, IV$^6_4$, and V$^6_5$ chords. Practice playing the left-hand accompaniment as block chords while you hum the melody. Then break the chords into arpeggios as shown below. Notice that the first four notes of the melody form an arpeggio of the C major chord.

ON TOP OF OLD SMOKY

Traditional

086 MIDI

■ Transpose to D major

Next, play *On Top of Old Smoky* using a waltz pattern in the left-hand accompaniment. Remember, the first beat is stressed and the second and third beats are played staccato.

Practice the arpeggio accompaniment in *Barcarolle* in the same way that you did for *Old Smoky*.

BARCAROLLE

Jacques Offenbach (1819–1880)

■ Transpose to A major

Another form of the arpeggio accompaniment is found in *Gaîté Parisienne*. First, try playing the melody with blocked chords throughout, then play the given accompaniment pattern while humming the melody. Finally, play the piece as written.

GAÎTÉ PARISIENNE

Jacques Offenbach (1819–1880)

Alberti Bass

The **Alberti bass** is an accompaniment pattern using a repeated arpeggio figure arranged with

- the lowest tone first,
- followed by the highest tone,
- then the middle tone,
- then a repeat of the highest tone.

It is named after the Baroque composer Domenico Alberti, who frequently used this kind of accompaniment in his music, as did later Classical composers. *Ah, Vous dirai-je, Maman?* uses an Alberti bass.

Sempre Staccato

Sempre staccato means "always staccato." Note that staccato dots are unnecessary with this instruction.

AH, VOUS DIRAI-JE, MAMAN? *(Ah, Shall I Tell You, Mama?)*

French

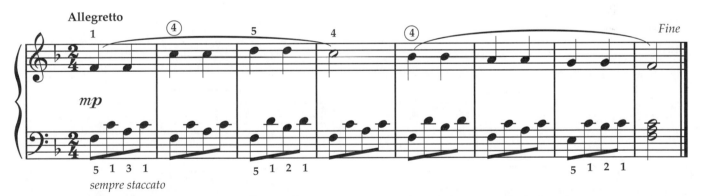
sempre staccato

SYNCOPATION

Syncopation is a rhythmic effect in which the stress is placed on the off-beats (weak beats) of the measure.

For example:

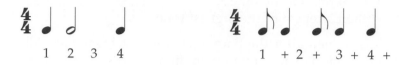

Play the following études which use syncopated rhythm in their melodies. Then transpose these études to other major keys of your choice.

ÉTUDES IN SYNCOPATED RHYTHM

Study 1

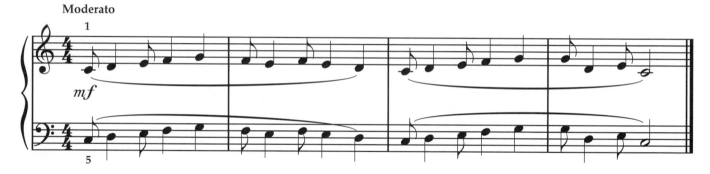

Study 2

In *Buffalo Gals*, the syncopation in the left-hand accompaniment begins with chords on the off-beats 2 and 4. Rests are found on the strong beats 1 and 3.

count   1   2   3   4   1   2   3   4

The right-hand melody uses syncopation by placing a longer note value on a weak beat (the second half of beat 1), so that the weak beat is stressed.

count: 1   +   2   +   3   +   4   +   1   +   2   +   3   +   4   +

BUFFALO GALS

American

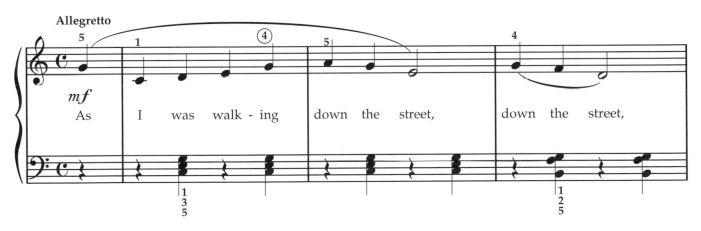

As   I   was   walk - ing   down   the   street,   down   the   street,

down   the   street, A   pret - ty   gal   I   chanced to   meet, oh,   she   was   fair   to

In *The Entertainer,* the right-hand melody uses syncopation by placing a longer note value on a weak beat (the second half of beat 1), so that the weak beat is stressed.

count: 1   +   2   +   3   +   4   +

The Entertainer also has a first ending and a second ending indicated by the marks shown below, first discussed on page 220.

Before playing the piece as written, block the broken-chord accompaniment in the left hand.

THE ENTERTAINER

Scott Joplin (1868–1917)

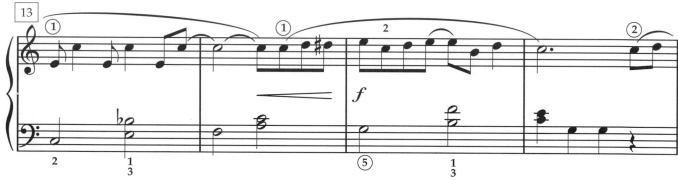

THE DAMPER PEDAL

As discussed in Unit 2, the damper pedal is the pedal farthest to the right. It is used to obtain more resonance and to connect and sustain tones that require legato playing. It works by releasing the felt dampers from the strings and allowing the strings to continue vibrating freely.

Push the pedal down with the right foot, hold as indicated by the markings below, and then release. Remember to keep your heel on the floor while pedaling.

down   up

Other standard markings are:

down   up-down   down   up   down   up

Direct Pedaling

Depress the damper pedal simultaneously with the chord, as indicated by the markings above. Release the pedal on one of the following beats. This type of pedaling is used primarily for resonance and to achieve a stronger feeling of legato. No attempt is made to bind all harmonies together.

Pedal Studies

Using direct pedaling, practice playing triads on the white keys only:

The Highlands and *Distant Horns* use direct pedaling.* Practice lifting the hands at the end of each phrase along with the pedal lifts.

THE HIGHLANDS

E. M.

* Other pieces that use direct pedaling are *Evening Tide* on page 95 and *Aaron's Song* on pages 136–137, both in Unit 2.

DISTANT HORNS

Elvina Pearce

OTHER ACCOMPANIMENT PATTERNS

Ostinato Accompaniment

An **ostinato pattern** is a constantly recurring figure usually found in the bass. *He's Got the Whole World in His Hands* uses an ostinato pattern called a *walking bass.* Notice how the four tones of the walking bass move either up or down scalewise, beginning or ending with the root of the appropriate chord.

HE'S GOT THE WHOLE WORLD IN HIS HANDS

Spiritual

Drum Roll Accompaniment

To play the drum roll accompaniment, place the left thumb, second, third, and fourth fingers on the keys and roll the whole hand quickly to the right.

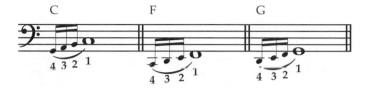

BATTLE HYMN OF THE REPUBLIC

William Steffe

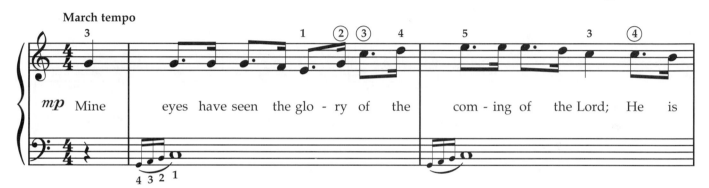

Mine eyes have seen the glo - ry of the com - ing of the Lord; He is

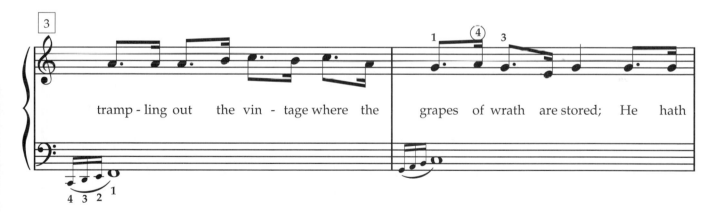

tramp - ling out the vin - tage where the grapes of wrath are stored; He hath

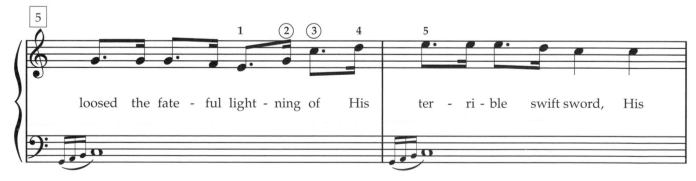

loosed the fate - ful light - ning of His ter - ri - ble swift sword, His

truth is   march-ing   on.   Glo - ry, glo - ry, hal - le-

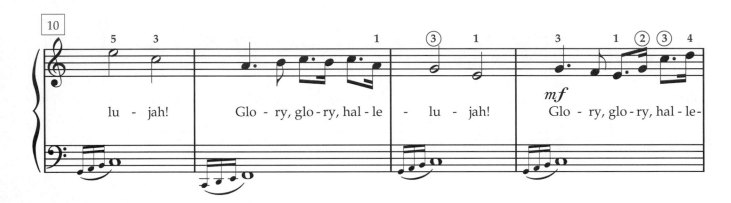

lu - jah!   Glo - ry, glo - ry, hal - le   - lu - jah!   Glo - ry, glo - ry, hal - le-

lu - jah! His   truth is   march-ing   on.

SECONDARY CHORDS

The **primary chords,** I, IV, and V, have been used in blues improvisation and in a variety of accompaniment patterns so far. The **secondary chords, ii, iii,** and **vi,** can also be used to accompany melodic lines. They are often referred to as substitute chords for I, IV, and V.

The ii Chord (Supertonic)

The **ii chord (supertonic)** is a minor triad constructed on the second degree of the major scale. It is sometimes substituted for the IV chord since the chords have two tones in common.

Note that the letter name of the ii chord is taken from the root of the chord.

Practice playing the following chord progressions using the ii chord in all major keys, noting common tones in the movement from one chord to the next.

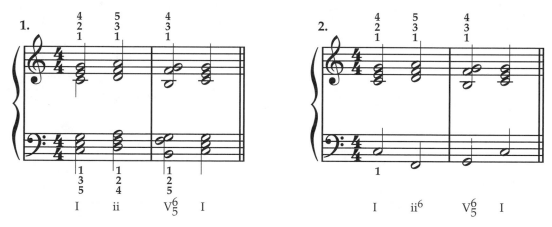

■ Transpose examples 1 and 2 to G major, D major, F major, and A major.

The iii Chord (Mediant)

The **iii chord (mediant)** is a minor triad constructed on the third degree of the major scale. It is sometimes substituted for the V chord since the chords have two tones in common.

Again, note that the letter name of the iii chord is taken from the root of the chord.

Practice playing the following chord progressions using the iii chord in all major keys, again noting common tones in the movement from one chord to the next.

Key of C Major

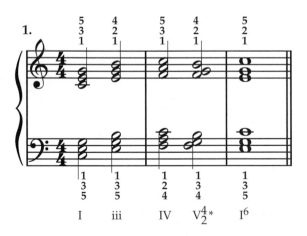

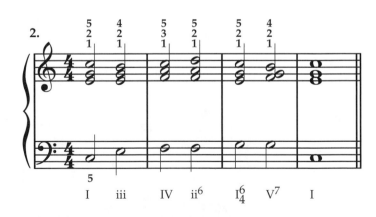

■ Transpose examples 1 and 2 to G major, D major, F major, and A major.

---

* Seventh chords and their inversions are discussed on page 317.

The vi Chord (Submediant)

The **vi chord (submediant)** is a minor triad constructed on the sixth degree of the major scale. It is sometimes substituted for the I chord since the chords have two tones in common.

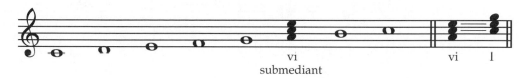

Again, note that the letter name of the vi chord is taken from the root of the chord.

Practice playing the following chord progressions using the vi chord in all major keys, again noting common tones in the movement from one chord to the next.

Key of C Major

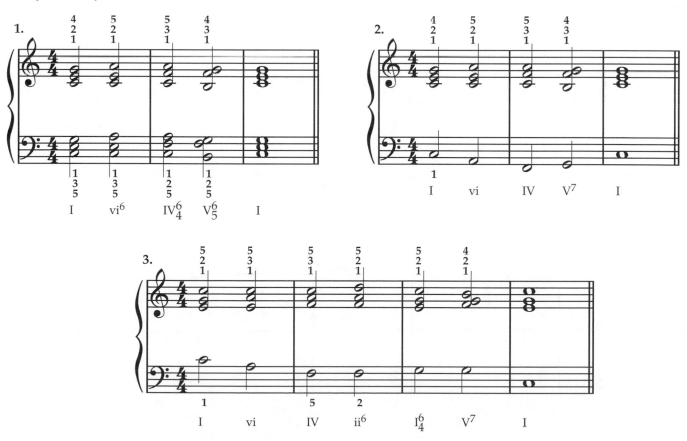

■ Transpose examples 1, 2, and 3 to G major, D major, F major, and A major.

Before playing *Every Night When the Sun Goes Down*, study the triads that make up the accompaniment pattern. Give the letter names (C, Dm, etc.) of the triads used in this piece.

EVERY NIGHT WHEN THE SUN GOES DOWN

American

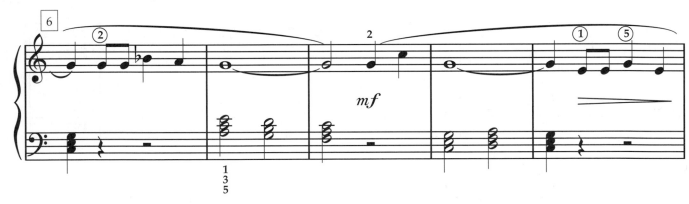

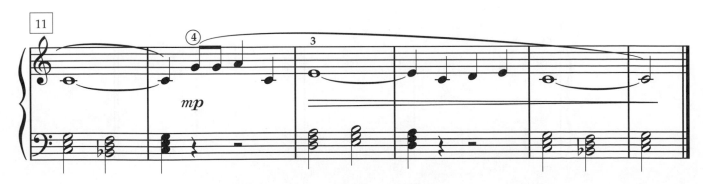

Stars of the Heavens uses the supertonic (ii) and the mediant (iii) chords in the accompaniment.

STARS OF THE HEAVENS *(Las estrellitas del cielo)*

Mexican Folk Song

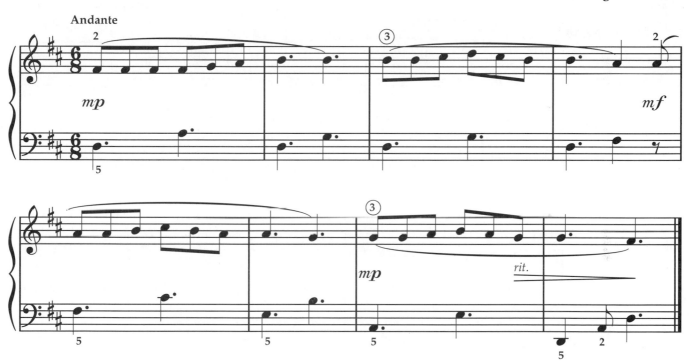

The Dreamer uses the supertonic (ii), mediant (iii), and submediant (vi) chords in the left-hand arpeggiated accompaniment.

THE DREAMER

Piano 1

Elie Siegmeister (1909–1991)
Arranged by E.M.

THE DREAMER

Piano 2

Ships Ahoy uses the mediant (iii) chord in the accompaniment.

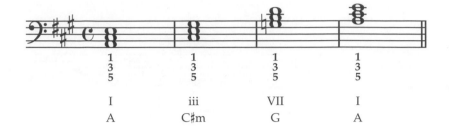

SHIPS AHOY

E. M.

Oregano Rock uses the supertonic (ii) and mediant (iii) chords in the right-hand part. Practice the triads below as a warm-up for this piece.

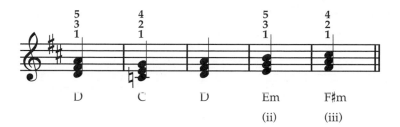

OREGANO ROCK

E. M.

INTERVALS WITHIN THE SCALE

The intervals formed between the tonic and the other degrees of the major scale are illustrated below.

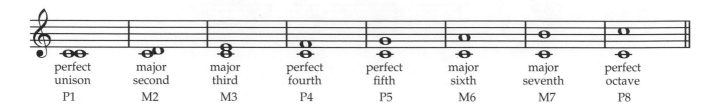

perfect unison	major second	major third	perfect fourth	perfect fifth	major sixth	major seventh	perfect octave
P1	M2	M3	P4	P5	M6	M7	P8

Perfect intervals: unison, fourth, fifth, octave

Major intervals: second, third, sixth, seventh

A **perfect interval** becomes **diminished** when the top tone is lowered a half step, or when the bottom tone is raised a half step.

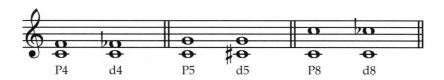

P4   d4   P5   d5   P8   d8

A **major interval** becomes **minor** when the top tone is lowered a half step, or when the bottom tone is raised a half step.

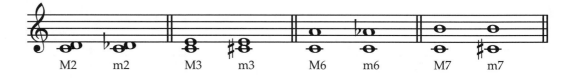

M2   m2   M3   m3   M6   m6   M7   m7

A major or perfect interval becomes **augmented** when the top tone is raised a half step.

Interval Diagram

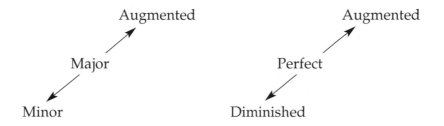

Practice Strategies

Practice building and playing melodic and harmonic intervals in various major keys of your choice. Name each interval.

MELODIC LINES WITH INTERVALS

Melodies using various intervals harmonically appear on the following pages.

Seconds

The Chase uses harmonic and melodic major seconds (a whole step apart) throughout the right hand.

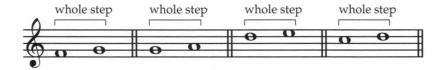

Notice that the right hand "chases" the left at the distance of a minor second (one half step) throughout.

Bitonal

The Chase is **bitonal,** which means that it is in two different keys simultaneously. The left hand is pentatonic, using only the five black keys, spelled here with sharps instead of flats. The right hand uses only the white keys in the five-finger pattern of C major. Note that a beam connects the eighth note in the left hand to the eighth note in the right hand.

$\frac{8}{8}$ Time

In $\frac{8}{8}$ **time,** there are eight beats to the measure with the eighth note receiving one beat.

THE CHASE

Stan Applebaum

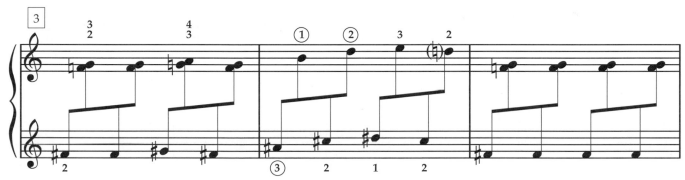

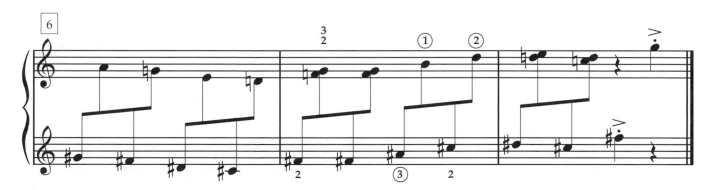

Thirds

Practice the following preparatory exercise containing thirds before playing *Carol of the Drum*.

CAROL OF THE DRUM

Katherine Davis

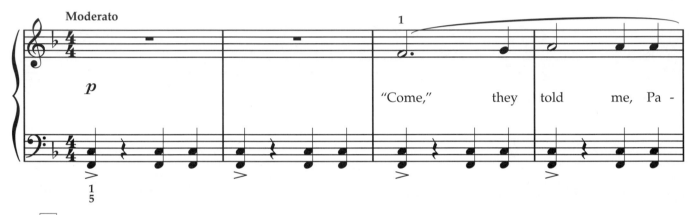

"Come," they told me, Pa-

rum-pa-pum - pum, _____ "Our new-born King to see! Pa-

rum-pa-pum - pum, _____ Our fin-est gifts we'll bring, Pa-

Thirds and Fourths

Saturday Smile uses major and minor thirds along with perfect and augmented fourths throughout, as illustrated in the following preparatory exercise.

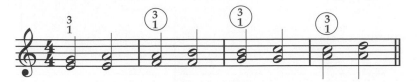

SATURDAY SMILE

Lynn Freeman Olson (1938–1987)

CHORD INVERSIONS

As discussed in Unit 2, a chord is **inverted** when a chord tone other than the root is in the bass.

Triads may be inverted twice.

When the third of the chord is in the bass, the chord is in **first inversion.**

When the fifth of the chord is in the bass, the chord is in **second inversion.**

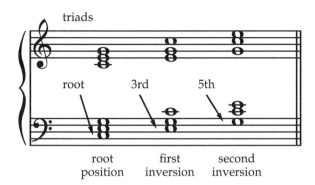

Seventh chords have three inversions:

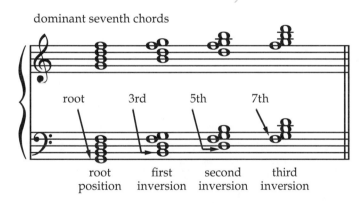

The numbers beneath the chords below represent the intervals that make up the chord, counting from the bottom note to the notes above.

For example, in the first inversion of the C major triad, the C$^6_3$, E to C is an interval of a sixth and E to G is an interval of a third.

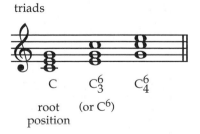

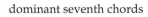

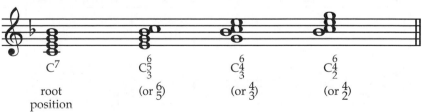

Chord Inversions—Blocked and Arpeggiated

Practice playing major chords in root position and in their inverted positions in all keys using correct fingerings. First play them blocked and then arpeggiated as illustrated below. They may also be played arpeggiated first and then blocked. Then play the chords in minor.

Root Position

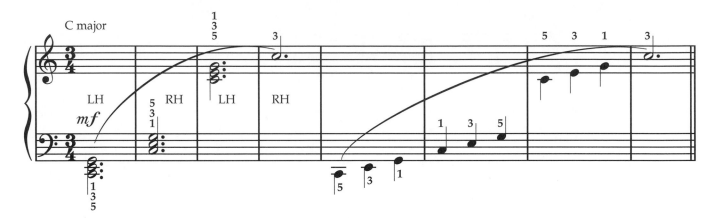

First Inversion

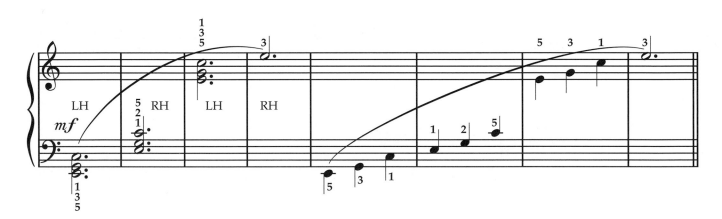

Second Inversion

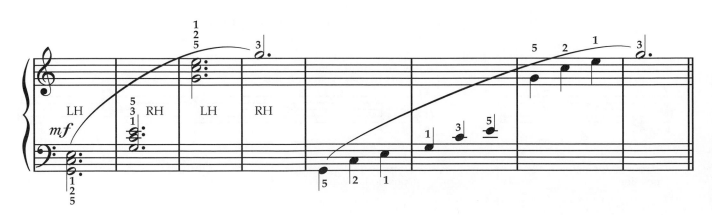

Root Position

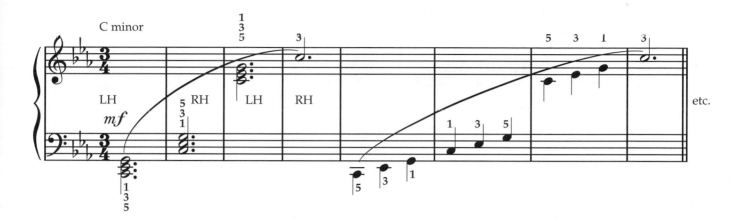

Next, practice playing chord inversions in all keys using correct fingerings, first with hands separately and then together. The inversions for the C, G, and D chords are given below. Continue in the order of the circle of fifths for the remaining keys.

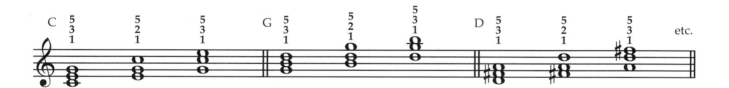

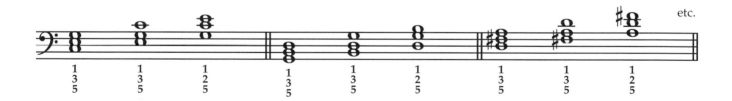

Triads are built in thirds. However, when a triad is inverted and there is an interval of a fourth, the top of those two tones is the root of the triad. Identify and play the following major triads using the chord symbols as illustrated:

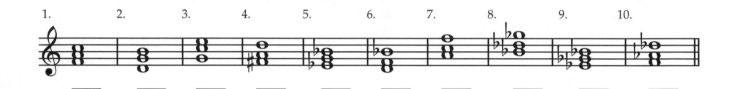

Practice the inverted triads in the right-hand part of *Steeplechase* before playing the piece.

Grazioso

Grazioso means graceful.

STEEPLECHASE *(from Opus 117)*

Cornelius Gurlitt (1820–1901)

Hemiola

Hemiola is a rhythmic device that shifts stresses from groups of two to groups of three, and vice versa.

TRIADS ON THE RUN

E. M.

THE DAMPER PEDAL (INDIRECT PEDALING)

Indirect or **legato pedaling** is used to obtain a very smooth connection of tones. This is created by depressing the damper pedal *immediately after* sounding the chord. As you play each subsequent chord, release the pedal quickly, then depress it immediately once again.

Pedal Studies

Using indirect pedaling, practice playing triads on the white keys only.

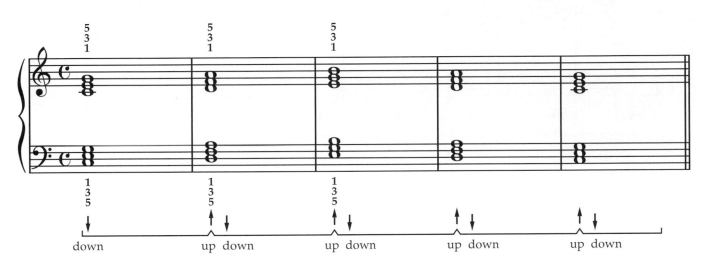

Practice the following two chord progressions in various keys.

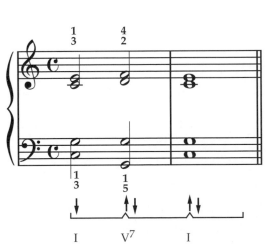

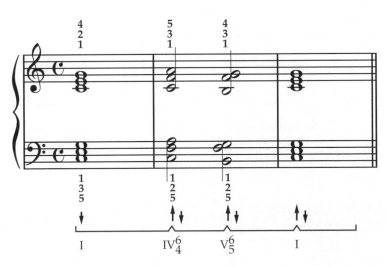

The right-hand part of *Big Ben* uses inverted triads throughout. Be sure to observe the legato pedal markings.

BIG BEN

E. M.

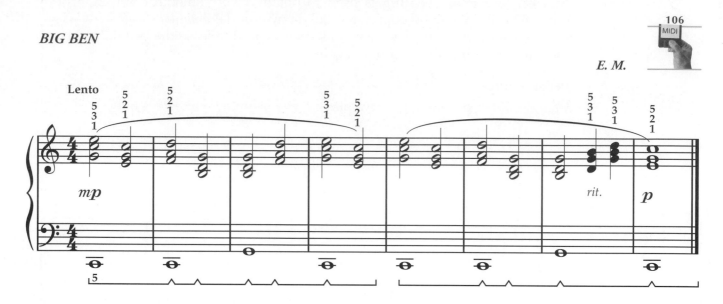

Twilight and *In Church* use indirect pedaling throughout. Be sure to carefully observe the pedal markings.

TWILIGHT

Lynn Freeman Olson (1938–1987)

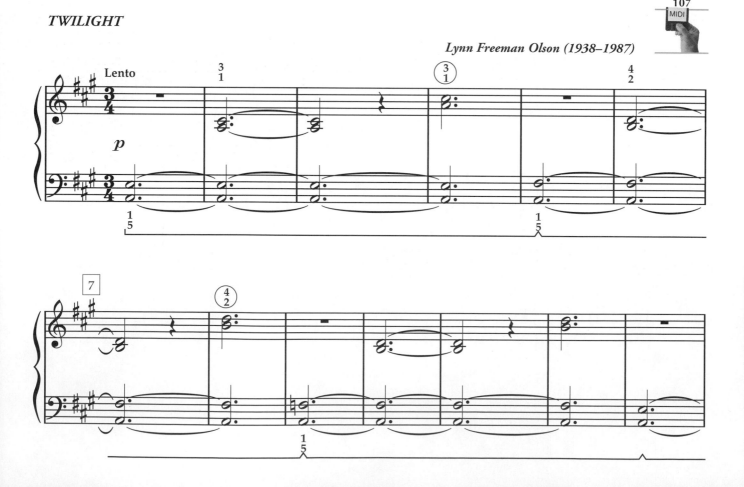

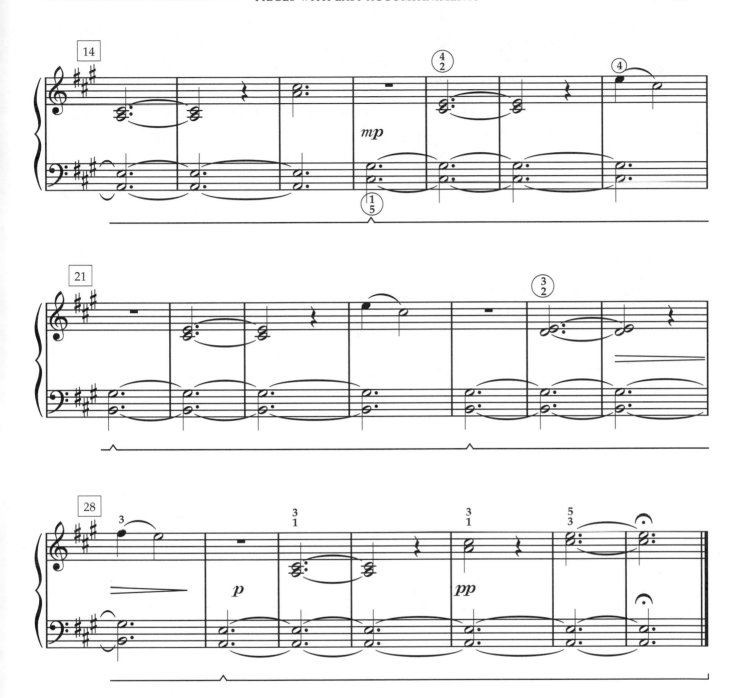

From *Piano for Pleasure: A Basic Course for Adults*, *1st edition, by Hilley/Olson © 1986. Reprinted with permission of Wadsworth, a division of Thompson Learning: www.thompsonrights.com. Fax 800-730-2215.*

HYMN STYLE

In **hymn style,** the melody is harmonized with chords divided between two hands. *In Church* and *Chorale* are written in hymn style.

Play these hymns with indirect pedaling, aiming for a perfectly smooth connection between the chords.

IN CHURCH

Jane Smisor Bastien

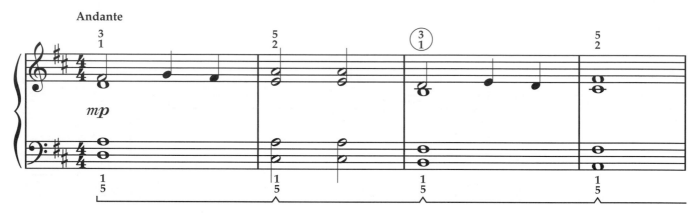

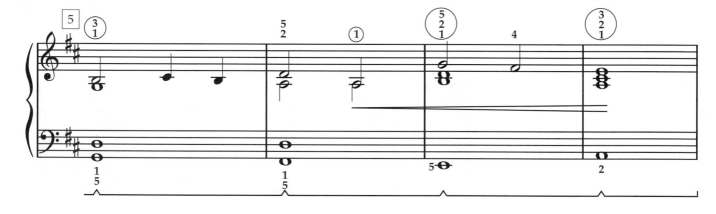

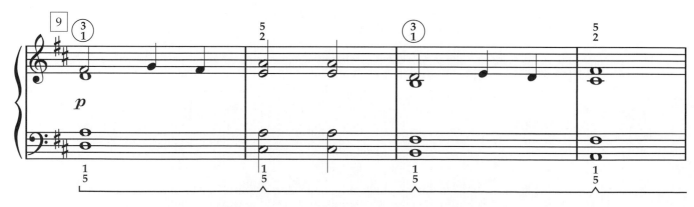

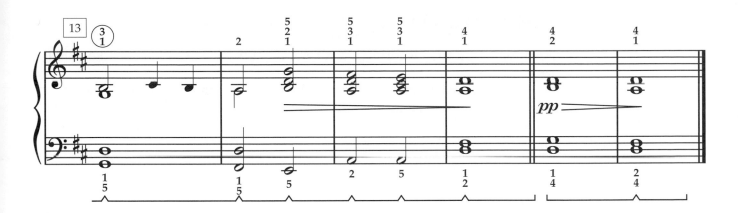

From Older Beginner Piano Course, Level 2, by James Bastion. Copyright © 1978 Neil A. Kjos Music Co., San Diego, California. International Copyright Secured. All Rights Reserved. Used with permission 2003.

CHORALE

Robert Schumann
(1810–1856)

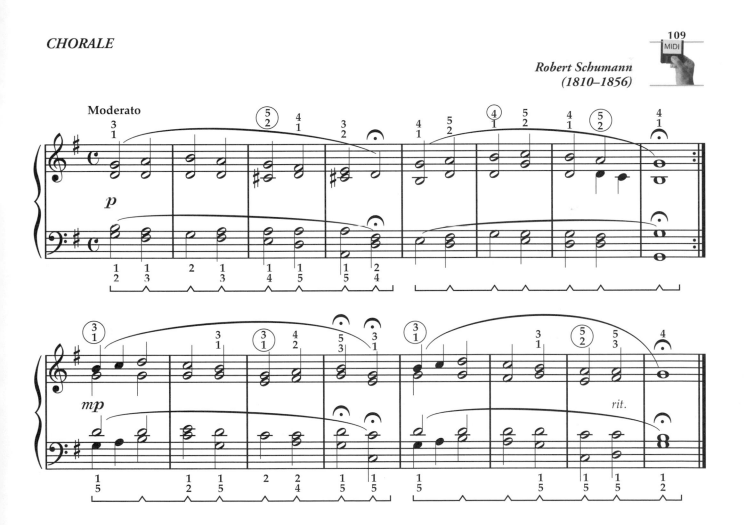

AUGMENTED AND DIMINISHED TRIADS

An **augmented triad** is formed by raising the fifth tone of a major triad one half step.

A **diminished triad** is formed by lowering the third and fifth tones of a major triad one half step.

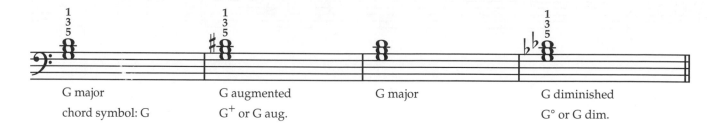

G major	G augmented	G major	G diminished
chord symbol: G	G⁺ or G aug.		G° or G dim.

Practice Strategies

Practice playing the four kinds of triads—major, augmented, minor, and diminished—using the following pattern in major keys of your choice. Practice with hands separately and then hands together.

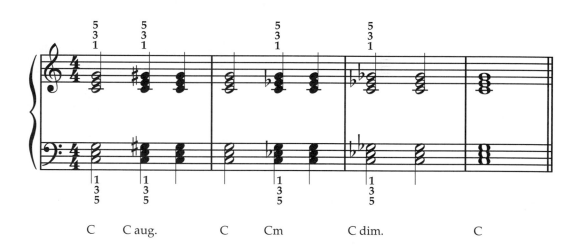

THEME FROM SYMPHONY NO. 5 ("From the New World")

Antonín Dvořák (1841–1904)

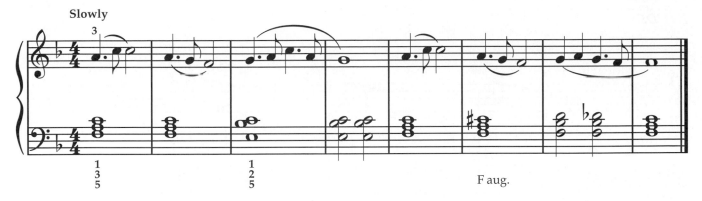

Marziale

Marziale means to play in the style of a march.

Identify the various triads and their inversions in this piece.

A NEW FANFARE

E. M.

REPERTOIRE

Ped. simile means to pedal in the same manner as previously marked.

ÉTUDE

Cornelius Gurlitt

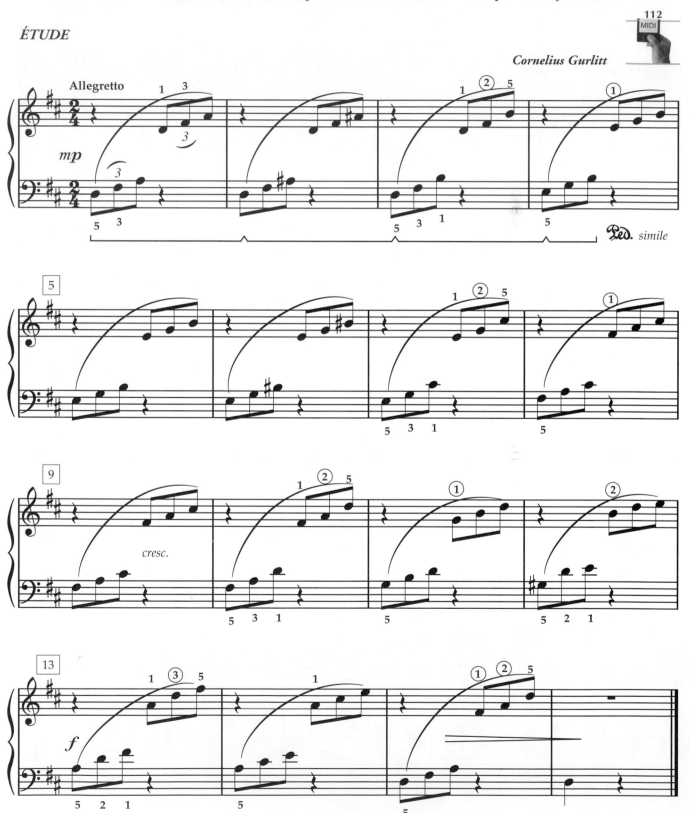

IMPROVISATION

Pentatonic Improvisation

PRACTICE DIRECTIONS

1. For a "bagpipe" sound using the pentatonic scale, improvise by playing open fifths with the left hand in $\frac{6}{8}$ or $\frac{3}{4}$ meter.
2. The open fifth G♭–D♭ seems to blend most easily with black-key melodies in this style.
3. Play the open fifth accompaniment in the lower register so the accompaniment will sound fuller.
4. An even better bagpipe sound will result with the addition of a grace note figure to the open-fifth accompaniment, as below. A *grace note* (♪) appears in smaller print, receives no note value, and is played quickly, almost together with the following note.
5. An effective way to get a good bagpipe sound is to play all three left-hand notes (the grace note and open fifth) *together*, and then lift up the second finger quickly.

Now improvise your own melodies over the open-fifth accompaniment. Look at some of the pieces in this book in $\frac{6}{8}$ or $\frac{3}{4}$ meter to give you ideas for various melody rhythms. The next piece, *Bagpiper's Strut*, is a good place to start.

BAGPIPER'S STRUT

E. M.

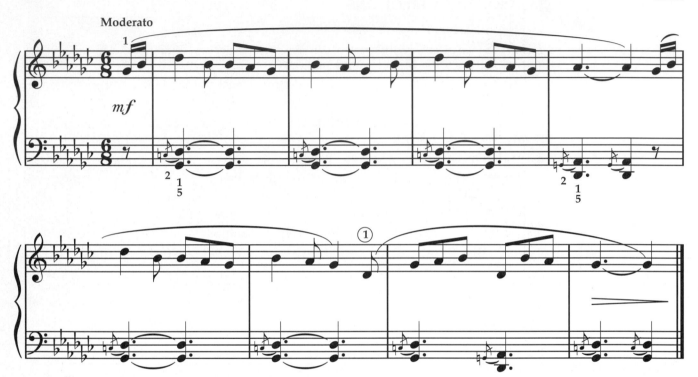

PRACTICE DIRECTIONS

1. For a "Western" sound, play one of the following ostinato accompaniment figures with the left hand.

2. In the pentatonic scale, two positions of this accompaniment are possible.

3. Here are two variations of the accompaniment in different meters:

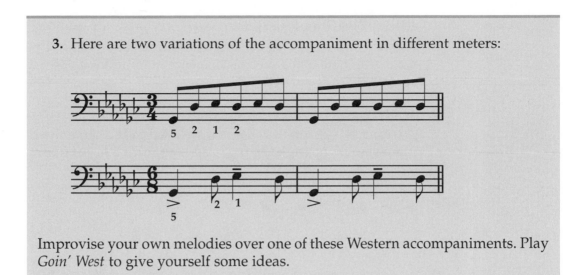

Improvise your own melodies over one of these Western accompaniments. Play *Goin' West* to give yourself some ideas.

GOIN' WEST

E. M.

12-Bar Blues Improvisation

Practice playing the 12-bar blues in various keys using rhythms such as a dotted eighth note followed by a sixteenth note, and with or without a *triplet* figure containing the blue note.

Triplet

A **triplet** is a group of three notes played in the same time as two notes of the same value. The triplet figure has a slur and a 3 either above or below it.

After playing *Step Along Blues,* which uses a triplet figure, improvise melodies using the same dotted note combination along with triplet figures.

To get the right rhythm for the triplet figure, chant "*step*-a-long" as you play each triplet in the piece.

STEP ALONG BLUES

Next, improvise melodies that extend the five-finger pattern. Let's begin with a scale as the melody. In *Scaling the Blues,* the major scales of C, F, and G are used.

Also try playing *Scaling the Blues* with a dotted rhythm for the scale melody:

SCALING THE BLUES

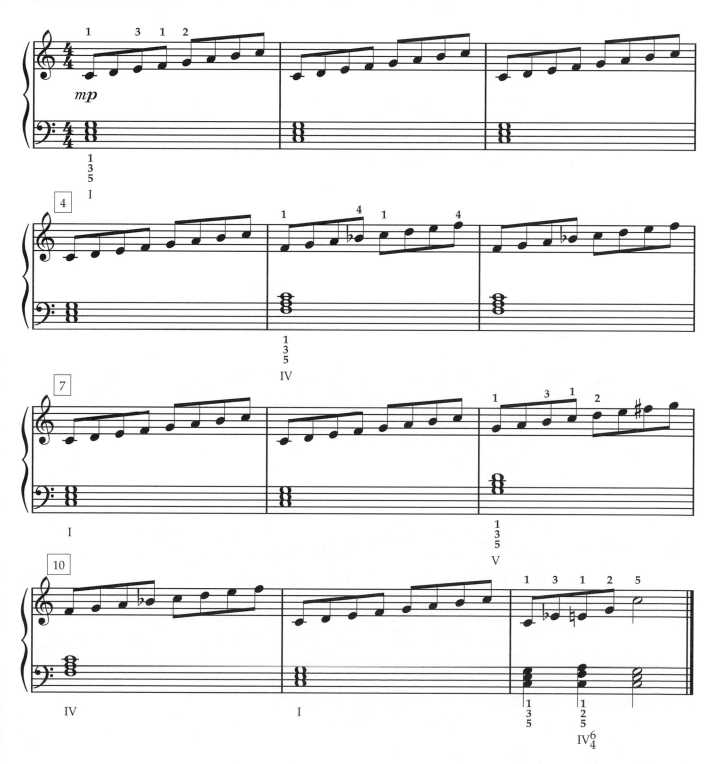

You can improvise a boogie-woogie pattern by using the

- basic triad of the accompaniment (tones 1, 3, 5)
- plus the *sixth* tone
- plus the *seventh* tone lowered by one half step.

If you add the lowered seventh tone to the accompaniment as well, you will have a V⁷ (dominant seventh) chord.

First play *Boogie-Woogie Blues.* Notice that the top tone of the dominant seventh chord in brackets is optional throughout.

BOOGIE-WOOGIE BLUES

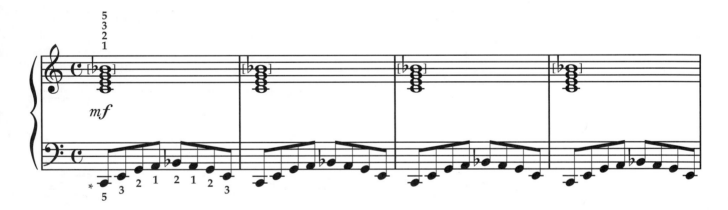

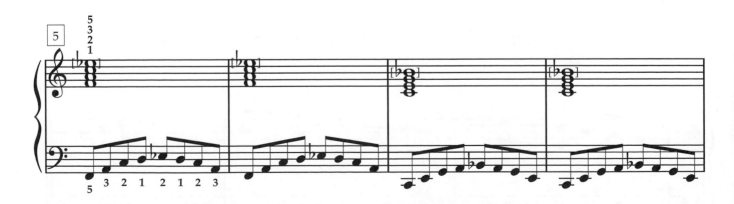

---

* Frequently played ( )

Next, try reversing the parts so that the right hand plays the boogie-woogie pattern while the left hand plays the chords.

etc.

Finally, start improvising your own melodies with different rhythmic patterns using the boogie-woogie pattern as a starting point.

There are many kinds of ostinato accompaniment patterns that are effective for blues improvisation. *Over Easy Blues* uses an ostinato pattern with I, vi^6, and a V^7 chord borrowed from another key. When moving from the vi^6 to the V^7, repeat the two bottom tones in the left hand and move the thumb tone up a *half step*.

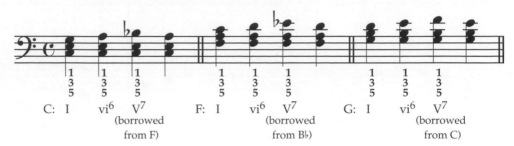

After practicing the accompaniment pattern, play *Over Easy Blues*. Then improvise your own melodies using this accompaniment pattern and some of the suggested patterns on page 339.

OVER EASY BLUES

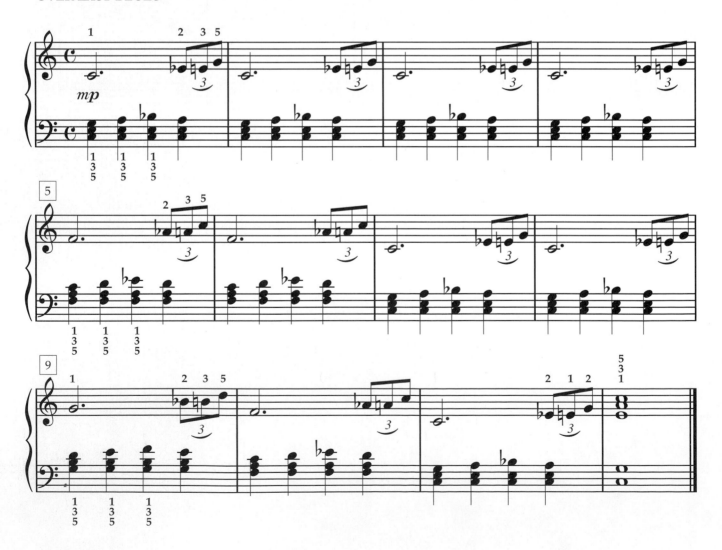

Ostinato accompaniment patterns

An ostinato pattern with a minor ii chord is effective for improvising blues melodies. Note the interval of a diminished seventh (dim. 7) in the second chord.

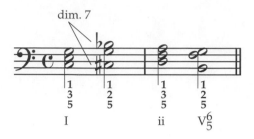

After practicing the accompaniment pattern, play *Step Around Blues*. Then improvise your own melodies using this accompaniment pattern.

STEP AROUND BLUES

Blues Scale

Now try improvising melodies using the **blues scale**, which is made up of

- scale degrees 1, 4, 5, and 8
- plus the *third*, *fifth*, and *seventh* tones, each lowered by one half step.

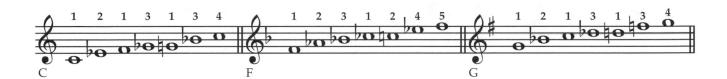

First get the "feel" of the blues scale by playing it ascending and descending in each key. Then begin accenting the *second* and *fourth* beats as you play *Up and Down Blues*. (Note that the top tone of the seventh chord may be omitted throughout if necessary.) Next try improvising your own melodies with different rhythmic patterns based on the blues scale.

UP AND DOWN BLUES

Now try improvising melodies based on the blues scale. *Conversational Blues* uses the ostinato accompaniment pattern I–I–V^7–IV$^6_4$–I to obtain a musical question-and-answer dialogue. The "question" is stated in the left hand:

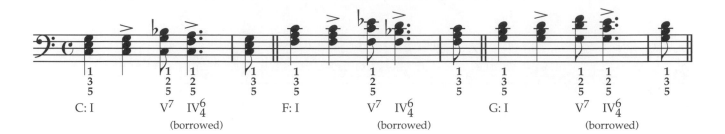

The "answer" is a free-style melodic line that differs both melodically and rhythmically each time it is stated. Try playing *Conversational Blues*, and then begin improvising your own free-style melodies. Finally, improvise blues-scale melodies with continuous left-hand accompaniment patterns.

CONVERSATIONAL BLUES

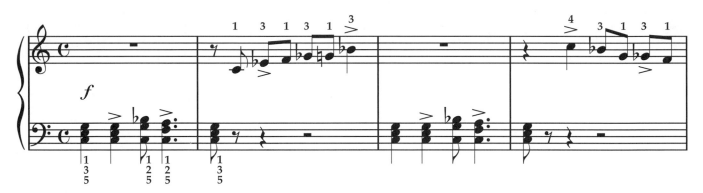

CREATIVE MUSIC AND HARMONIZATION

1. The following two phrases extend beyond the five-finger position. Improvise matching phrases for each, using an extended range. Write the phrases on the staves provided, then add fingerings to the phrases and circle those that extend the range using extension, substitution, crossing, and contraction. Consider tempo, dynamics, and kinds of phrasing as well.

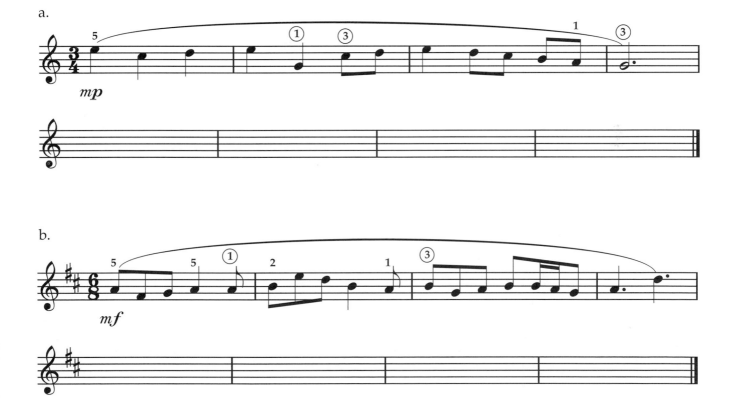

2. Improvise matching phrases in extended range for each of the following phrases and harmonize with I, IV$_4^6$, and V$_5^6$ chords. Write the phrases, chords, and the chord numbers on the staves provided.

a.

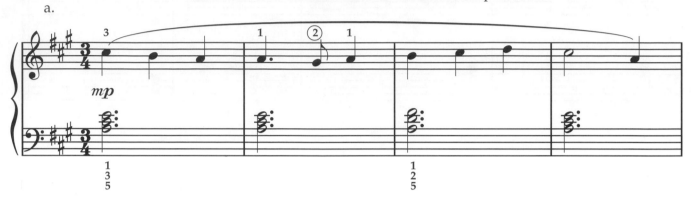

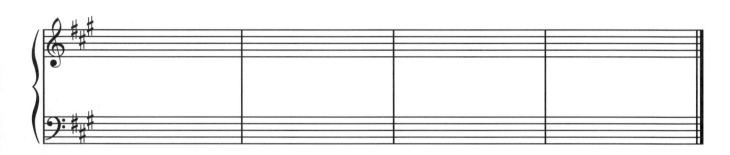

b.

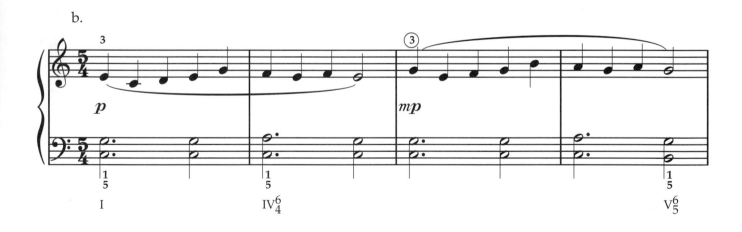

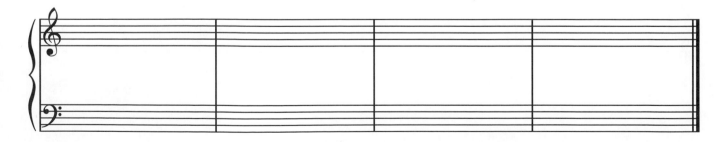

3. Add the indicated accompaniment pattern to the melodies below. Play the first melody with the waltz pattern (a), then with the arpeggio pattern (b).

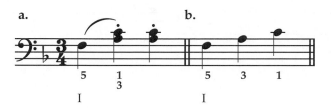

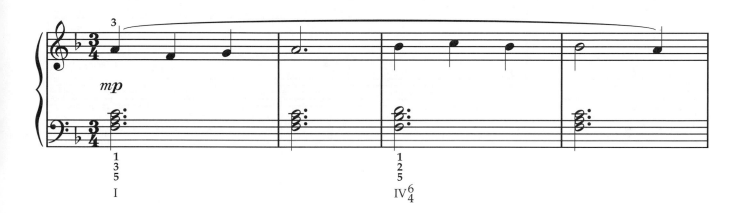

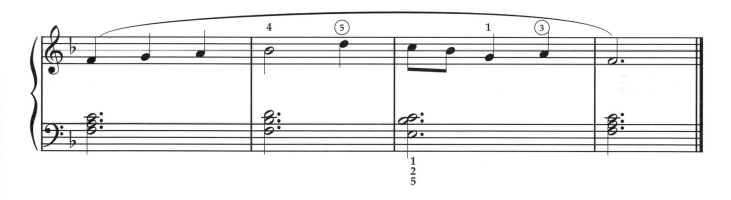

Play the second melody with the Alberti bass pattern (a), then with the extended-arpeggio pattern (b).

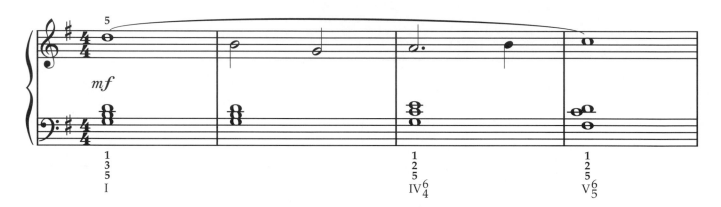

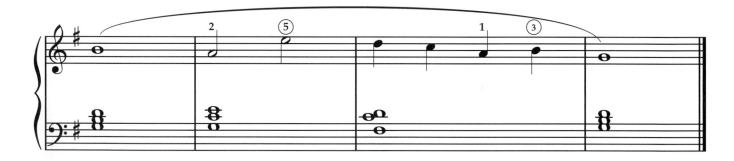

Play the last melody with a broken-chord pattern.

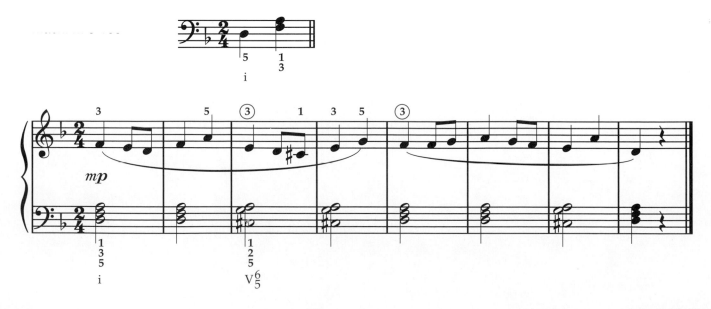

4. Harmonize the following melody with I, IV$^6_4$, and V$^6_5$ chords in the same accompaniment style as in the first measure, and add chord numbers below each as indicated.

Next, try replacing some of the I, IV$^6_4$, and V$^6_5$ chords in the accompaniment with the secondary chords ii, iii, and vi for added color.

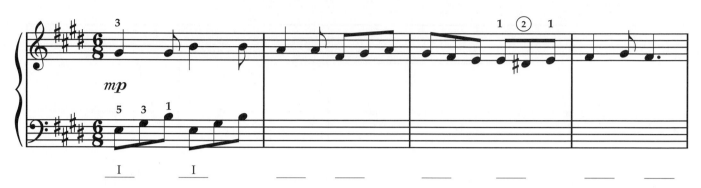

5. Use the melody tones given to help you improvise melodies to the blues-style accompaniment that follows.

6. A melodic skeleton and one possible completed version of it are given below. Use this as an example for improvising your own version of melodic skeleton 1 and to help you complete melodic skeleton 2.

Melodic skeleton 1

Melodic skeleton 1 completed

Melodic skeleton 2

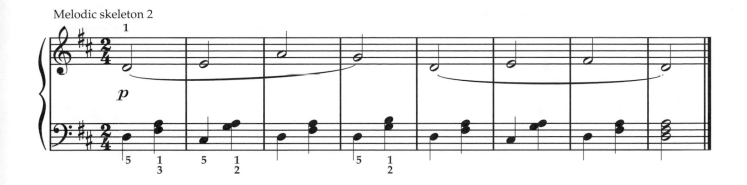

Improvise some completions for melodic skeleton 2 and write down your favorite one.

Melodic skeleton 2 completed

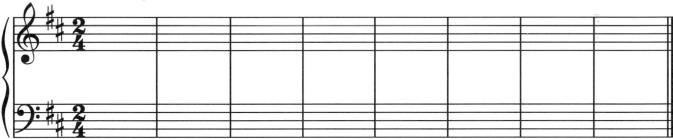

7. Write your own composition in two-part song form (AB) or three-part song form (ABA). Select a key, meter signature, accompaniment style, tempo, expression and dynamic markings, and pedal markings (if pedal is desired). Indicate any fingering changes. First notate the music in pencil and then make any necessary corrections before writing the final version. Be sure to give your composition a title.

SIGHTREADING STUDIES

PRACTICE DIRECTIONS

1. Determine the key of the study.
2. Observe the meter signature, then quickly scan the example to look at rhythmic and melodic patterns and any harmonic patterns.
3. Note changes of fingering where they occur.
4. Observe all dynamic and expression markings.
5. Look ahead in the music as you play.
6. Be sure not to look down at the keys!

Melodies in Parallel Motion

1.

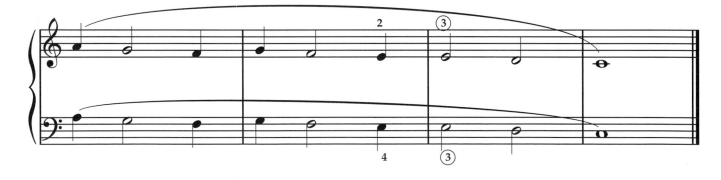

2.

3.

Accompanied Melodies

4.

5.

6.

7.

8.

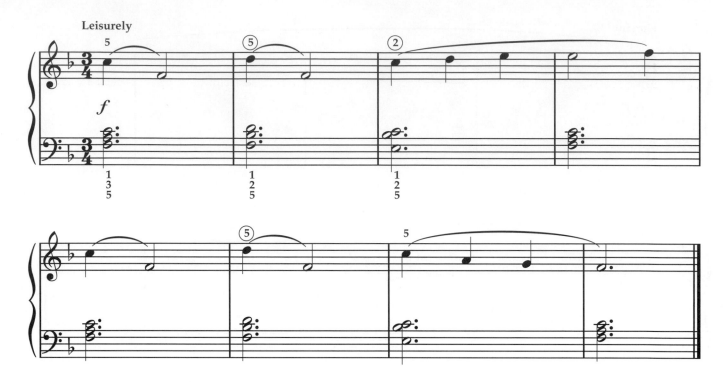

9.

10.

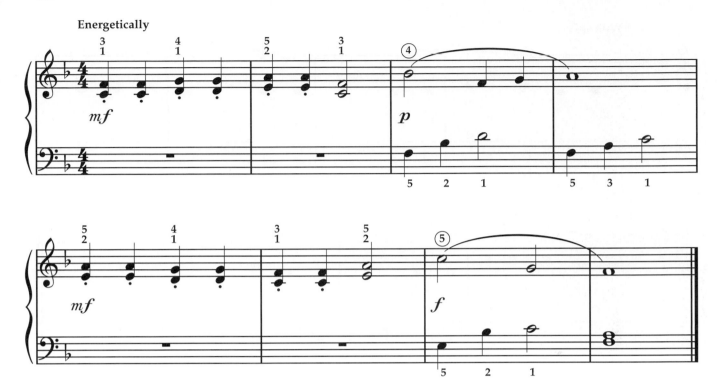

11.

12.

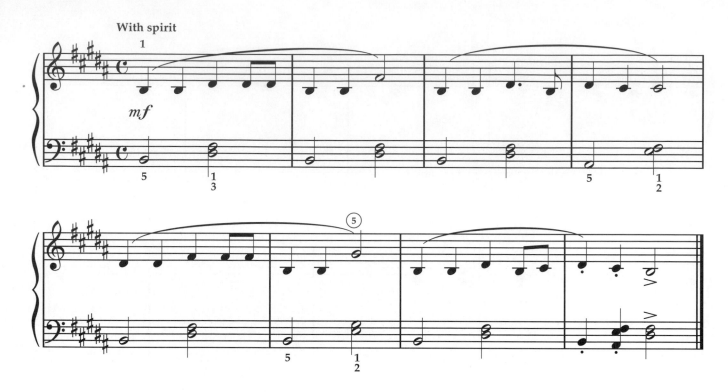

Pedal Studies

13.

14.

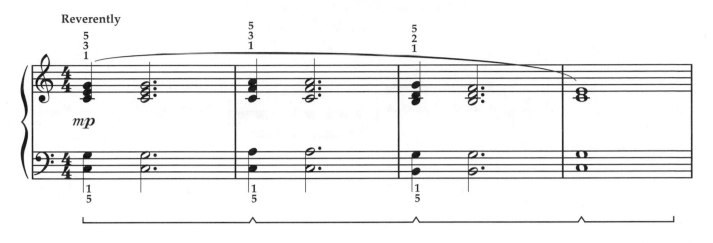

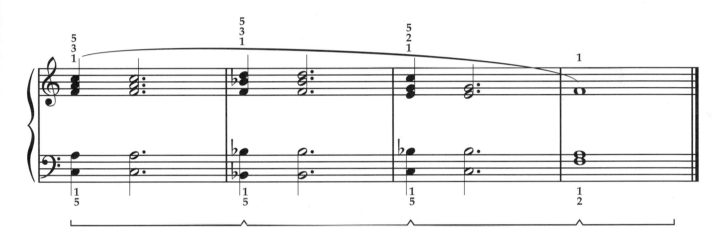

RHYTHMIC STUDIES

Tap and count the following rhythmic exercises with both hands.

1.

2.

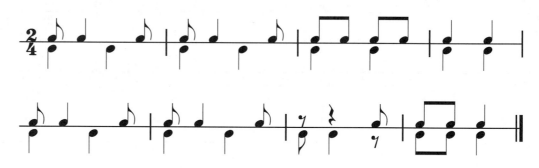

3.

4.

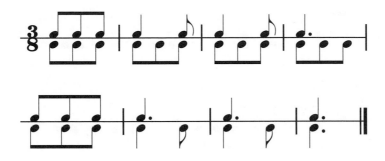

5.

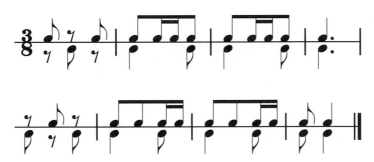

6.

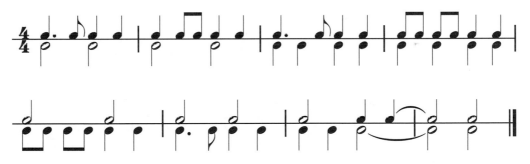

7.

8.

9.

10.

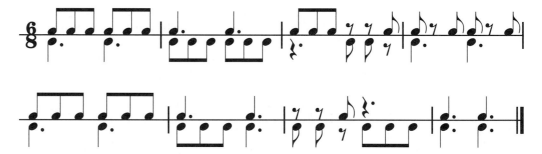

11.

TECHNICAL STUDIES

1. Play the following Hanon fingerbuilder exercise in various tempos. Alternate tempos by playing every other measure at twice the speed. This exercise can also be practiced legato, staccato, in various slur groupings, and with various changes of dynamics.

FIVE-FINGER EXERCISE

Charles-Louis Hanon (1819–1900)

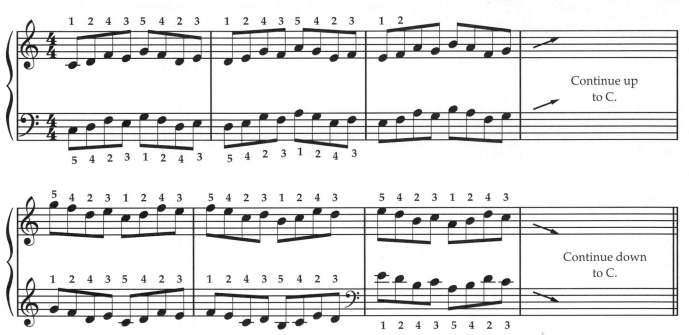

2. Practice the following fingerbuilder exercise in the keys of C and G.

Friedrich Wieck (1785–1873)

3. The Romantic composer and pianist Franz Liszt wrote the finger-strengthening exercise below specifically for one of his young piano students.

    Practice this exercise with both hands in the keys of C, G, and F. Play the left-hand part one octave below what is written. Next, play the exercise in contrary motion with both hands.

Franz Liszt (1811–1886)

Continue up through the rest of the scale.

4. Practice the following two-octave scale in contrary motion in keys of your own choice.

5. Practice the following exercise in keys of your own choice. Do not twist the wrists back and forth as you practice this study.

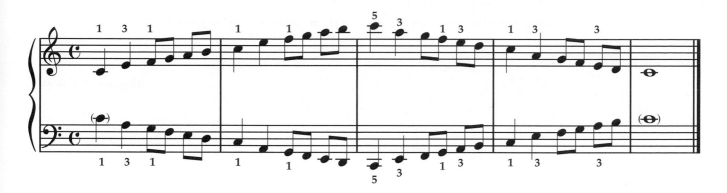

6. Practice the following inversion exercise in various keys. Try not to look down at your fingers as you go through this study.

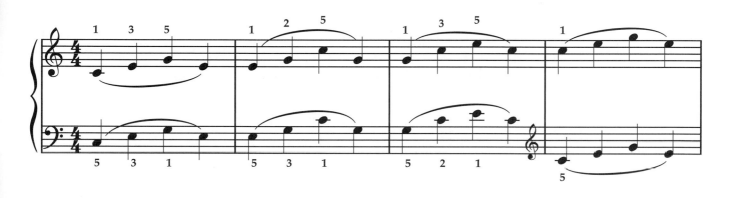

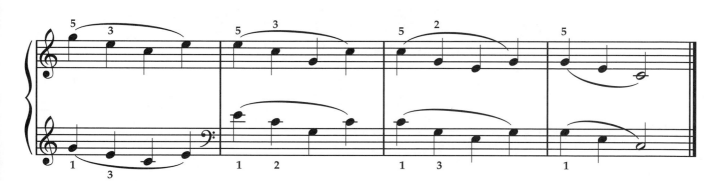

ENSEMBLE PIECES

Student-Teacher Duets

Student plays one octave higher than written if at one piano.

BOOGIE WOOGIE TREAT

Student

Margaret Goldston

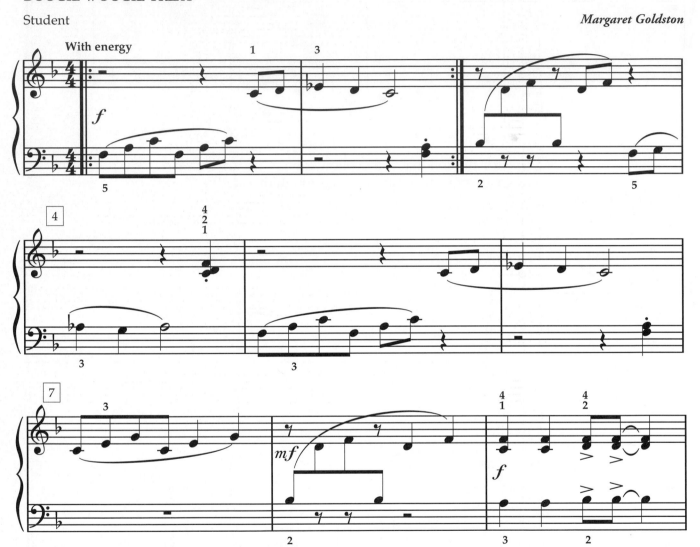

From Simply Jazzy—Book 1 © *Alfred Publishing Co., Inc.*

BOOGIE WOOGIE TREAT

Accompaniment

Margaret Goldston

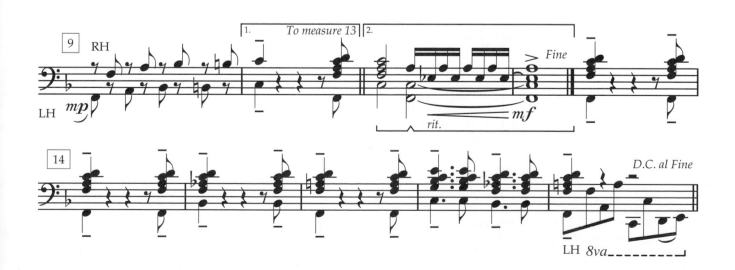

SUNSET*

Student

Dennis Alexander

*Student plays one octave higher than written when playing at one piano.

SUNSET

Accompaniment

Dennis Alexander

Student Ensemble Pieces

LULLABY

Louis Kohler (1820–1886)
Arranged by E.M.

THIS TRAIN

African-American Spiritual
Arranged by E.M.

POLOVETZIAN DANCE (*from the opera* Prince Igor)

Alexander Borodin (1833–1887)
Arranged by E.M.

NAME _____

DATE _____

SCORE _____

1. Give the name of the *sixth* degree in each of the following major scales:

F _____   A _____   E♭ _____

G _____   B♭ _____   D♭ _____   B _____

D _____   C♯ _____   A♭ _____

2. Analyze the following major, minor, augmented, and diminished triads given below:

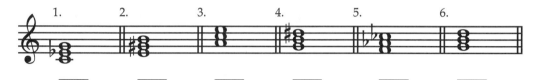

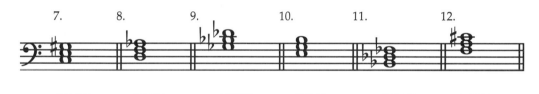

3. Identify the following major and minor triads and their inversions.
(Use chord symbols, e.g., C [root position]
C6 [first inversion]
C$_4^6$ [second inversion])

4. Build the following major scales using letter names.

D __ __ __ __ __ __ __

F __ __ __ __ __ __ __

B♭ __ __ __ __ __ __ __

G♭ __ __ __ __ __ __ __

C♯ __ __ __ __ __ __ __

5. Build the triads indicated by the letter-name symbols given.

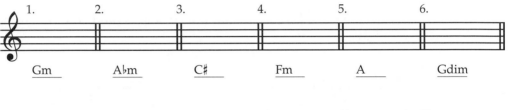

Gm   A♭m   C♯   Fm   A   Gdim

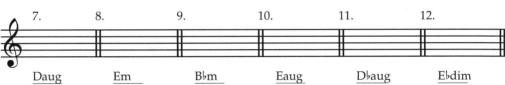

Daug   Em   B♭m   Eaug   D♭aug   E♭dim

6. Build *perfect fourth* intervals (either melodically or harmonically) *upward* from the given pitch. Write the names of the pitches on the lines provided.

Matching

Write the numbers from Column A to correspond to the given answers in Column B.

COLUMN A	COLUMN B
1. syncopation	_____ play in the style of a march
2. mediant	_____ 3 notes played in the same time as 2 notes of the same value
3. direct pedaling	_____ a constantly recurring figure
4. con moto	_____ name of the 6th degree of a major scale
5. hymn style	_____ a shifting of stresses from groups of 2 to groups of 3
6. sempre	_____ when the 5th of the chord is in the bass
7. indirect pedaling	_____ depressing the pedal simultaneously with the chord
8. ostinato pattern	_____ name of the 2nd degree of a major scale
9. submediant	_____ a melody harmonized with chords divided between two hands
10. second inversion	_____ depressing the pedal immediately after sounding the chord
11. marziale	_____ when the 3rd of the chord is in the bass
12. supertonic	_____ name of the 3rd degree of a major scale
13. first inversion	_____ stressing the off-beats of the measure
14. triplet	_____ always
15. hemiola	_____ play with motion

Tonality and Atonality

MINOR SCALES

This unit introduces minor scales, scales of other modes, the chromatic scale, and the whole-tone scale, together with pieces based on these scales. Bitonality, atonality—including twelve-tone technique—and additional innovative notations are also introduced.

Relative Major and Relative Minor

Each minor scale is built from a corresponding major scale with the same key signature; this major scale is referred to as the **relative major**. For example, the F major scale is the relative major of the D minor scale (and the D minor scale is the **relative minor** of the F major scale) because both scales have one flat in their key signatures.

F major scale

D minor scale

Natural Minor Scale

The **natural minor scale** is formed by beginning on the sixth tone of its relative major and continuing up an octave. The natural minor scale can also be formed by beginning *three half steps down* from its relative major key (see p. 379).

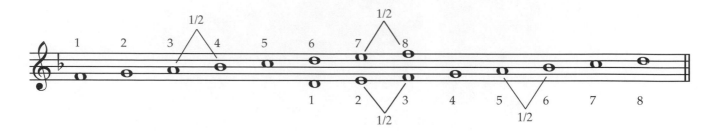

Note that while the half steps occur between tones 3 and 4 and between tones 7 and 8 in the major scale, they occur between tones 2 and 3 and between tones 5 and 6 in the natural minor scale.

Harmonic Minor Scale

Besides the natural form, there are two other forms of the minor scale—the harmonic and the melodic. The **harmonic minor scale** is probably the most frequently used form of the three. It is the same as the natural minor scale with the exception of the seventh tone, which is raised one half step with the use of an accidental.

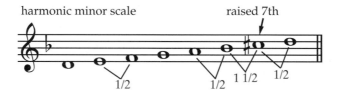

Note that the half steps in the harmonic minor scale occur between tones 2 and 3, between tones 5 and 6, and between tones 7 and 8. The raised seventh tone creates an interval of a step and a half between tones 6 and 7.

Melodic Minor Scale

The **melodic minor scale** is the same as the natural minor scale, except that the sixth and seventh tones are raised one half step in its ascending form. The descending melodic minor scale is identical to the natural minor form:

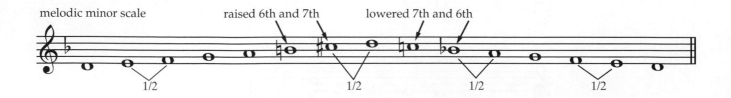

Note that the half steps in the melodic minor scale occur between tones 2 and 3 and between tones 7 and 8 ascending, and between tones 2 and 3 and tones 5 and 6 descending.

MINOR KEY SIGNATURES

Since each minor scale and its relative major scale have the same key signature, the key of a piece cannot be determined by looking only at the key signature.

Therefore, be sure to do the following:

1. Look at the final tone of the piece (particularly the lowest tone of the final chord), which will usually be the key tone, or tonic.
2. Look for tones 1, 3, and 5 of the tonic triad at the beginning and end of the piece.
3. Your ear can also help determine whether the piece has a major or a minor sound to it.

If you know the major key signatures, but are not completely certain of the minor key signatures, remember this:

- The minor key is *three half steps down* from its relative major key.
- For example, if the key signature has two sharps, the piece is either in D major or, counting down three half steps, B minor.

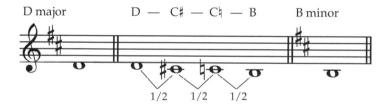

Here is a list of all major-minor key signature pairs:

Relative key signatures

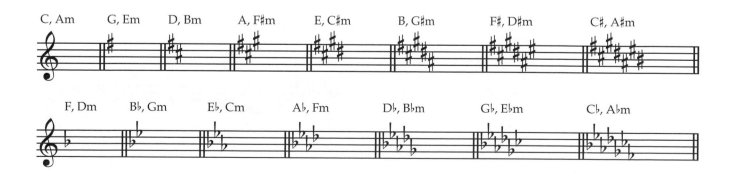

NATURAL MINOR SCALES IN TETRACHORD POSITIONS

Begin practicing the natural minor scales using sharp keys in tetrachord positions starting with A natural minor and continuing clockwise in the circle of fifths through A♯ natural minor. Notice that the upper tetrachord of the A natural minor scale, E–F–G–A, becomes the lower tetrachord of the E natural minor scale by raising the *second* degree one half step, E–F♯–G–A. This procedure is continued from one natural minor scale to the next. The harmonic and melodic forms of the minor scales can be worked out from the natural minor scales given.

Sharp keys

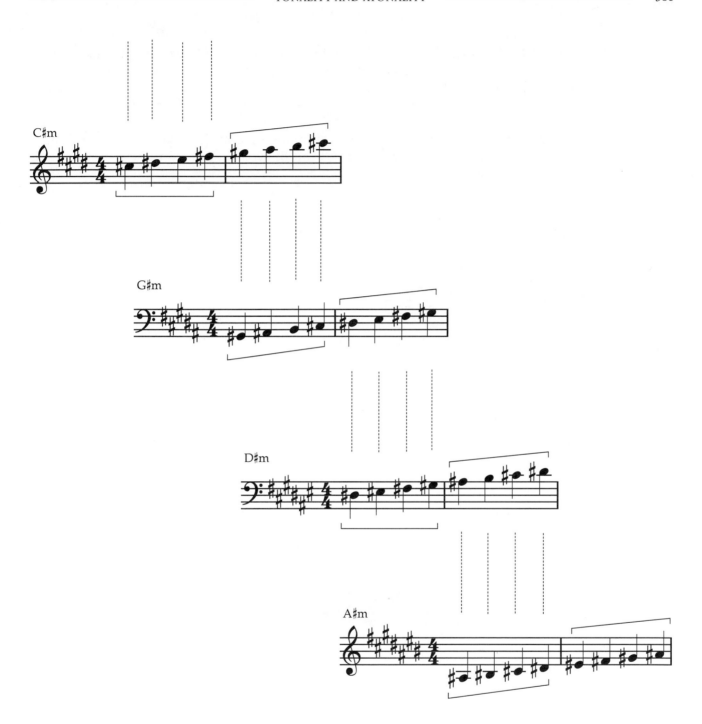

Begin practicing the natural minor scales using flat keys in tetrachord positions starting with A♭ natural minor and continuing clockwise in the circle of fifths through A natural minor. Notice that the upper tetrachord of the A♭ natural minor scale, E♭–F♭–G♭–A♭, becomes the lower tetrachord of the E♭ natural minor scale by raising the *second* degree one half step, E♭–F–G♭–A♭. This procedure is continued from one natural minor scale to the next. The harmonic and melodic forms of the minor scales can be worked out from the natural minor scales given.

Flat keys

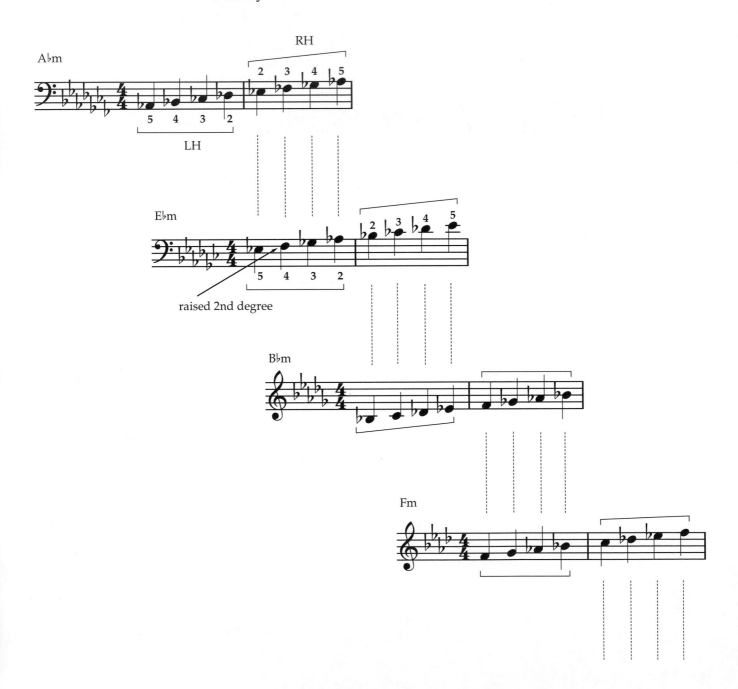

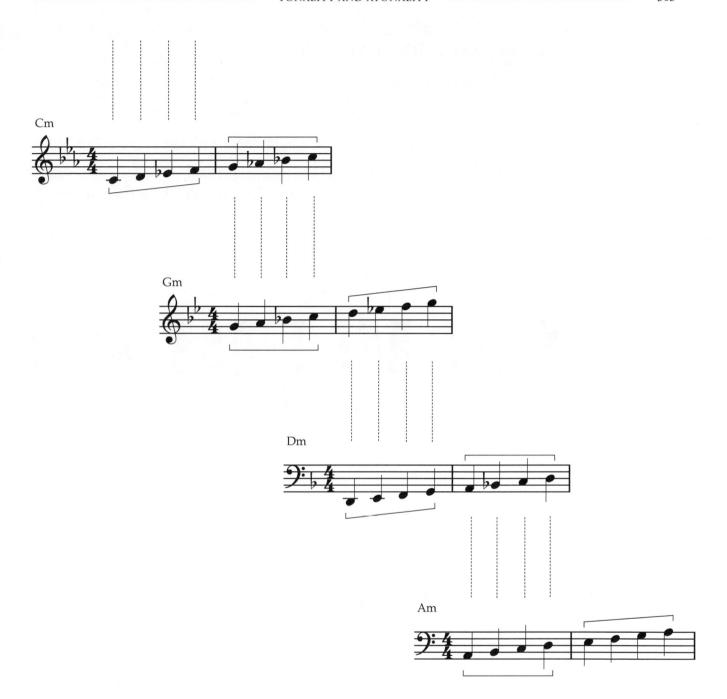

HARMONIC MINOR SCALES

The following chart illustrates each minor scale in harmonic form with fingerings for both hands. (The natural and melodic minor scale forms can be worked out from the harmonic scales given.)

1. Practice playing the scales, first with hands separately, then with hands together.
2. Be sure to observe the fingerings provided. The places where both hands use the same finger numbers are bracketed to help you learn your fingerings more quickly.
3. The keyboard diagrams give the locations of scale tones and help you to visualize the entire scale pattern at once.

Harmonic minor scales and fingerings*

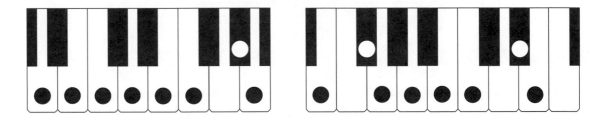

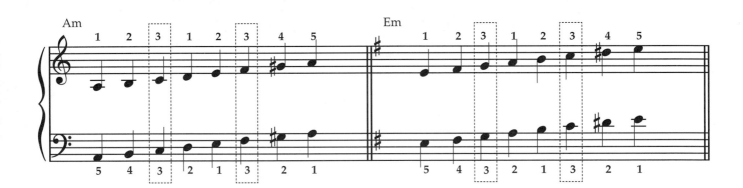

---

* Harmonic minor scales and their fingerings in two octaves are given in Appendix B, on pages 532–536.

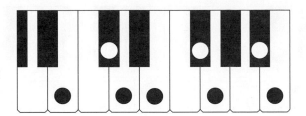

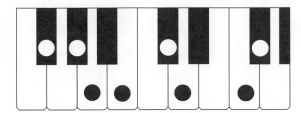

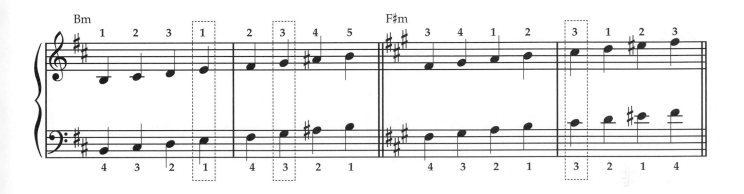

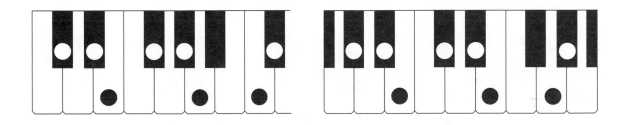

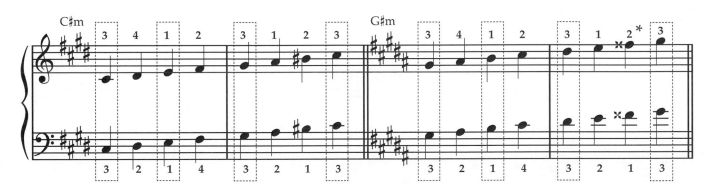

* A double sharp (×) raises a tone two half steps or one whole step.

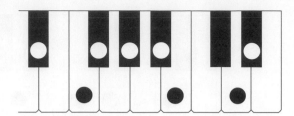

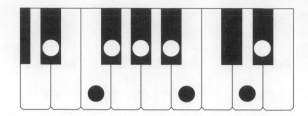

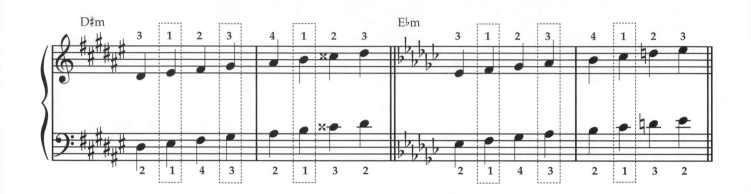

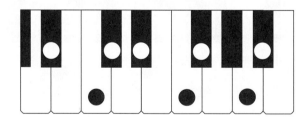

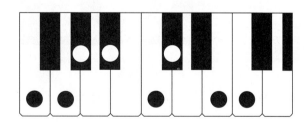

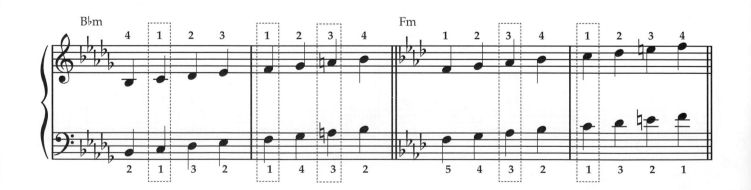

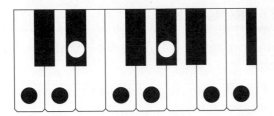

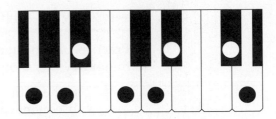

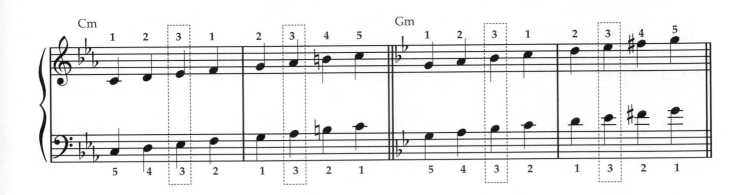

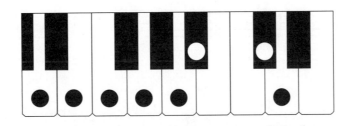

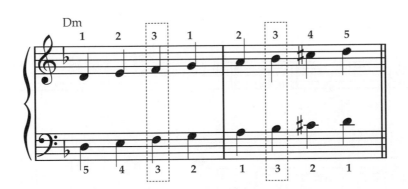

i–iv$_4^6$–i–V$_5^6$–i CHORD PROGRESSION

Practice playing the chord progression i–iv$_4^6$–i–V$_5^6$–i with the left hand in all minor keys, as shown below.

1. Use the fifth tone of the five-finger pattern as the first tone (tonic) of each subsequent chord progression.
2. Remember not to look at the keys.
3. Develop a feel for the progression and anticipate the changing of chords.

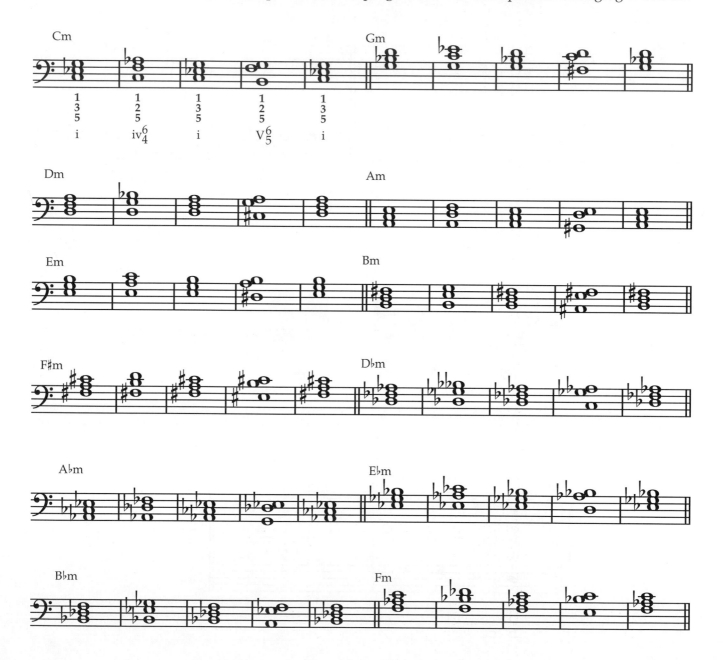

Another way of practicing the i–iv$^6_4$–i–V$^6_5$–i chord progression is to play the chords with the right hand while playing the root (or letter name) of each chord with the left hand, as shown next.

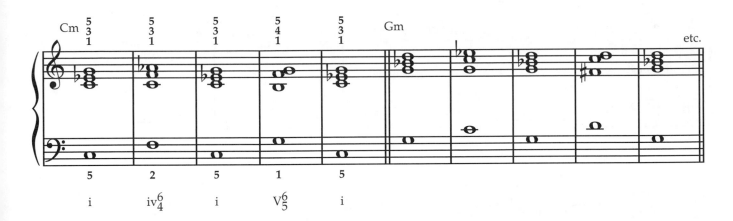

Volga Boatman and *Joshua Fought the Battle of Jericho* use the natural form of the C minor scale and the harmonic form of the D minor scale, respectively.

VOLGA BOATMAN

Russian

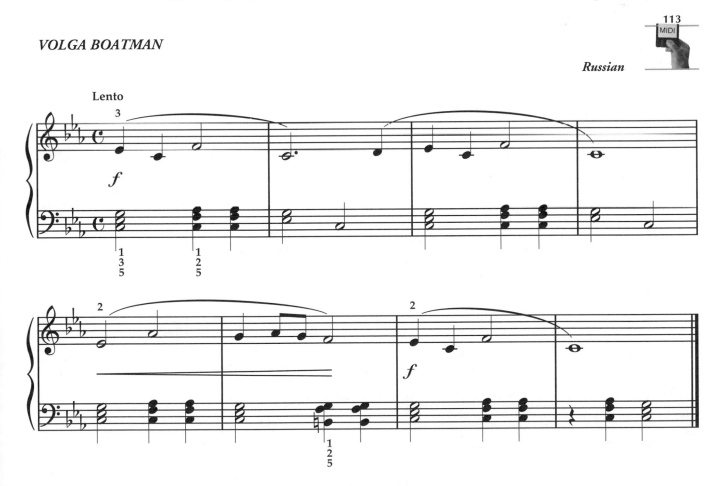

JOSHUA FOUGHT THE BATTLE OF JERICHO

Spiritual

Hatikvah, the Israeli national anthem, uses the natural form of the D minor scale.

HATIKVAH

Israeli

A *Sea Chantey* uses the natural form of the E minor scale. Practice playing the left-hand accompaniment as a block chord on the second beat of each measure before playing the piece as written.

A SEA CHANTEY

Chantey

116
MIDI

What minor key is *Moroccan Caravan* written in, and what form of the minor scale does it use?

MOROCCAN CARAVAN

E.M.

Name and then write down the letter names of the chords on the lines provided. Next, play the triads in the left-hand part of *Greensleeves,* and then play the piece as written. What forms of the minor scale are used in the piece and in what minor key is it played?

GREENSLEEVES

English

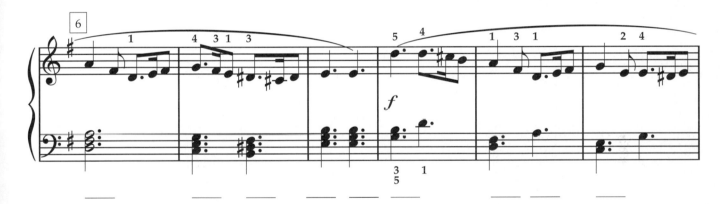

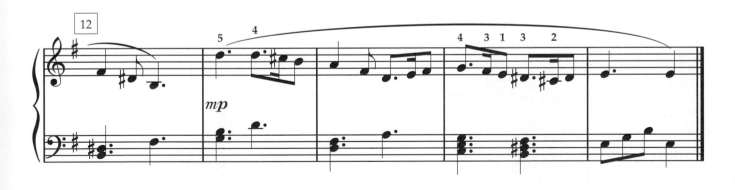

PARALLEL MAJOR AND MINOR SCALES

When the *third* and *sixth* tones of a major scale are lowered, that scale's parallel harmonic minor scale is obtained. Since both scales begin with the same tonic, the reverse is also true. By raising the third and sixth tones of the harmonic minor scale, its parallel major scale is obtained. There is no other relationship between parallel scales. Unlike relative scales, parallel scales do not share the same key signature.

C major

C harmonic minor

G major

G harmonic minor

Modulation

A **modulation** is a change of key within a composition.

Scaling Pyramids and *Venetian Waltz* each contain a **modulation,** or change of key. Both pieces begin in a minor key and modulate to their respective parallel major keys.

SCALING PYRAMIDS

E. M.

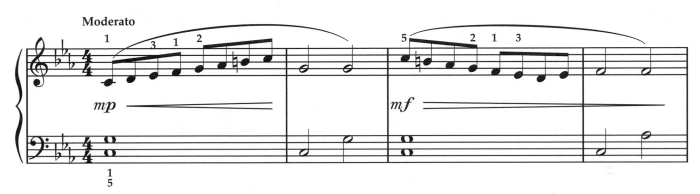

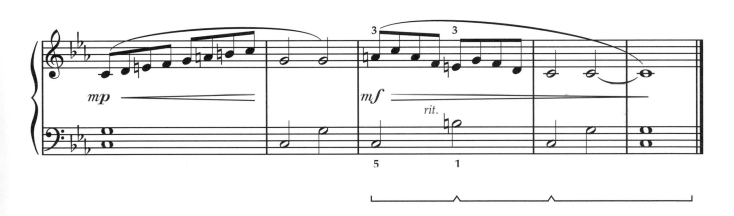

VENETIAN WALTZ

E. M.

OTHER SCALE FORMS (MODES)

The word **mode** has a meaning similar to the word *way*; that is, a particular mode is a particular way of arranging whole steps and half steps in scale form. For roughly the last three hundred years, most Western music has used the major and minor modes or scales. But there are other modes, some of which are used in American folk tunes and in the music of other cultures. Each mode has its own arrangement of whole steps and half steps, and each can be constructed on the white keys alone, as illustrated below. (*When the scales of these modes are transposed to the various sharp and flat keys, accidentals must be added to preserve the half-step arrangement.*)

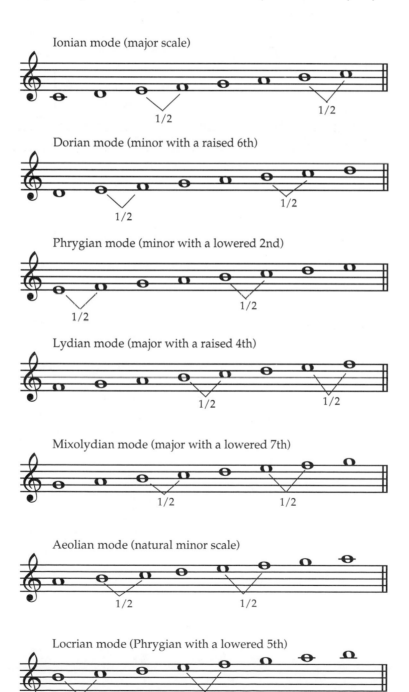

Both *Sakura*, a Japanese tune, and *Aeolian Lullaby* use the Aeolian mode (the natural minor scale).

Poco Ritardando

Poco ritardando means to gradually slow down the tempo a little.

SAKURA

Japanese

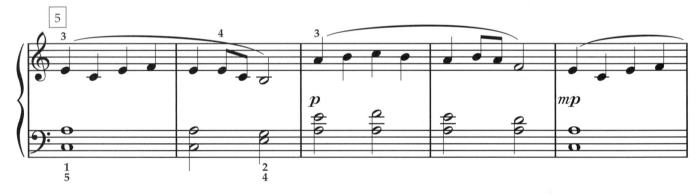

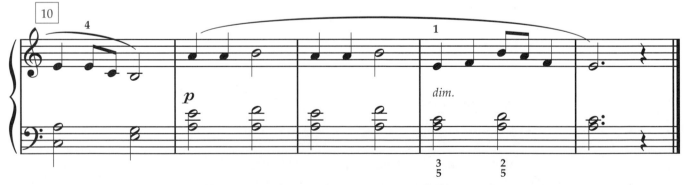

AEOLIAN LULLABY

Joan Hansen

Scarborough Fair uses the Dorian mode, beginning on E.

SCARBOROUGH FAIR

English

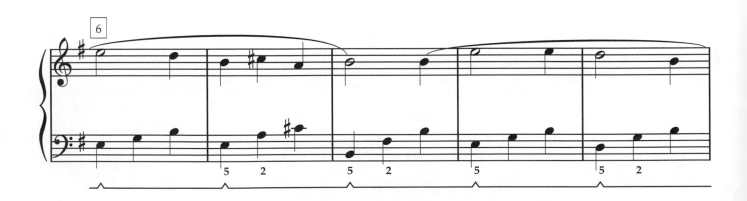

High Noon is in the Mixolydian mode, which sounds like the major scale with a lowered seventh degree. This mode is frequently used in the jazz idiom.

HIGH NOON

E. M.

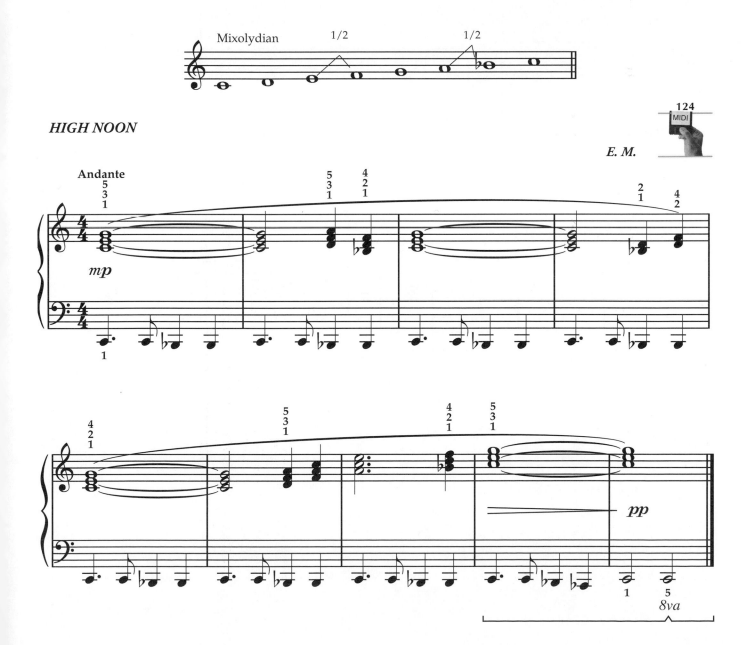

Spanish Folk Melody uses the Phrygian mode, which sounds like the natural minor scale with a lowered second degree. The Phrygian mode is frequently used in Spanish flamenco music.

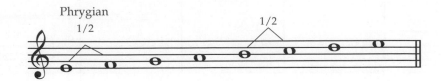

SPANISH FOLK MELODY

Spanish

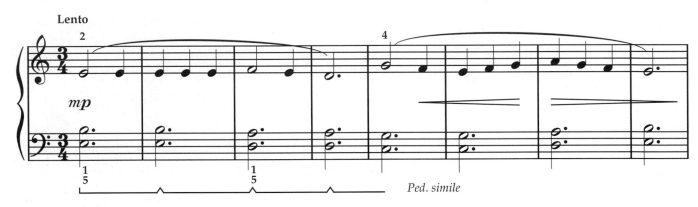

Sharp Four and *Lydian March* are both in the Lydian mode, which sounds like the major scale with a raised fourth degree.

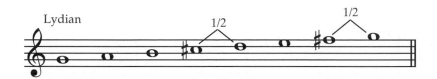

Note that in *Sharp Four* the Lydian mode begins on G and accidentals are required to preserve the half-step arrangement.

SHARP FOUR

Arthur Frackenpohl (born 1924)

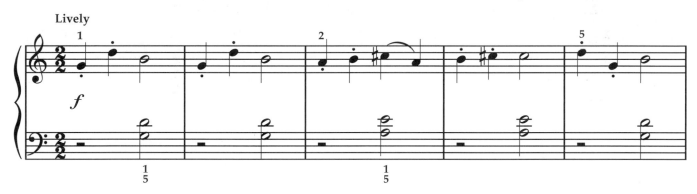

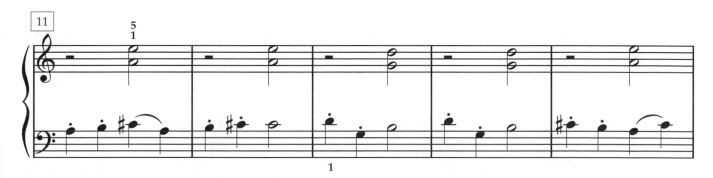

Used by permission.

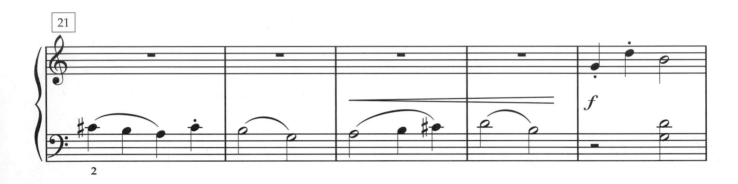

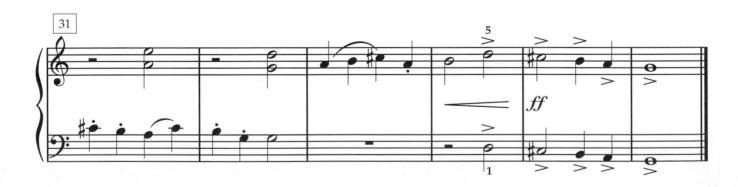

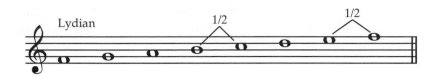

LYDIAN MARCH

David Duke

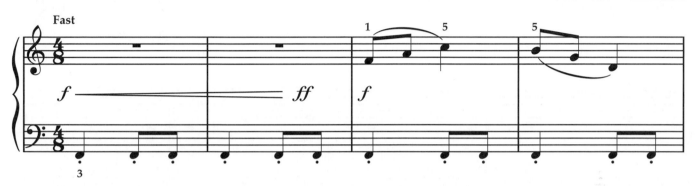

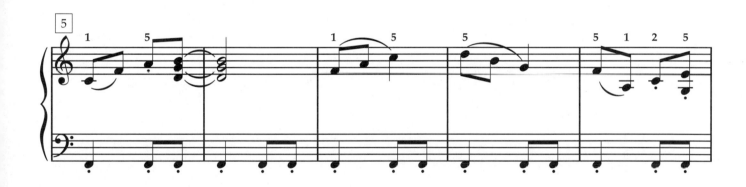

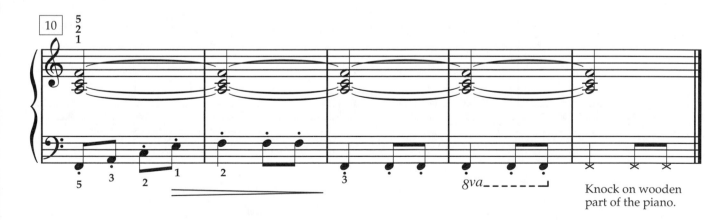

Knock on wooden
part of the piano.

Marche Slav uses the **Byzantine scale** (also called the Hungarian minor scale), which is the harmonic minor scale with a raised fourth degree. This scale is often used by Russian composers.

MARCHE SLAV

Peter Ilyich Tchaikovsky (1840–1893)

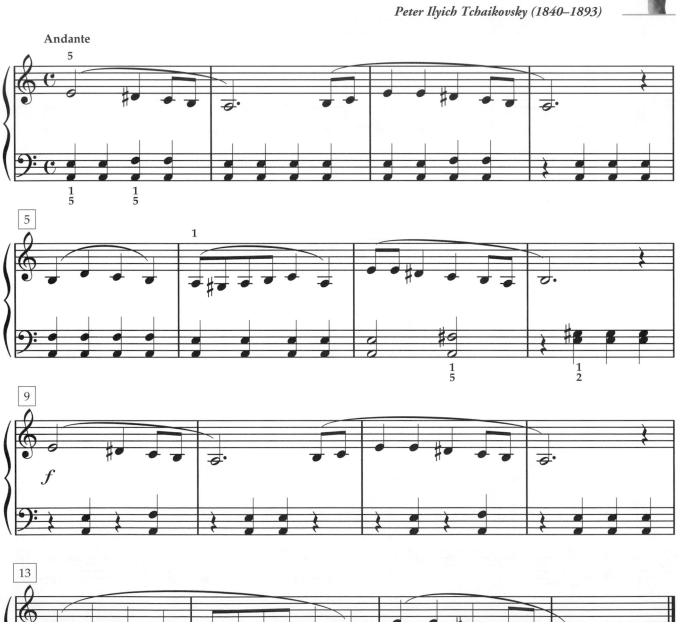

THE CHROMATIC SCALE

The **chromatic scale** contains all twelve tones and is constructed by using half steps only. Notice the fingering for this scale as given below.

- The *third* finger is used on the black keys.
- The *thumb* is used on most of the white keys.
- The *second* finger is used for the notes F and C in the right hand and for the notes E and B in the left hand.

Practice Strategies

First, play the following preparatory chromatic scale exercises.

1. Using the middle finger (3), first, in the right hand, then the left, and then with both hands, play lightly upward and then downward on the black keys only, beginning on F♯ and ending upward one or more octaves on an F♯.

2. Play the same black keys with the third finger of each hand, but add lightly the thumb. When you come to a pair of white keys (B–C, E–F), play the first one and omit the second white key.

3. Next, practice the following chromatic scale warm-up exercises that use the pair of white keys with RH 1–2, LH 2–1 finger combinations.

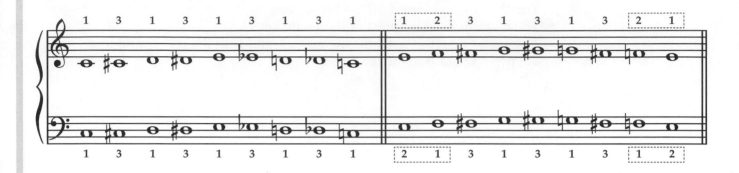

4. Finally, practice the chromatic scale ascending and descending, first with each hand separately, then with hands together. Be sure to observe the correct fingering.

THE CHROMATIC SCALE

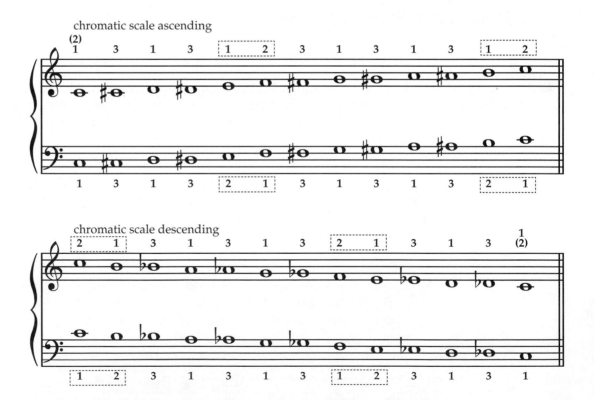

Chromatic Blues and *Navy Blues* use chromaticism in their melodies.

Molto Rit.

Molto rit. is a term indicating a marked slowing of the tempo.

CHROMATIC BLUES

E. M.

NAVY BLUES

E. M.

JAZZ

Jazz has been one of the most influential musical styles in the twentieth century. *Just Struttin' Along* uses some of the basic style elements of jazz, which include syncopation, off-beat accents, and chromaticism.

JUST STRUTTIN' ALONG

Martha Mier

PANDIATONICISM

Pandiatonicism is a technique that gained prominence early in the twentieth century as an alternative to the chromaticism of well-known composers such as Richard Wagner, Maurice Ravel, and Claude Debussy. Most of the tones are taken from one scale, frequently major and often C major, with no (or very few) accidentals, as illustrated by *Andantino*. From this lack of accidentals comes the term "white-note writing," as pandiatonicism is often called.

Another twentieth-century practice illustrated by this piece is the use of irregular phrase lengths to accommodate rhythmic patterns.

❜

❜ is a symbol that means to take a short breath or pause before continuing with the music.

ANDANTINO *(from* Les Cinq Doigts*)*

Igor Stravinsky (1882–1971)

THE WHOLE-TONE SCALE

The **whole-tone scale** contains six tones and is constructed by using whole steps only. Some early twentieth-century music, notably that of Debussy (1862–1918), uses the whole-tone scale.

Veiled, atmospheric effects can be produced by using the damper pedal to sustain whole-tone groupings, as in *Morning Mist*. Play this whole-tone piece with a very light touch.

Metronome Marking

♩ = 126 is a **metronome marking.** A metronome is a time-keeping instrument which produces a ticking sound at any desired speed. This particular marking means to set the metronome at 126, with the resultant ticking sound equivalent to the duration of a quarter-note beat, 126 beats a minute.

MORNING MIST

E. M.

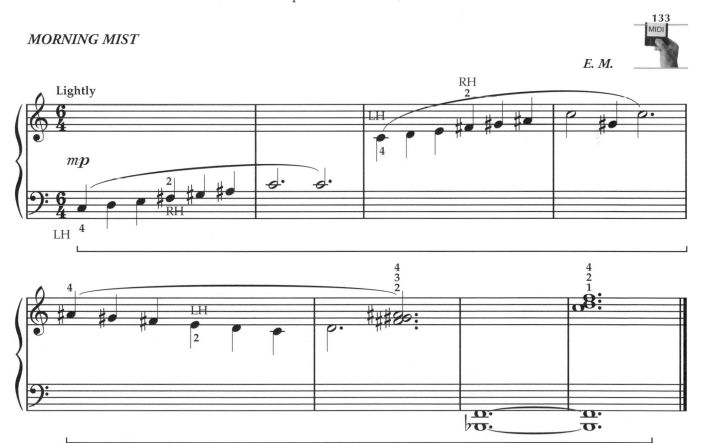

For fun, try rewriting a familiar tune using the whole-tone scale. It will sound somewhat changed! Here is an example:

NAME THAT TUNE

E. M.

Take other familiar tunes and arrange them in whole-tone settings by altering tones to fit the whole-step pattern. Then try improvising melodies that use the whole-tone scale.

BITONALITY

As mentioned in Unit 3, a *bitonal* piece uses two keys simultaneously. *Pomp* and *Two Tone* are examples. In *Pomp*, the right hand is in the key of A, and the left hand is in the key of C.

Before playing these two pieces, identify the various triads and practice them first with each hand separately and then with both hands together.

Allegro con brio

Allegro con brio is a tempo marking that means to play quickly and with vigor; briskly.

Intenzionato

Intenzionato means to play in a deliberate manner.

𝄐𝓟𝓮𝓭.

𝓟𝓮𝓭. refers to use of the damper pedal.

Con forza

Con forza means to play with forcefulness; stressed.

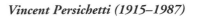

POMP

Vincent Persichetti (1915–1987)

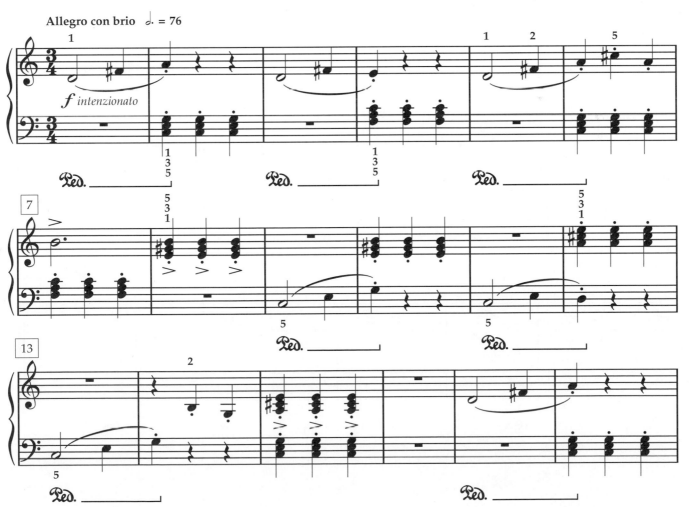

In *Two Tone*, the right hand is in the key of D and the left hand in the key of G. This piece can be played as a duet by having one player take the treble clef part with two hands, and another player take the bass clef part with two hands.

TWO TONE

Joan Hansen

"Two Tone" by Joan Hansen from Music of Our Time, *© 1977, Waterloo Music Co. Ltd., Waterloo, Ontario, Canada. Reprinted by permission.*

ATONALITY

An **atonal** piece does not have a tonal center—that is, it has no key, and no one tone seems more important than any other.

Some atonal music is written with the use of **twelve-tone technique,** in which all twelve tones of the chromatic scale are arranged in a particular **series** or **tone row.** These tones have no key or tonal center. The entire row is usually heard in full before it or any of its tones is repeated. After the row has been introduced, it may be varied in a number of ways; it may be used in **inversion** (upside down), in **retrograde** (backward), or in **retrograde inversion** (upside down and backward).

The tone row in *Row, Row, Row Your Tone* sounds nothing like the familiar tune to which the title alludes. The row is stated and then repeated without any variation.

After playing this piece, try writing a new melody to familiar words, using a tone row of your own.

A tone row or series

ROW, ROW, ROW YOUR TONE

Walter and Carol Noona

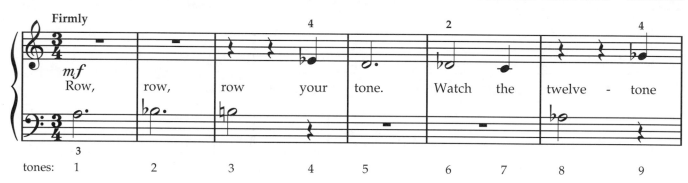

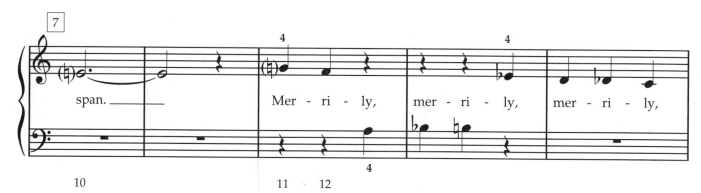

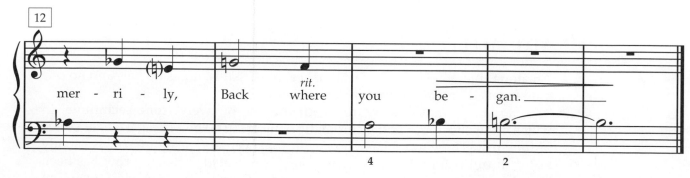

INNOVATIVE NOTATIONS

An innovative notation is any notation invented by a composer to indicate special effects and how they should be performed.

In *5-White-Note Clusters*, the white stemmed rectangles are half-note clusters. In *Seashore* they are dotted half-note clusters. The number 5 that appears above the rectangles specifies the number of tones, and the positions of the rectangles on the staff specify the exact pitches.

Play the clusters in the following pieces with your fingers or your fist. As mentioned earlier, clusters can also be played with the knuckles, the palm of the open hand, or the arm. Sometimes clusters are even played with pieces of wood or other devices.

5-WHITE-NOTE CLUSTERS

Ross Lee Finney (1906–1997)

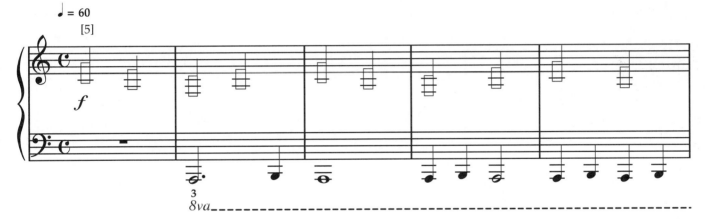

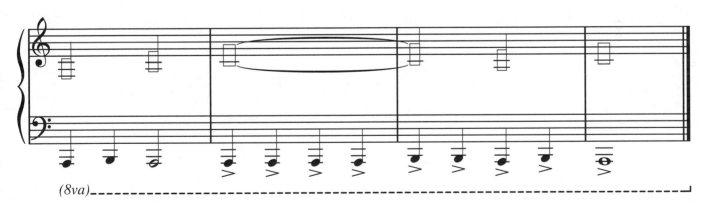

15ma

15ma means to play 15 notes (two octaves) higher than written.

Six components make up the piece called *Seashore*. First, study and play each of these components. Next, tap out the rhythms of the piece, and then play it as written.

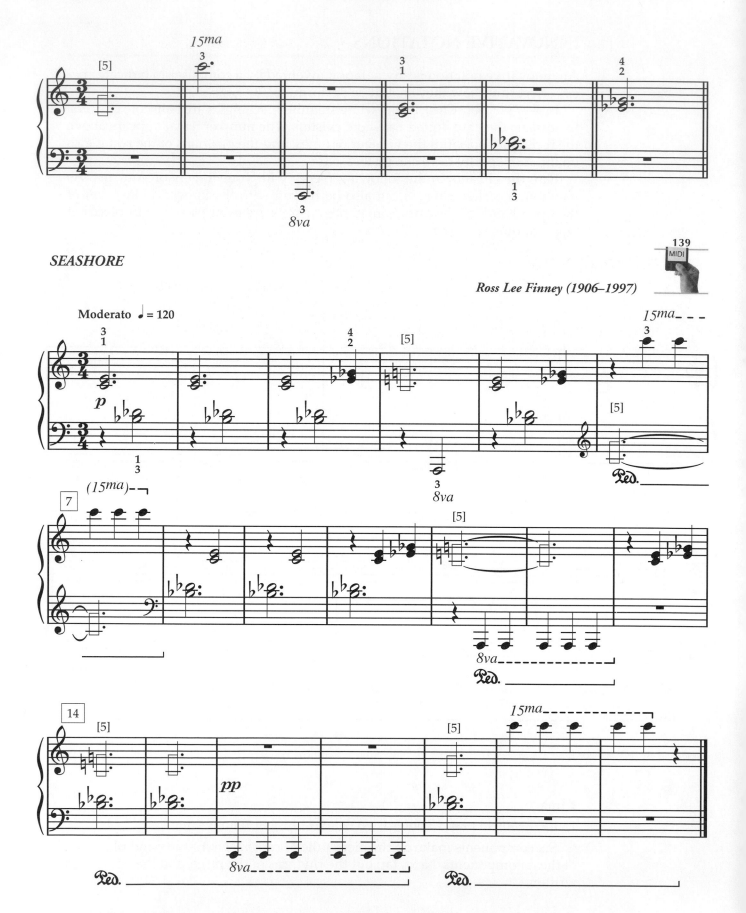

SEASHORE

Ross Lee Finney (1906–1997)

In *Winter,* the composer has used several innovative notations in addition to clusters:

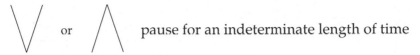 pause for an indeterminate length of time

make a ritardando as indicated by the increasingly wide distance between the notes

Finney has also omitted meter signature and bar lines, to give the performer the freedom to interpret the music in his or her own way.

Tremolo

A **tremolo** is a quick alternation from one cluster to the other, and is indicated by the parallel lines between the clusters.

WINTER

Ross Lee Finney (1906–1997)

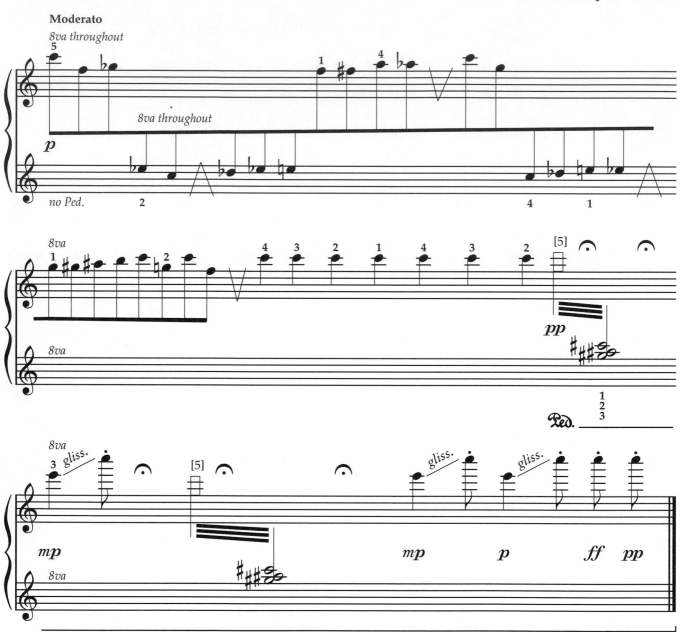

QUARTAL HARMONY

Some contemporary composers use **quartal harmony,** which is based on chords built in fourths rather than in the traditional thirds. In *The Cathedral in the Snow,* which uses an old Christmas chant, the whole-note figures are in quartal harmony. Other contemporary features are the omission of meter signature and bar lines, and the use of tones that are blurred together for effect by holding the pedal down for the duration of the piece.

THE CATHEDRAL IN THE SNOW (A Gregorian Christmas chant)

David Duke

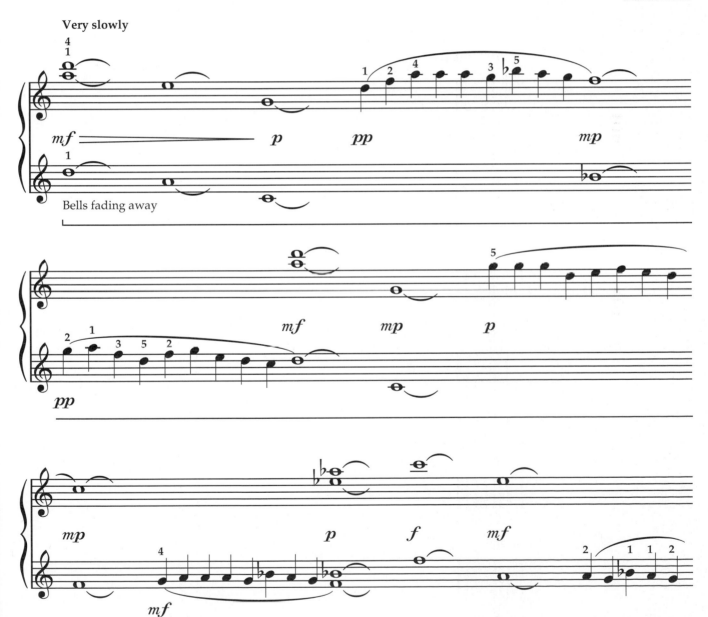

REPERTOIRE

ÉTUDE

Ludvig Schytte (1848–1909)

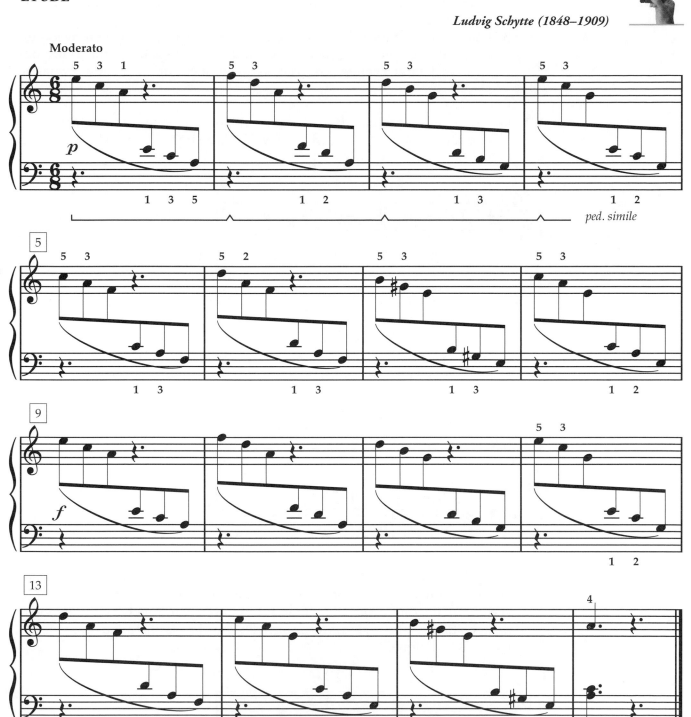

BITONAL IMPROVISATION

1. First play the following examples.
2. Then improvise your own melodies using the left-hand accompaniment patterns given.
3. Finally, create new left-hand patterns to accompany your own melodies. Also think of changing meters, using different registers, and trying out various tempo changes as well as experimenting with new dynamic shadings.

1. Improvise a bitonal melody with the right hand to the left-hand accompaniment of open fifths, which is in the key of C. The right-hand melody is in the key of E.

2. Using a black-key ostinato pattern as the left-hand accompaniment, improvise white-key melodies with the right hand.

3. Using black-key open fifths in the left hand, improvise white-key melodies and harmonic intervals with the right hand. Use the **toccata** style below to start with. Toccata (from the Italian word *toccare*, "to touch") is a keyboard composition in the style of an improvisation that is intended to exhibit a player's technique.

4. Using a left-hand pattern based on the whole-tone scale, improvise melodies that will blend with the accompaniment. Use the pattern below as a model.

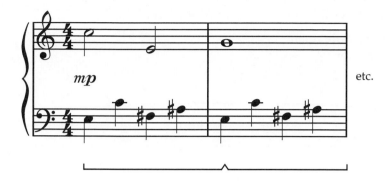

5. Improvise melodies to a chromatic left-hand accompaniment such as the one started below.

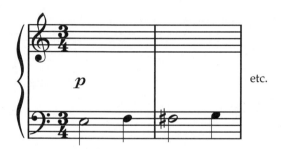

SIGHTREADING STUDIES

As you sightread these studies, *do not slow down* to find the notes or correct mistakes. If you encounter difficulties, isolate the passage later and work out the problem with careful study and practice.

1. Harmonic form
E minor

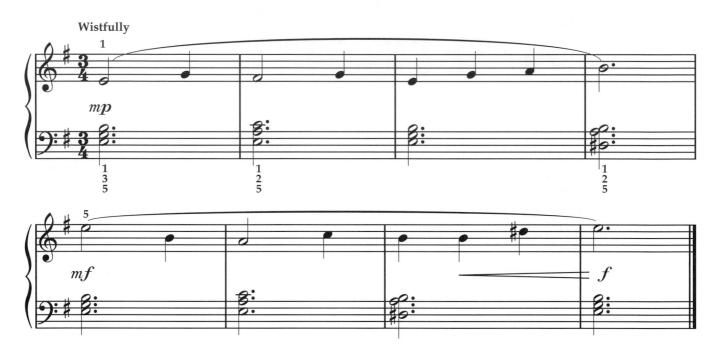

2. Parallel keys

3. Harmonic form
A minor

4. Relative keys

5. Aeolian

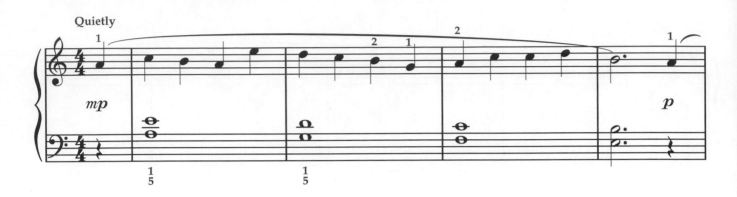

6. Phrygian

7. Dorian

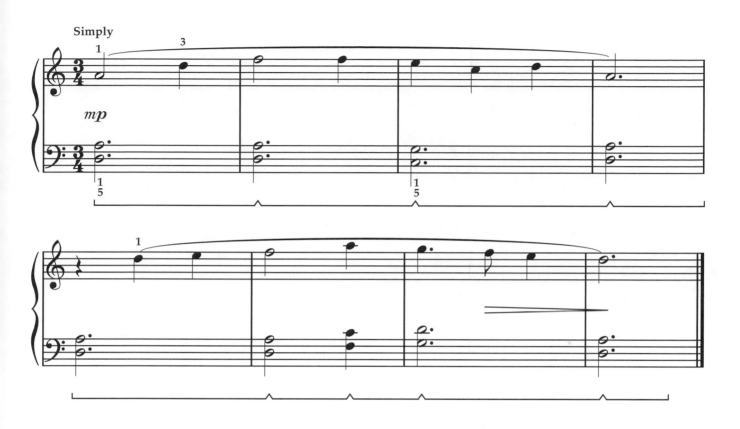

8. Lydian

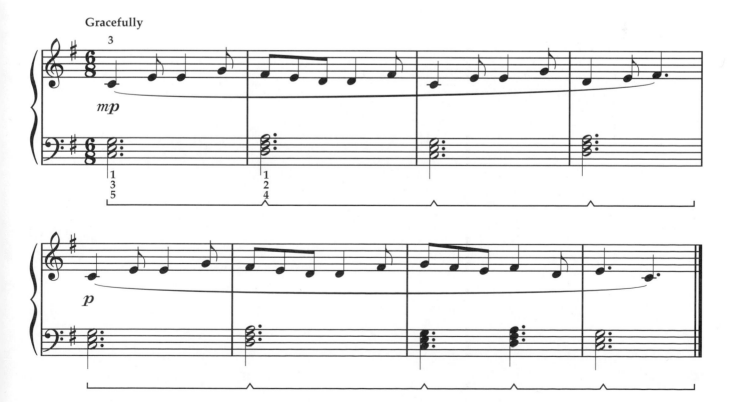

9. Mixolydian

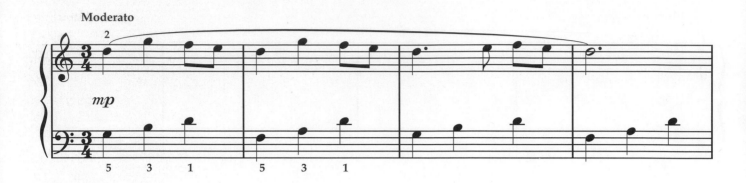

10. Byzantine (Hungarian minor)

ENSEMBLE PIECES

Rallentando (Rall.)
Rallentando (rall.) indicates a gradual slowing of tempo.

Student-Teacher Duets

STORY TIME

Norman Dello Joio (1913–)
Arranged by E.M.

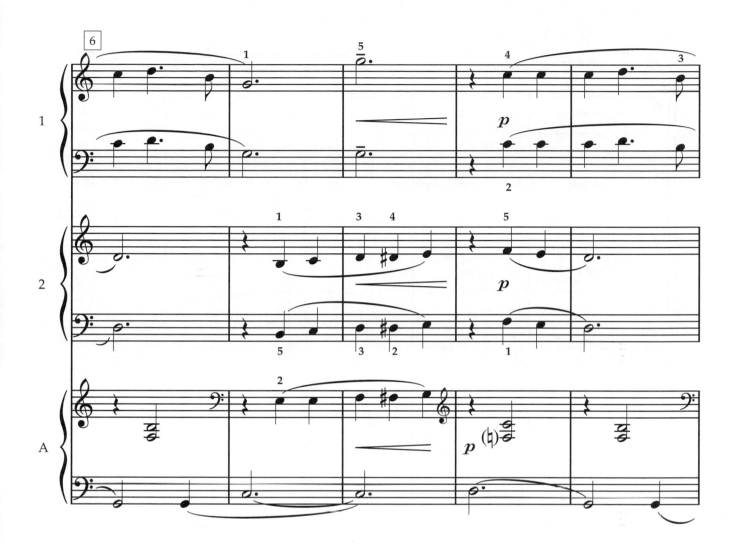

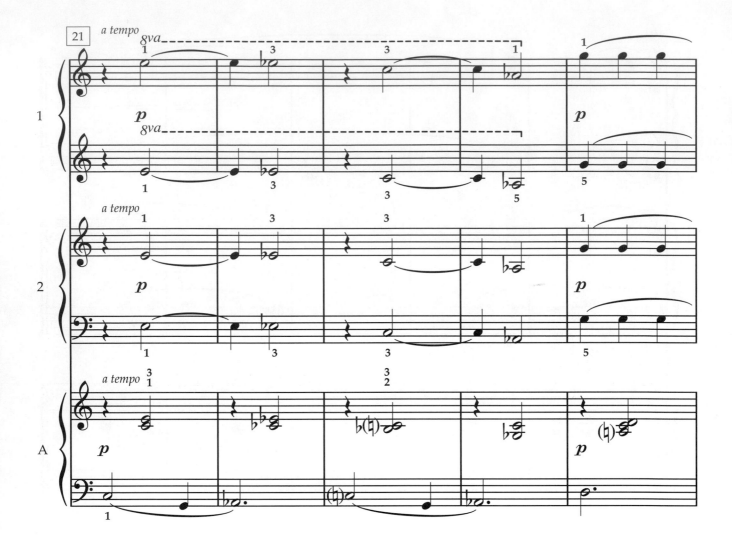

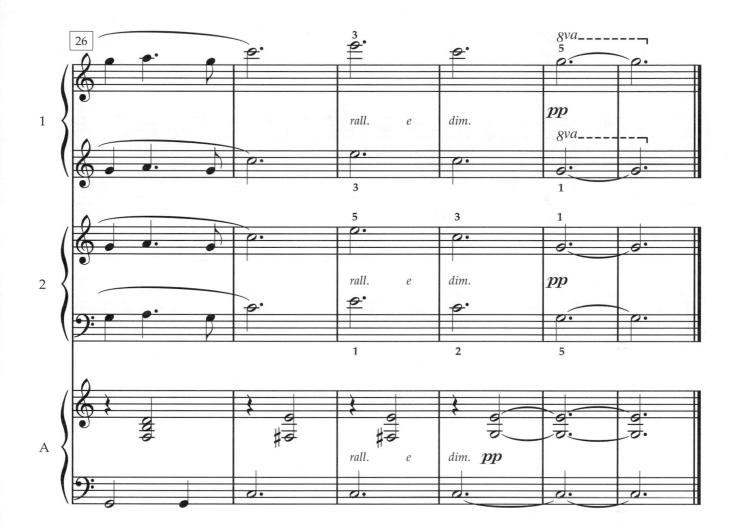

SPANISH INTERMEZZO

Student

Dennis Alexander

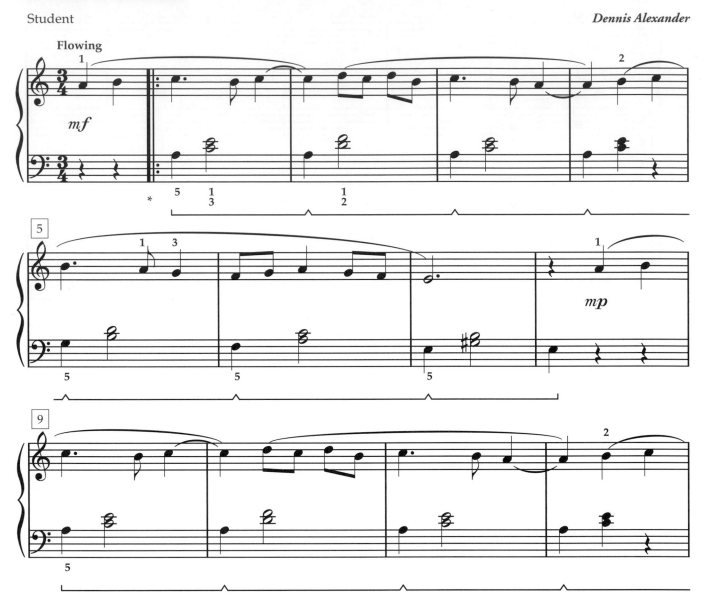

From Alfred's Basic Adult Duet Book, Level I. Copyright © 2000 by Alfred Publishing Co. Used with permission of the publisher.

---

* Pedaling is optional.

SPANISH INTERMEZZO

Accompaniment

Dennis Alexander

Student

Accompaniment

Student Duets

SUGARLOAF MOUNTAIN

Everett Stevens

FOR THE KID NEXT DOOR

Soulima Stravinsky (1910–1994)

NAME _____

DATE _____

SCORE _____

Short Answer

1. Give the name of the *sixth* degree in each of the following minor (natural form) scales:

Cm _____   C♯m _____   Am _____

Em _____   Fm _____   Dm _____

Gm _____   Bm _____   F♯m _____

2. Name the major and relative minor keys that share the following key signatures. Write the major key first, followed by its relative minor key.

3. Identify the following chords by letter names. If the chord is inverted, be sure to use numbers indicating the inversion.

Construction

4. Build the following minor scales in harmonic form using letter names.

Gm   ___   ___   ___   ___   ___   ___   ___

Cm   ___   ___   ___   ___   ___   ___   ___

B♭m   ___   ___   ___   ___   ___   ___   ___

Dm   ___   ___   ___   ___   ___   ___   ___

Em   ___   ___   ___   ___   ___   ___   ___

5. Construct a chromatic scale ascending and descending one octave upward and then downward in both bass and treble clefs. Then indicate the right- and left-hand fingerings on the lines provided above and below the treble and bass clefs. The beginning notes and fingerings have been provided to get you started.

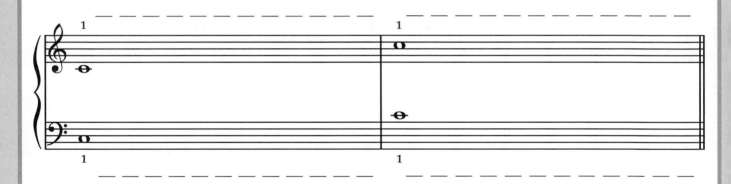

Matching

Write the numbers from Column A to correspond to the given answers in Column B.

COLUMN A	COLUMN B
1. Phrygian mode	_____ a modal scale that has half steps between the 2–3 and 6–7 degrees
2. atonal	_____ a modal scale that has half steps between the 1–2 and 5–6 degrees
3. bitonal	_____ a piece written in 2 keys simultaneously
4. Dorian mode	_____ a harmonic minor scale with a raised fourth degree
5. whole-tone scale	_____ a piece having no specific key
6. parallel scales	_____ a natural minor scale
7. con brio	_____ refers to use of the damper pedal
8. pandiatonicism	_____ to play with forcefulness
9. quartal harmony	_____ "white-note" writing
10. 15ma	_____ backwards
11. Byzantine scale	_____ a metronome marking
12. 𝄢𝆏𝆒𝆓.	_____ play 2 octaves higher than written
13. retrograde	_____ a major scale with a raised fourth degree
14. Aeolian mode	_____ a mode frequently used in the jazz idiom
15. Lydian mode	_____ to play with vigor
16. con forza	_____ scales which begin with the same tonic
17. Mixolydian mode	_____ a scale using only whole steps
18. ∨ ∧	_____ a major scale
19. ♩ = 80	_____ an innovative notation meaning to pause
20. Ionian mode	_____ chords built in fourths

Letter-Name Chord Symbols

Many printed versions of folk tunes and popular songs do not include any accompaniment; instead, chords are identified merely by letter names. Letter names are used instead of Roman numerals because they are much simpler and faster to read. In this unit (and in other printed songs), the letter-name chord symbols are meant to serve as a guide for improvising your own accompaniments.

It is important to know that letter-name chord symbols indicate root position only of the given chord, not inversions. Depending on the accompaniment pattern you choose, you have the option of using any chord in its root position or in one of the inversions studied earlier—particularly the second inversion of IV (IV$^6_4$) and the first inversion of V^7 (V$^6_5$).

LETTER NAMES OF I, IV, AND V⁷ CHORDS

Remember that the I, IV, and V^7 chords are named for their position in the scale.

I chords are constructed on the *first* degree of the scale.
IV chords are constructed on the *fourth* degree of the scale.
V^7 chords are constructed on the *fifth* degree of the scale.

In the key of C, for example, the letter names of these three chords are C, F, and G^7.

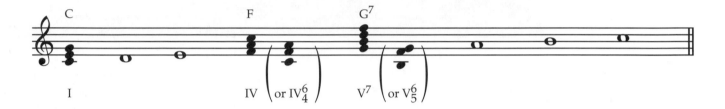

The following chart gives the letter names of the I, IV, and V^7 chords in all major keys along with the IV_4^6 and V_5^6 inversions.

Key	I	IV	IV_4^6	V^7	V_5^6
C	C	F	F/C	G^7	G^7/B
G	G	C	C/G	D^7	D^7/F♯
D	D	G	G/D	A^7	A^7/C♯
A	A	D	D/A	E^7	E^7/G♯
E	E	A	A/E	B^7	B^7/D♯
B	B	E	E/B	$F♯^7$	$F♯^7$/A♯
F♯ ⎫	F♯ ⎫	B ⎫	B/F♯ ⎫	$C♯^7$ ⎫	$C♯^7$/E♯ ⎫
G♭ ⎭	G♭ ⎭	C♭ ⎭	C♭/G♭ ⎭	$D♭^7$ ⎭	$D♭^7$/F ⎭
C♯ ⎫	C♯ ⎫	F♯ ⎫	F♯/C♯ ⎫	$G♯^7$ ⎫	$G♯^7$/B♯ ⎫
D♭ ⎭	D♭ ⎭	G♭ ⎭	G♭/D♭ ⎭	$A♭^7$ ⎭	$A♭^7$/C ⎭
A♭	A♭	D♭	D♭/A♭	$E♭^7$	$E♭^7$/G
E♭	E♭	A♭	A♭/E♭	$B♭^7$	$B♭^7$/D
B♭	B♭	E♭	E♭/B♭	F^7	F^7/A
F	F	B♭	B♭/F	C^7	C^7/E

MELODIES WITH LETTER-NAME CHORD SYMBOLS

Letter names rather than Roman numerals have been used for the I, IV, and V^7 chords in the melodies that follow. Refer back to the section in Unit 3 titled Broken-Chord Accompaniment Patterns (page 278) as a guide for choosing appropriate patterns for improvising left-hand accompaniments to some of these melodies, using the indicated harmonies.

WILLIAM TELL OVERTURE

Gioacchino Rossini (1792–1868)

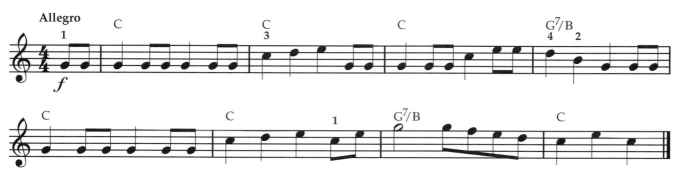

THE WASHINGTON POST MARCH

John Philip Sousa (1854–1932)

NEW RIVER TRAIN

American

ALOHA OE

Queen Liliuokalani of Hawaii

CAMPTOWN RACES

Stephen Foster (1826–1864)

De Camp-town la - dies sing dis song, Doo - dah, Doo - dah. De

Camp-town race - track five mile long, Oh! doo - dah day.

Gwine to run all night, Gwine to run all day, I'll ___

bet my mon-ey on de bob - tail nag, Some-bod - y bet on de bay.

ARKANSAS TRAVELER

American

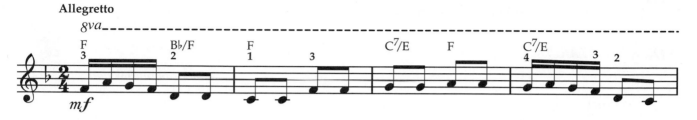

OVER THE WAVES

Traditional

In addition to I, IV, and V^7, the following melodies include the secondary chords ii, iii, and vi, as well as augmented and diminished chords. Follow the same procedure in improvising accompaniments for these melodies, using the indicated harmonies.

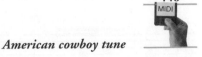

STREETS OF LAREDO

American cowboy tune

* first inversion

SAINT ANTHONY CHORALE

Franz Joseph Haydn (1732–1809)

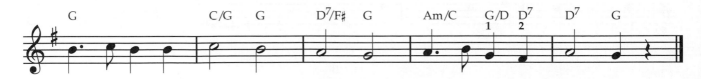

WALTZING MATILDA

Australian

JACOB'S LADDER

Spiritual

ALL THROUGH THE NIGHT

Welsh

TAKE ME OUT TO THE BALL GAME

Albert Von Tilzer
Words by Jack Norworth

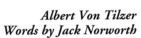

Take me out to the ball game, Take me out with the crowd. ____

Buy me some pea-nuts and crack - er - jack, I don't care if I nev - er get

back, Let me root, root, root for the home team, If they don't win it's a shame. __

__ For it's one, two, three strikes you're out, At the old ball game. ____

* second inversion

JESU, JOY OF MAN'S DESIRING

Johann Sebastian Bach (1685–1750)

* first inversion

AULD LANG SYNE

Scottish

FAMOUS THEMES

THEME FROM BRIDAL CHORUS (*from* Lohengrin)

Richard Wagner
(1813–1883)

FÜR ELISE

Ludwig van Beethoven
(1770–1827)

THEME FROM DON GIOVANNI (*La ci darem la mano*)*

Wolfgang Amadeus Mozart
(1756–1791)

* "Give me your hand" (translation from Italian)

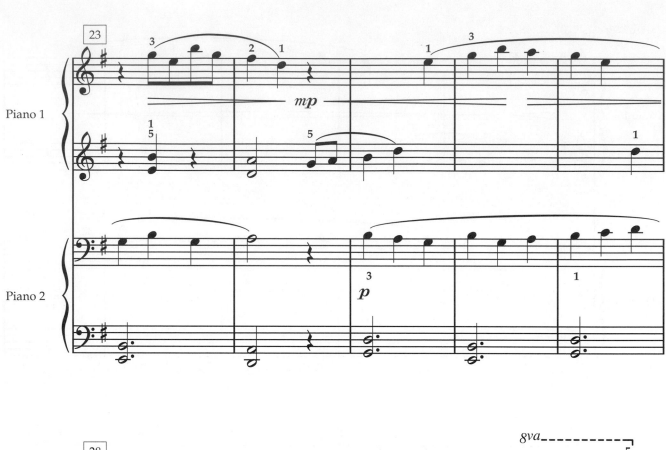

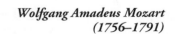

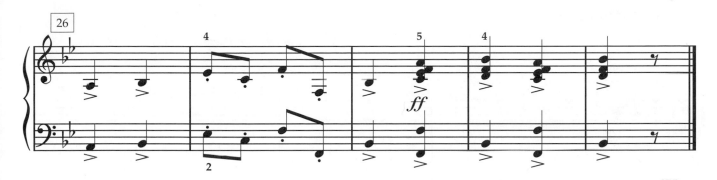

10. MINUET IN C

Wolfgang Amadeus Mozart (1756–1791)

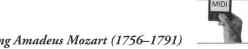

11. GERMAN DANCE

Ludwig van Beethoven (1770–1827)

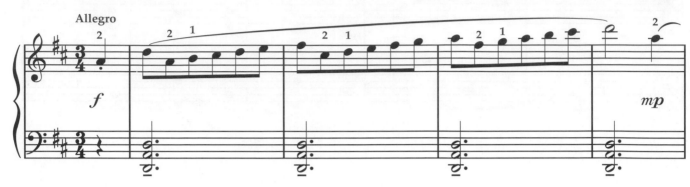

12. *MELODY* *(from* 43 Piano Pieces for the Young, *Op. 68)*

Robert Schumann (1810–1856)

13. *THE BEAR*

Vladimir Rebikoff (1866–1920)

14. *SPRINGTIME SONG* (No. 2 from For Children, *Vol. 1*)

Béla Bartók
(1881–1945)

15. *HOMAGE TO BARTÓK*

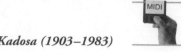

Pál Kadosa (1903–1983)

Poco allegro

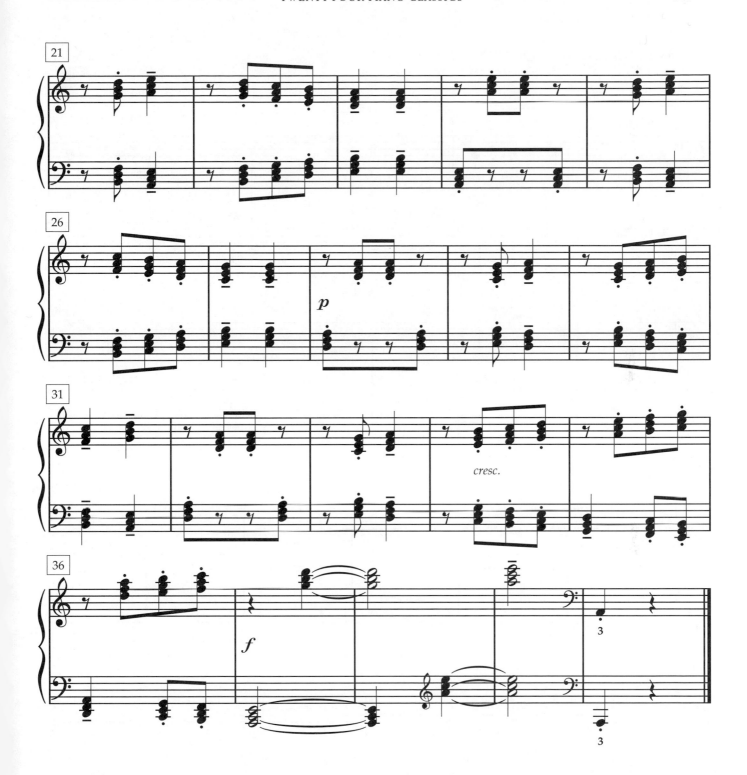

16. *A CONVERSATION* (Op. 39, No. 7)

Dmitri Kabalevsky
(1904–1987)

17. *MOON DANCE* *(No. 2 from* Mountain Idylls*)*

Alan Hovhaness (1911–2000)

18. *EVENS AND ODDS*

Robert Starer (1924–2001)

19. *AUTUMN IS HERE*

William L. Gillock

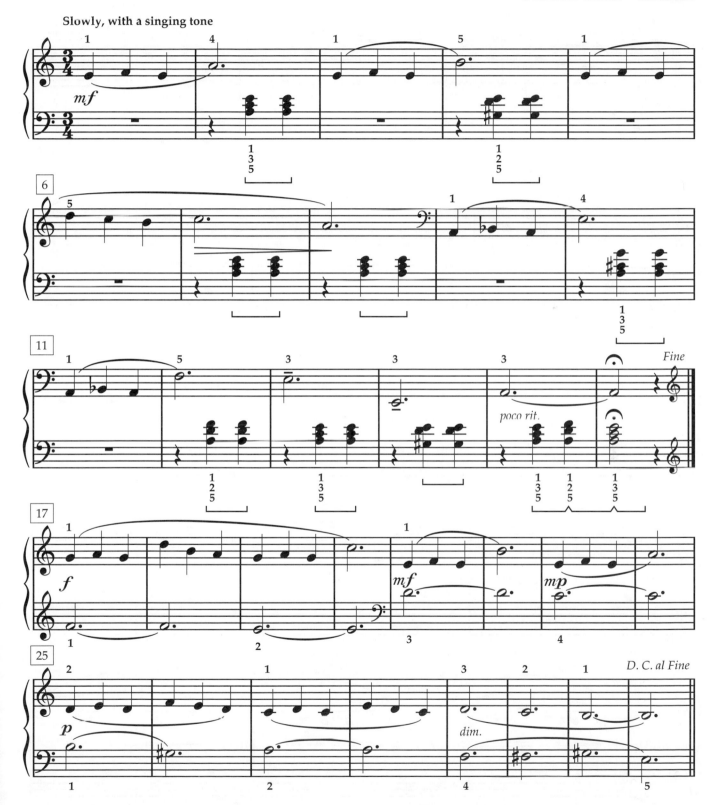

20. *MOONLIT SHORES*

Randall Hartsell

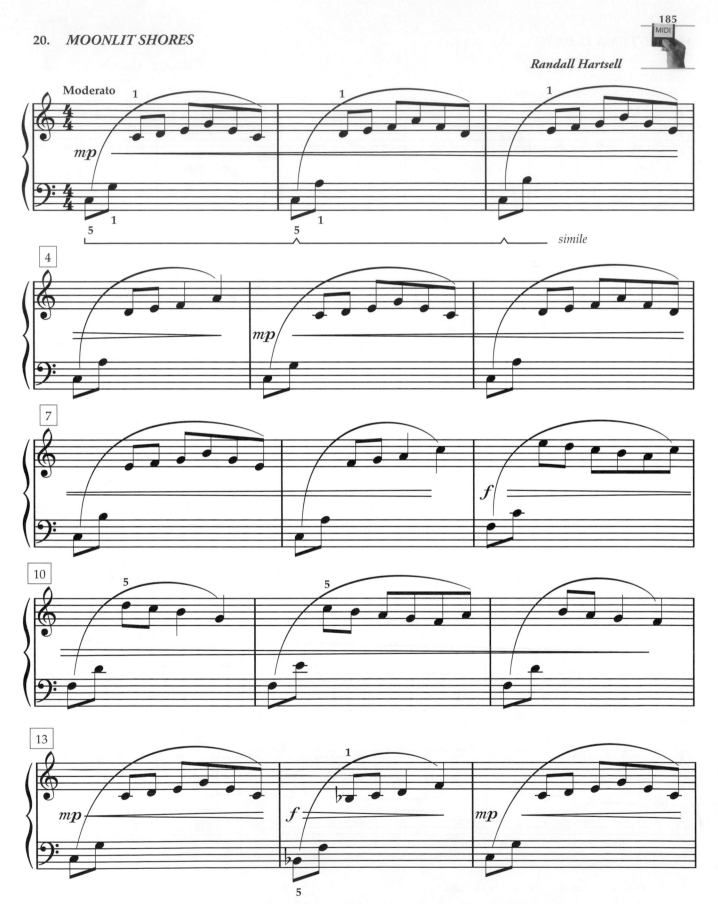

21. *SNEAKY BUSINESS*

Martha Mier

22. *DREAMSCAPE*

George Peter Tingley

23. *EARLY SPRING*

George Peter Tingley

24. *FESTIVE DANCE*

Carolyn Miller

* *Coda* means "a tail."

$\mathcal{S}$core Reading

THREE-PART TEXTURE

Score reading involves the ability to read music from several staves simultaneously as well as the ability to read music written in clefs other than treble or bass.

Various examples of score reading are provided here to acquaint you with the basics of the technique.

The following exercises appear in three-part texture. Play the upper two parts with the right hand and the lower part with the left hand. Practice with hands separately, then hands together.

1.

3.

4.

FOUR-PART TEXTURE

The following exercises appear in four-part texture. Play the upper two parts with the right hand and the lower two parts with the left hand. Practice with hands separately, then hands together.

1.   *HUSH, LITTLE BABY*

American

2. *RED RIVER VALLEY*

American Folk Song

3. *LONDONDERRY AIR* *(O Danny Boy)*

Irish Folk Tune
Arranged by Ken Iversen

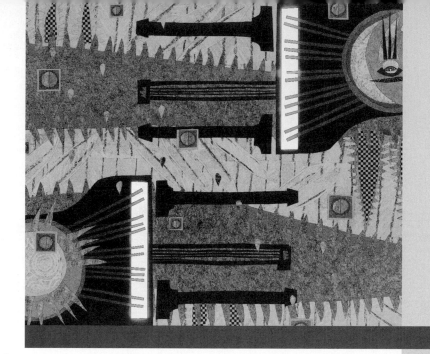

Major and Harmonic Minor Scales in Two Octaves

*P*lay the major and harmonic minor scales in two octaves, first with hands separately, then with hands together. Also try practicing these scales using cluster techniques as illustrated earlier on pages 252–253.

Other ways of playing these scales are with shifting accents such as ♩♩♩♩ groupings and ♩♩♩♩. Then play the scales using various slur groupings like ♩♩♩♩♩♩. Other suggestions would be to play one hand louder than the other, and then the reverse. Or play the right hand legato while playing the left hand staccato, and then the reverse.

MAJOR SCALES IN TWO OCTAVES

A Major

E Major

B Major (or C♭ Major)

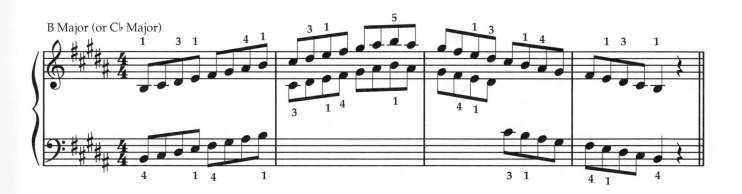

G♭ Major (or F♯ Major)

D♭ Major (or C♯ Major)

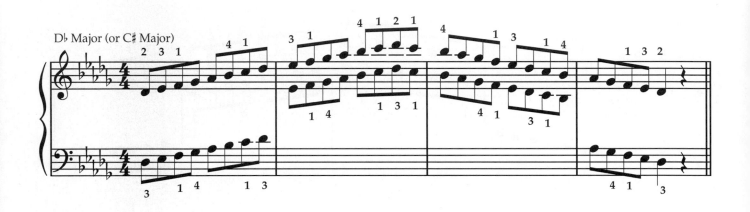

A♭ Major

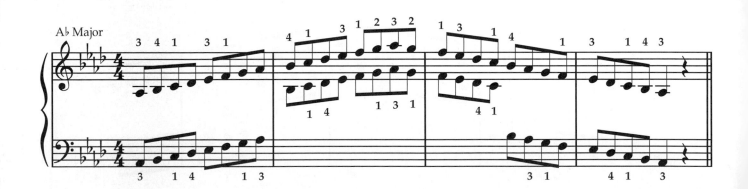

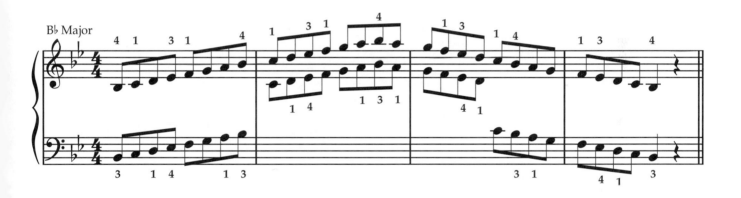

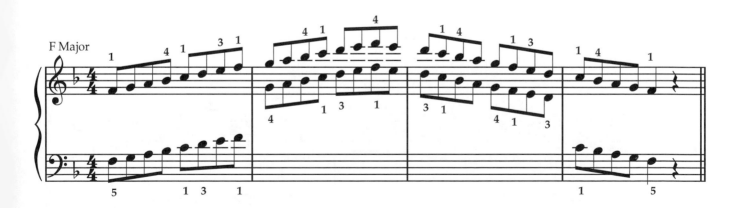

HARMONIC MINOR SCALES IN TWO OCTAVES

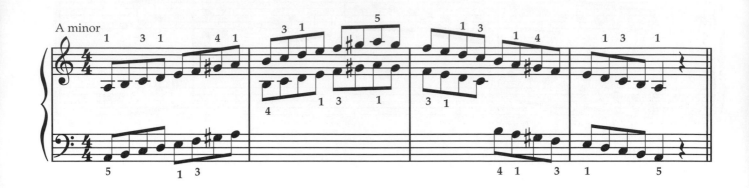

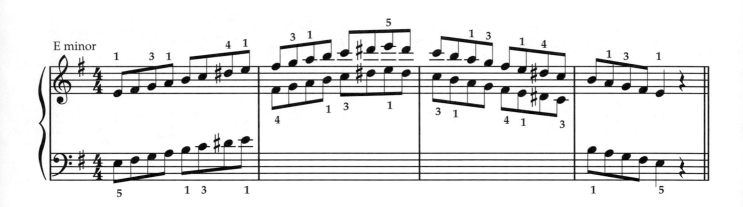

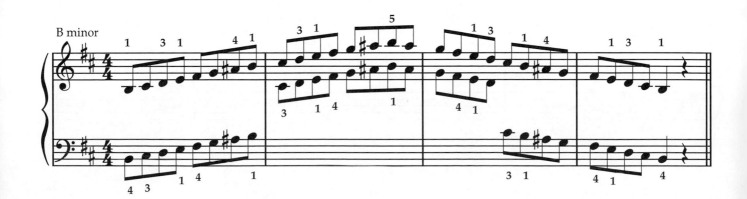

F# minor (or G♭ minor)

C# minor (or D♭ minor)

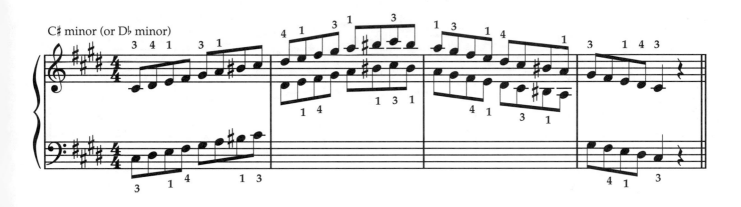

G# minor (or A♭ minor)

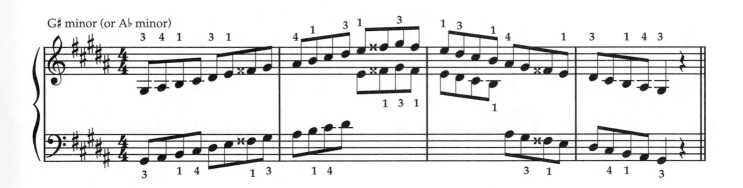

Eb minor (or D# minor)

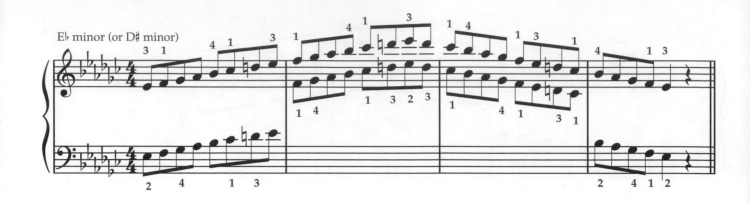

Bb minor (or A# minor)

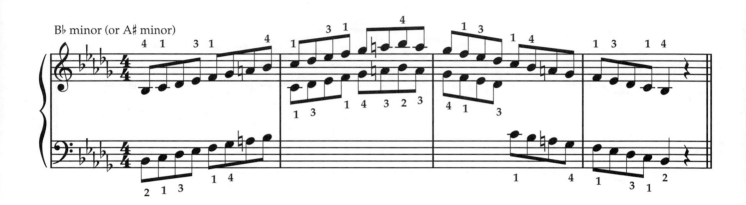

F minor

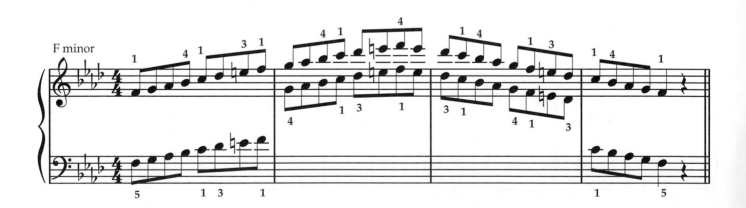

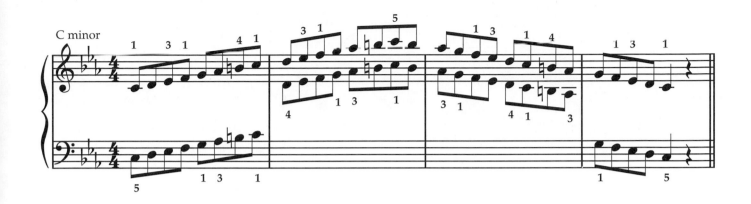

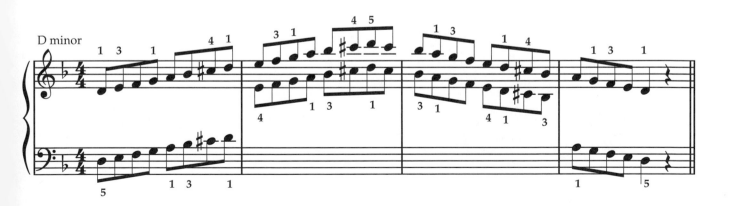

Three Patriotic Song Arrangements

*E*asy-to-play arrangements of three patriotic songs, *America, America the Beautiful,* and *The Star-Spangled Banner,* appear in this section.

For students who will be working in the classroom, these pieces are essential to learn to play.

AMERICA

Henry Carey

AMERICA THE BEAUTIFUL

Words by Katharine Lee Bates
Music by Samuel A. Ward

THE STAR-SPANGLED BANNER

Words by Francis Scott Key (1779–1843)
Music by John Stafford Smith (1750–1836)

Performance Terms and Symbols

TEMPO TERMS

Presto   very rapidly
Vivace   quickly; spirited
Allegro   fast; lively
Allegretto   moderately fast; slower than Allegro
Moderato   moderately
Andantino   somewhat faster than Andante
Andante   at a walking pace
Adagio   rather slow; leisurely
Lento   slow
Largo   slow; broad
Grave   very slow; solemn

CHANGE-OF-TEMPO TERMS

A tempo   return to original tempo
Accelerando (accel.)   gradually increasing in
   tempo
Meno mosso   with less movement or motion
Più mosso   with more movement or motion

Rallentando (rall.)
Ritardando (rit., ritard.) } gradually slowing in tempo
Ritenuto (riten.)   immediately slowing in tempo; also used synonymously
   with rallentando and ritardando

DYNAMIC TERMS

Crescendo (cresc.)   gradually becoming louder
Decrescendo (decresc.)
Diminuendo (dim., dimin.) } gradually becoming softer
*Pianissimo (**pp**)*   very soft
*Piano (**p**)*   soft
*Mezzo piano (**mp**)*   moderately soft
*Mezzo forte (**mf**)*   moderately loud
*Forte (**f**)*   loud
*Fortissimo (**ff**)*   very loud
*Sforzando (**sf**, **sfz**)*   strongly accented; with an emphatic stress

OTHER TERMS

Animato   animated; with spirit
Cantabile   in singing style
Coda   a concluding section of a few measures at the end of a
   composition
Con forza   with forcefulness; stressed
Con moto   with motion
Da capo (D.C.)   repeat from the beginning
Da capo al coda   repeat from the beginning and play to the coda sign (⊕);
   then end with the coda
Da capo al fine (D.C. al fine)   repeat from the beginning to *Fine,* the finish
   or end
Dal segno (D.S.)   repeat from the sign 𝄋
Dal segno al coda   repeat from the sign 𝄋 to the *Coda*
Dal segno al fine   repeat from the sign 𝄋 to *Fine*
Dolce   sweetly; delicately
Espressivo   expressively
Fine   at the end of a composition
Giocoso   humorously; playfully
Grazioso   gracefully
Intenzionato   in a deliberate manner
Legato   smoothly; connected
Leggiero   lightly; nimbly
Lunga   long
Maestoso   majestically; with dignity
Marcato   marked; stressed
Marziale   in a march-like manner
Meno   less
Molto   much
Mosso   with agitated motion
Pesante   heavily
Più   more
Poco   little; a little

Risoluto   boldly
Scherzando   playfully
Sempre   always
Senza   without
Simile   in the same manner; similarly
Sostenuto   sustained
Subito   suddenly, at once
Troppo   much; too much
Una corda   soft pedal

SYMBOLS AND SIGNS

> – V   *accent mark*—a sign placed over or under a note to indicate stress or emphasis

arpeggio—a sign placed before a chord to indicate that the notes are to be quickly rolled, one after the other, from bottom to top; harplike

'   *breath mark*—indicating a brief pause before resuming

a cluster of notes to be played simultaneously, usually with the palm of an open hand, or the arm

crescendo—gradually becoming louder

decrescendo or *diminuendo*—gradually becoming softer

first and second endings

fermata—indicates a hold or pause

gliss.   *glissando*   a sweeping sound produced by pulling one or more fingernails rapidly over the keys

C   a meter signature standing for common time; same as $\frac{4}{4}$

¢   a meter signature standing for cut time (alla breve); same as $\frac{2}{2}$

♩ = 126   metronome marking

Ped.   pedal markings

repeat bar line

staccato mark—a dot placed under or over a note to indicate that the note is to be played detached, nonlegato

staccato mark—indicates a very short staccato note

tremolo—a rapid alternation of two pitches of an interval larger than a second

tr   *trill*—an even alternation of two adjacent tones

triplet—a group of three notes played in the same time as two notes of the same value

8va- - - - ⌐   ***8va octava***—means to play eight notes higher than written

15ma   ***quindecima***—means to play 15 notes, or two octaves, higher than written

Title Index

Composer Index

$\mathcal{S}$ubject $\mathcal{I}$ndex